EARLY
CHILDREN'S
BOOKS

A Collector's Guide

"Oh nurse, what tales you told me!
To school I hardly would go,
And yet we have been so merry
How could you frighten me so?"

"The master was kind, like my father,
We laughed and sang and could play,
And instead of hating it, nursie,
I wish it had lasted all day."

"And bags full of goodies he gave us;
The largest of all was for me,
I'll run home so quick to dear mother
And give her the biggest I see!"

M. SCHERER & H. ENGLER
Registered.

Printed by Rommler & Jonas, Dresden.

EARLY CHILDREN'S BOOKS

A Collector's Guide

Eric Quayle

DAVID & CHARLES
Newton Abbot   London
BARNES & NOBLE BOOKS
Totowa, New Jersey

(Frontispiece) An illustration from Childhood's Golden Days *(1880), a folio published by Dean & Son, London. The photo-lithographic plates were prepared in Dresden, Germany. 33 × 26cm*

NOTE
If the date given after the title of any work quoted is enclosed in parentheses, this biblio-graphical device indicates that it was published in that year but appeared without a date of issue on its title-page or elsewhere in the book. Unless otherwise stated, all dates quoted are first editions. All the illustrations are from books in the author's collection, except in a few instances.

British Library Cataloguing in Publication Data

Quayle, Eric
  Early children's books.
  1. Children's literature—Collectors and
  collecting
  I. Title
  028.5′34   PN1009.Al

  ISBN 0 7153 8307 8

Library of Congress Cataloguing in Publication Data

Quayle, Eric.
  Early children's books.

  Bibliography: p.
  Includes index.
  1. Children's literature—Bibliography.   2. Children
  —Books and reading—Bibliography.   I. Title.
  Z1037.Q39 1983 [PN1009.A1] 016.82′08′09282 82-13863
  ISBN 0-389-20331-9

This edition first published in 1983
in Great Britain by
David & Charles (Publishers) Limited
Brunel House Newton Abbot Devon

First published in the USA 1983 by
Barnes & Noble Books
81 Adams Drive, Totowa, New Jersey, 07512

Typesetting by A.B.M. Typographics Ltd., Hull
and printed in Great Britain
by Butler and Tanner Ltd., Frome

CONTENTS

For SACHIKO

INTRODUCTION

'Once upon a time. . .' The lost delights of childhood are immediately conjured back from a past now far away whenever those magical words are heard. Do any of us ever forget the stories learned in early childhood? The plots and blood-curdling details of the fairy-tales and folklore contained in the first books we read for ourselves etched indelible pictures in our memories and, long after most of the novels and romances of adult life have become merely a pot-pourri of scenes and incidents, can still be recalled in the minutest fashion. The nursery rhymes and fairy-tales we first heard in the tucked-up-in-bed security of early youth can be repeated almost word for word, taking us back to the lost delights of childhood to a time when all make-believe was real. *Jack and the Beanstalk, Goldilocks and the Three Bears, The Sleeping Beauty, Cinderella, Puss in Boots, The Constant Tin Soldier, Little Red Riding Hood,* each of us has his or her own particular favourite, just as, generations earlier, our grandparents and their grandparents before them knew by heart *The Butterfly's Ball, The Adventures of a Pincushion* or *The History of Little Goody Two-Shoes.*

Perhaps this is one of the reasons why so many collectors feel the urge to possess copies of first and early editions of books whose stories and tales have stood the test of critical juvenile applause, or of even earlier volumes depicting the history of the genre from its first beginnings in the sixteenth century up to the days of their own childhoods. The scope of this present work embraces this entire period, from the time when books specially conceived for the young made their first appearance in the time of Queen Elizabeth I of England, didactic and puritanical aids to youthful piety for the most part, full of threats of Hell Fire and Everlasting Damnation for any child who dared to stray from the path of strict obedience, until the mid-eighteenth century saw the emergence of specialist publishing houses whose aim was to creat a juvenile market for their wares. For the first time publishers set out to amuse and interest their potential customers, the bindings themselves seeking to attract youthful eyes so that parents and uncles and aunts might be persuaded to hand over the prize.

The vast majority of the titles discussed and illustrated here can still

An early edition of Charles Perrault's fairy tales, 1700, first published in 1697. The words 'Tales of Mother Goose' are shown in the frontispiece, although the printed title now reads 'Stories or Tales of Bygone Times'. 13 × 7.5cm

be purchased, if and when found, at prices that enable the novice to compete with collectors who have spent the best part of a lifetime book-hunting—though certainly not for the pence and shillings of *their* early days. There is, however, one proviso: namely that the 'high-spots' and world-famous titles of acknowledged rarity are sighed for rather than pursued. Works such as these will either empty a very long pocket or be stumbled on in true fictional fashion for practically nothing. There is no half-way house; the seller either knows what treasure he is offering on his shelves, on his stall or in his hands, or he remains blissfully ignorant that the book he is about to part with for a few pounds could, and should, command a ransom. No one bookseller's knowledge, which must be wide enough to make valid decisions as to value across the entire spectrum of literary and scientific endeavour, can at all times compete with the specialist collector who can aspire

8

Two pages of hand-coloured pictures, captioned in three languages, from Neuer Bildersaal (New Picture Gallery) *(1815), published by F. Fechner, of Guben, Germany. 14.5 × 9.5cm*

to be a world expert, providing his field is narrow enough. But few, if any, antiquarian booksellers of repute will fail to price a title well known in the trade at other than its full market value. In this decision they will take full account of the volume's condition and format, both of which readers of this present work will be considerably better informed about by the time they reach the final pages.

The gradual acquisition of a well chosen selection of early children's books, dating from the days of one's own childhood to as far back in time as luck and your financial resources allow you to go, becomes a hobby of increasing fascination and reward. My own collection stands in serrated rows of talls and shorts, some stout and important-looking or elegantly thin, some plain and unadorned as befits their period, others blazoned with gold blocking and brightly coloured in a spectrum of blind-stamped cloth bindings. Some hide in miniature slip-cases less than five centimetres tall, while the late-nineteenth-century annuals tower over their shelf-mates and announce their volume numbers with the glint of gold stars on their spines. The most extravagantly dressed as regards their eye-catching bindings are always to be found on shelves housing collections of boys' adventure stories written by authors

(Above) *A group of children's books published by John Harris in the 1820s. His format of printed paper-covered boards with leather spines blocked with horizontal gold lines was quickly copied by his rivals. Average size: 17 × 11cm*

Vide humilitatem meam, & laborem meum: &
dimitte universa delicta mea.   Psalm. 24.
                                           IV.

(Left) *One of the forty-five full-page woodcut illustrations from* Pia Desideria Emblematis, 1628, by Herman Hugo, *an emblem book beloved by children of the day. 12.5 × 8.5cm*

contemporary with the pre-war decades when G. A. Henty was at his prolific best. Author collections of works by him and his many rivals-in-trade are discussed at length in a later chapter, as are the magazines and annuals where many of these stories first appeared.

A love and understanding of the often ephemeral little volumes that brought pleasure to countless children of past ages must surely be a prime requisite for successful book-hunting and the gradual building of a library whose specialist interest opens the way to research and scholarship. In my own early days as a collector there was no printed guide that set out the points and pitfalls to watch for and inevitably I burned my fingers on more than one occasion. Often, in fact; for although the vast majority of booksellers and dealers were helpful with their advice there were times, after experience had taught me to collate both plates and text, when disappointments led to expensive discards. Issue points came later: the original quest was for first editions of authors for whom there was often no bibliographical guide and the experience and know-how which all collectors accumulate in time was often dearly bought. It is to be hoped that the facts and figures set out in the following pages will enable beginners and seasoned collectors alike to avoid many of my own early mistakes.

The illustrations used are almost all of books in the juvenile section of my library, a collection which now numbers several thousand volumes. I add additional volumes whenever time and finances permit, and hope to continue until I myself fill a final shelf.

1

FROM WILL SHAKESPEARE TO WILL WYCHERLEY

The percentage of children who could read or look at picture books in the Middle Ages was minutely small, and even these favoured few could seldom have been allowed to handle personally the illuminated manuscripts which depicted, often in graphic and exciting form, the myths and legends of earlier days in religious history. One can imagine a kindly monk lifting up a wondering boy as he turned the vellum leaves and told the story they unfolded . . . A fanciful picture of a scene more likely to have been enacted between a pedagogue and his pupil in the latter half of the fifteenth century, the boy being taught his alphabet and figures by repeating the letters from his horn-book.

Reading for pleasure was practically unknown for the young of those days, and, not surprisingly, few, if any, juvenile manuscripts that may have passed from hand to hand have survived. After the invention of printing with movable metal type about 1456, and the setting up of William Caxton's press at Westminster about twenty years later, there was still to be a long wait before any work remotely interesting to children made its appearance. Then, on 26 March 1484, 'in the first year of the reign of King Richard the Third', Caxton finished his translation from the French of Aesop's *Fables. The book of the subtyl hystoryes and Fables of Esope,* with its woodcut illustrations, was not in any way intended by Caxton as a text for the young, but, since this first translation into English nearly five hundred years ago, the work in various forms and illustrated by scores of artists has remained in print almost exclusively for a juvenile audience.

One of the most popular collections of tales of the Middle Ages was *Gesta Romanorum,* compiled in Latin, almost certainly in England, around 1300, which appeared in manuscript in English during the fifteenth century. *The Acts of the Romans,* as it was usually called, is believed to have been written in order to supply a series of entertaining stories for regaling the brothers of an unidentified abbey and was probably compiled by one of their number to lighten the long nights of winter. The earliest manuscript versions differ widely in the tales they

William Caxton, the first English printer, in his workshop in Westminster Abbey, London, in the 1480s. A bas-relief from the entablature, Jerusalem Chamber, in the Abbey. The boy on the right acted as inker and was known as the 'printer's devil'.

tell, but all are romances of chivalry and legends of saintly deeds, and to each of the stories a moral is attached. They supplied material for many subsequent authors, and in modified form provided the sort of adventure story reading beloved of children. Long before the invention of printing the youth of the fourteenth and fifteenth centuries must have thrilled to the accounts of Roman heroes dressed as they were in the garb of early medieval knights, slaying Greeks and dragons with equal impunity. Caxton's successor, Wynkyn de Worde, who had joined the master in London in 1477, and who inherited Caxton's press on his death in 1491, was the first to print *Gesta Romanorum*. Versions of his text, in abbreviated form and illustrated with crude little woodcuts, were read by children for their own amusement throughout the next four centuries, many carrying little homilies on their title-pages, such as:

> The Story's pleasant, and the moral good,
> If read with Care, and rightly understood.

13

Another favourite with children must have been the various *Bestiaries,* described by M. R. James in his treatise on the subject, *The Bestiary*, 1928, as 'one of the leading picture-books of the twelfth and thirteenth centuries in this country'. These were early natural history, with many of the animals depicted being fabulous, but none the less fearsome for that. *The Voiage and Travaile of Sir John Maundevile, Kt,* a purely fictitious work written originally in French, purported to be a guide to pilgrims to the Holy Land, and must have proved extremely entertaining to youth from the middle of the fourteenth century onwards with its tales of ant-hills of gold dust; tribes of one-footed men 'and the foot so large that it shadeth all the Body against the Sonne when they lye down and raze it'; of wells whose water changes colour at the stroke of every hour; trees which bear honey and whose sap is wine; a one-eyed tribe, with the orb in the centre of their foreheads; and much more in the same vein with pictures to prove the statements true.

One of the many strange woodcut illustrations from The Voiage and Travaile of Sir John Maundeville, Kt, *composed in the fourteenth century, and printed in 1725 and again in 1839. A purely fictitious account, whose pictures children found most amusing. 7 × 6.7cm*

None of these works was in any way intended for children, either in manuscript or in later book form, and we have to wait until the final quarter of the sixteenth century, to a time when William Shakespeare was a boy of sixteen, before the first purpose-made picture book for children made its appearance.

Kunst und Lehrbüchlein was first published in Germany in 1578, but this issue was merely a hotch-potch of illustrations culled from a variety of works which the publisher, Sigmund Feyerabend (1528–90), had commissioned during the previous decade. *Book of Art and Instruction for Young People*, to give the work its English title, was re-issued in 1580 as a book specially prepared for the youth of the day.

The title-page of the earliest known picture book for children, Kunst und Lehr-büchlein, *1580, the first part of the translation reading: 'A Book of Art and Instruction for young people, wherein may be discovered all manner of merry and agreeable drawings'. 16.5 × 13cm*

The finely executed woodcut illustrations, of which several are displayed here, were the work of Jost Amman (1539-91), who lived the early part of his life in Zurich, Switzerland. As an artist, he had designed and drawn the pictures to appeal to young people, and his success in this is measured by the fact that new editions continued to appear until the 1670s.

'These [illustrations] have been published for the benefit of all who wish to profit by them, and it is my sincere hope that this book will confer particular benefits upon the young,' wrote Sigmund Feyerabend in his preface. He was one of the pioneers of book production, a forward-thinking man who headed the profession of printers and publishers that made the name of Frankfurt world-famous in this sphere. The fact that the present-day Frankfurt Book Fair is held annually in that city owes much to Feyerabend's drive and determination to make a success of his business back in the sixteenth century so that sons, partners and others in his employ proliferated in the same trade in the years after his death.

He can now be awarded the laurels for publishing the first picture book ever produced for juveniles, and possibly the first specifically children's book ever printed. 'We have a duty to our children, no matter what our standing or profession,' he told his readers, addressing his remarks to the parents, relatives or friends of the young people for whom the book was primarily intended, for no child of the age could have afforded such a lavishly illustrated quarto as *Kunst und Lehrbüchlein*. 'The setting and publishing of books during these years has not been accomplished without incurring considerable expense,' Feyerabend added, in mitigation of the price he was forced to charge. A glance at the magnificent series of woodcut illustrations, depicting almost every aspect of European everyday life at that time, makes one appreciate that this statement was something more than a mere puff to stimulate sales. As the first book aimed at the totally unexplored juvenile market, it set a standard hard to equal—and all this some eight or ten years before the invincible Spanish Armada set sail up the English Channel bound for Flanders.

The work is also important in that it contains a fine early example of a young scholar using a horn-book, and also a very early printed picture of a little girl holding a doll. Both these illustrations, reproduced in this present work, are outstanding examples of Jost Amman's observant attention to detail and a tribute to his masterful skill as both artist and draughtsman.

Horn-books, such as the one which the young man is so diligently using, consisted of a piece of paper or parchment let into a recess in a tablet of wood, leather or, in rarer cases, metal or bone. There may

Woodcut illustration by Jost Amman for Kunst *und* Lehrbüchlein, *1580, showing one of the earliest printed pictures of a child using a horn-book. With his fescue he is ringing the letters or numbers as he reads them. 16.5 × 13cm*

have been ivory examples, but I know of none which have survived, although several set in silver—probably given to mark a special birthday and not meant for school use—can be seen in the show-cases of one or two museums. No two examples seem to be identical, and a child about to start school may have had one carved specially for his use. The name derives from the fact that a slice of thin transparent horn was used to cover the paper, thus protecting it from the grubby fingers of its owner, rather in the manner in which a slip of plastic sheeting might be used today. On the sheet of paper or parchment the letters of the alphabet, a set of Roman numerals and perhaps the words of the Lord's Prayer were written or printed. These were then studied and learned in the manner which the boy in Amman's picture is applying himself.

Of particular interest to students of the period and educational historians is the manner in which he is reading his horn-book. Presumably Amman used a model or sketched from life and his accurate representation and close attention to detail let us see that earlier theories of the way these personal teaching aids were used were wrong. The projection at the top did not start life as a handle to hold the horn-book: that was a later development. If we look at the picture we can see that in his right hand the boy holds a fescue, a short metal or wooden rod with a hook at one end and a ring at the other. When not being used it hung from the child's belt, as did the horn-book itself, being secured by a loop of string or a thin leather thong which passed through a small hole in the projection shown at the top. With the ring of his fescue the boy is circling individual letters and figures, reading them out aloud and repeating their names so that they are learned by rote, the most simple series of letters being replaced under the translucent horn by actual sentences as he progresses. Amman completes this amble home from school with a background of youngsters carrying school-books and riding imaginary horses, while the youngest child feeds with a spoon from a dish as the cat waits patiently.

Horn-books may have come into use as early as the fourteenth century, although the first printed pictures of pupils using them date from the 1490s. Those used in the seventeenth and eighteenth centuries often had handles (in place of the small projection shown in the illustration) and were used the other way, the handle being at the bottom. Boys used them as bats, nicknaming them 'battledores', and bat and ball games evolved that finally gave birth to our very English game of cricket.

The illustration of the little girl with her doll is taken from the same 1580 edition of Amman's work. She represents a figure familiar in children's books from that time onwards, but, as far as I am aware, this is the earliest printed picture of a child holding a doll or puppet of any sort. The child herself is shown by Amman dressed in clothing almost identical to that which would be worn by her mother and other female relatives, just as the little doll is itself wearing a dress in the same style as its young mistress. Children, even as late as the first quarter of the nineteenth century, invariably wore scaled-down versions of the dresses and clothes used by their elders, with boys in tricorn hats and girls wearing crinolines depending on the adult fashions of the time.

The rest of the woodcuts of *Kunst und Lehrbüchlein*, totalling ninety-four full-page illustrations, provide an intimate picture of the late-sixteenth-century society in which Jost Amman lived and worked, as well as a rich store of legends, fables and folk-tales popular with children at that time. It seems more than likely that potential young artists used the book as an aid to draughtsmanship, as Sigmund Feyerabend primarily intended they should, emphasising this aspect in his preface. The figures were probably traced over, coloured, cut out

18

One of the earliest printed pictures of a child holding a doll, taken from Kunst und Lehrbüchlein, *1580. 16.5 × 13cm*

for scrap-books, disfigured by rude and humorous alterations, stiffened with backing and used for cardboard soldiers and citizens of model towns, and, in the final stages of the volume's disintegration, carefully folded for boats and paper darts. Children, from the time of Amman onwards, have committed affectionate outrages on the picture books which have brought them the greatest pleasure, rating the book's value only in direct proportion to the practical enjoyment it brought them. It is certain that children of the day made use of Feyerabend's *Book of Art and Instruction for Young People* in similar fashion and its mortality in the first fifty or so years of its life must have been extremely high. By the eighteenth century it was already a sought-after collector's piece, but the few copies that managed to survive until then had a more than sporting chance of lasting to the present day. Most would be carefully preserved in private collections, museums or national libraries, and the one displayed belongs to the handful still complete with all text and illustrations. Such a volume would today be beyond the reach of all but the wealthiest, but a finely produced collotype facsimile of this landmark in the annals of children's books was published in the form of a limited edition in 1971 by the Eugrammia Press, London.

Picture books, with their simple text and (hopefully!) graphic illustrations, afford one of the most fruitful ways by which young children can increase their knowledge of the world and extend their vocabulary to include a diverse and exotic mixture of places and things to which they would otherwise remain strangers. John Locke, in *Some Thoughts concerning Education*, 1693, believed that pictures riveted the attention of the young in a way which could be exploited for their own good: 'As soon as he begins to spell, as many pictures of animals should be got him as can be found, with the printed names to them, which at the same time will invite him to read, and afford him matter of enquiry and knowledge.' Locke was not the first to expound this theory: Johannes Amos Comenius (1592-1670), a philosopher as well as an educationalist, had compiled and illustrated an instructional book for children as early as 1654. *Orbis Sensualium Pictus* was published in Nuremberg, Germany, the author expressing the hope in his preface that his little book might 'entice knowedgeable children . . . to read more easily than hitherto'. *The World around us in Pictures*, as its title translates, first appeared in English as translated by Charles Hoole in 1658. He titled the English edition *Visible World; or, A Nomenclature, and pictures of all the chief things that are in the world, and of Men's employments therein; in above 150 cuts. . . .* , and it was an immediate success as an illustrated school textbook, new editions continuing to be called for until well after the end of the eighteenth century.

Jan Amos Komensky was born in Moravia and was orphaned in early childhood, his name being Latinised to Comenius while at school, this being a common practice at that time. Later in life he became Bishop of Leszno, Poland, by which time his educational books had become so well known especially his *Janua Linguarum Reserata* (*The Gate of Tongues Unlocked*), 1631, that he was invited by Parliament to assist in reforming the British educational system. The outbreak of the Civil War made this impossible and he remained in Amsterdam, where he had fled when the Swedes overran Poland and, amongst other outrages, looted and burned his library at Leszno.

I have stressed his importance as being one of the very first to seek to make learning more attractive to children. 'Boyhood is distracted for years with precepts of Grammar, infinitely prolix, perplexed and obscure,' he stated. 'For children, pictures are the most easily assimilated form of learning they can look upon.' His theories were put into practice with the publication of *Orbis Sensualium Pictus,* whose primary purpose was the instilling of the Latin tongue into the heads of youth to whom it was a tortuous and infinitely boring foreign language.

The pictures which accompanied the text showed many aspects of life at that time, the subjects ranging from 'God' to 'crawling vermin'. Sports and pastimes were not forgotten, and typical of the vernacular text which stood beside the Latin versions, in this case against the picture entitled *Ludus Pilae,* or 'Tennis Play' in Charles Hoole's English version, is the extract: 'In a Tennis-Court they play with a Ball, which one throweth, and another taketh, and sendeth it back with a Racket: and that is the sport of Noble-men to stir their body.'

The crudely drawn miniature woodcut illustrations accompanying Comenius' text measured less than 5 × 4cm in the early editions, not much bigger than some modern postage stamps. The artistic ability and technical merit so fluently displayed in Jost Amman's woodcuts three-quarters of a century earlier is totally absent, and it seems possible that the drawings were originally made by Comenius himself. Nevertheless, a fresh start had been made in an attempt to amuse children while teaching them how to read. Like Sigmund Feyerabend a century earlier, Comenius had recognised that an element of enjoyment was a necessary factor in endeavouring to reach into the minds of the young. Both men were far ahead of their time in their educational ideas in an age when books were usually written at children rather than for them.

For the literate youngsters of the seventeenth century there was little reading available that could in any way be described either as enjoyable or amusing. Latin and Greek grammars abounded, but who would read school books in the few permitted leisure hours? For the rest there was only the heavy brigade of 'suitable' works they were allowed to peruse openly with freshly washed hands while paying due regard to decorum. These were opened on Sunday afternoons in respectful silence if parents or tutors were present, in the pious hope of an English rather than a Latin text with perhaps a picture or two to dwell on, then consumed in leaf-turning boredom in a gloom deepened by the thought of the 'now let us see how much you have learned' catechism that would probably follow.

On fortunate occasions, when alone in the library, the children of the house undoubtedly discovered other volumes not always meant for their eyes. There were the delights of John Foxe's *Actes and Monuments,* 1563, affectionately known as *The Book of Martyrs,* a work filled with a crackling inferno of full-page copperplate engravings of dead and dying Christians being helped on their way to everlasting damnation by equally fervent Christians of a slightly different persuasion. The work was constantly reprinted in the form of massive folio volumes and delightfully chilled the youth of Britain from the sixteenth century onwards as 'X'- certificate wide-screen presentations or late-night horror movies do in the present day.

The History of
the Life of JESUS CHRIST.

There were in the Field Shepherds Abiding by their Flocks.........
And ye Angel of ye Lord came upon them....And said, Behold I Bring you good
Tidings Unto you is Born a Saviour which is CHRIST the Lord. Luk. 2.

The Evangelical

HISTORY:
OR, THE

LIFE of our Bleſſed Saviour

JESUS CHRIST,
Comprehenſively and Plainly Related.

WITH

Practical Inferences & Diſcourſes
THEREUPON.

In Four BOOKS.

I. Of the Birth of *John the Baptiſt*. Of the Conception and
Birth of *JESUS CHRIST*; with an Account of what
paſſed to his Entrance upon the Miniſterial Function.

II. The Hiſtory of the Acts and Miracles of our Saviour,
in the firſt Two Years of his Miniſtry.

III. A Relation of his Acts and Miracles, in the Third
Year of his Preaching.

IV. An Account of his Acts and Preaching, from the triumphant Entrance into *Jeruſalem*. Of his Crucifixion, Reſur-
rection, Apparitions and glorious Aſcenſion into Heaven.

With a Large Practical Introduction, by way of Preface.

Written in French by the Learned L. E. du Pin, and Engliſh-
ed by a Divine of the Church of *England*, with Additions.

Adorn'd with Copper Cuts.

LONDON: Printed for *Abel Swall* and T. Childe, at the
Unicorn at the Weſt-End of S. Paul's Church-yard. 1694.

Typical of the religious works produced during the seventeenth century in a style which made them attractive to children is this example translated from the French of L. E. du Pin. It contained six full-page copperplate engravings, and a simple but comprehensive index. Size of title-page: 17.4 × 11.2cm

They felt genuine affection for at least one of the works of John Bunyan: but not perhaps for such titles as *A Few Sighs from Hell, or the Groans of a Damned Soul,* 1658, or *The Strait Gate, or, Great Difficulty in Going to Heaven,* 1676. These brought a pleasant sense of mortification in the minds of many of their elders, but a glance at the title-pages of these and others of Bunyan's well-meaning tracts must have been more than a little off-putting to those in their early teens.

But a work young people quickly discovered and took to their hearts was Bunyan's novel *The Pilgrim's Progress,* published in 1678. The book is remarkable for the beauty and almost childish simplicity of its language, the whole permeated with the author's insight into nature and evident sense of humour. The many luridly illustrated and abbreviated editions that continually appeared during the two centuries which followed, and which appear in more muted tones even in the present day, had a particular appeal to children, and there could have been few nursery shelves that were unable to boast at least one drastically abbreviated, but excitingly illustrated, well read copy. It was a work which every literate child in the late seventeenth century, and more especially in the eighteenth century, knew, and most would have been able to recite the plot by heart.

Bunyan had not intended *The Pilgrim's Progress* for a juvenile audience, any more than Defoe with *Robinson Crusoe* or Swift with *Gulliver's Travels,* but children took to it with a surety of instinct that led each succeeding generation to endorse their choice. In essence it is an adventure story, a romance bristling with dangerous escapades and peopled with giants, ogres and fabulous monsters; a world through which the hero threads his way to the happiest of all endings. In various shortened forms it has been in the hands of children ever since, yet when its author purposely addressed himself to the young he failed to make an impact.

Lured by its attractive title, many young people must have opened its pages expectantly; but very few ploughed their way through the morass of pious platitudes and moral precepts in which the puritan writer clothed his finger-shaking chapters. *A Book for Boys and Girls; or, Country Rhimes for Children* first appeared in 1686, some two years before its author's death, and he stated his purpose in his introductory lines to his readers:

> The Title-page will show, if there thou look,
> Who are the proper Subjects of this Book.
> They'r Boys and Girls of all Sort and Degrees,
> From those of Age, to Children on the Knees.

The work was priced at sixpence, and appeared again in 1701 with an altered subtitle; and again in 1724, but this time with cuts to illustrate the text and with the title altered to read *Divine Emblems; or, Temporal Things Spiritualized,* its publishers having abandoned further attempts to pretend it had attractions for the young. The 1686 first edition is known by only two copies, but a facsimile was published in 1889, and again in 1928; these latter are the only quarry for present-day collectors and even these may prove elusive.

Bunyan made no pretence of having written the work for the amusement of children: he was determined to save their souls by whiffing brimstone through the nursery and rooting out every thoughtless pleasure indulged in by the young. He set out to show them:

> . . . how each fingle-fangle,
> On which they doting are, their souls entangle.

Unfortunately for the children of the day Bunyan was by no means the only inspired divine soul-saving in the playgrounds and school-rooms, nor was he by any means the most fearsome of the moralising oppressors of youthful spirits who stalked the pages of juvenile literature in the seventeenth and early eighteenth centuries. James Janeway (1636 ?-74) helped set the trend with his *A Token for Children: being an Exact Account of the Conversion, Holy and Exemplary Lives, and Joyful Deaths of Several Young Children,* issued in two separate parts in 1671/2, followed a few years later by his equally menacing *Token for Youth.* To stand any chance of winning a place in Heaven, he warned his young readers, they must live lives of religious ecstasy before dying joyfully with their Saviour's name on their lips. Satan and his legions from hell were always waiting to swoop on any child whose thoughts wandered to earthly pleasures, but to give them a chance of redemption the author set out rules to be strictly observed. Toys of any shape or form were forbidden; whipping tops in the playground only brought the Devil another recruit; secular enjoyment in any form was only for the hell-bent; pious children must strive to prevent their companions from enjoying amusements and have the courage to rebuke all frivolity, while constantly reminding themselves of their own inherent tendency to live sinful lives. 'I would fain do what I can possibly to keep thee from falling into everlasting Fire,' he informed them, and promised that God would reward good young Protestants with a joyful death at an age too early to have allowed them time for more than a modicum of sin.

Janeway's books provide a classic example of the morbid and gloating piety and preoccupation with death of a consumptive fanatic, his works appearing when his own health was undermined by the progressive disease which finally killed him 'in the 38 yeare of his age', and at a time when he must have known that he was doomed to an early, and let us hope, joyful death.

The Latin word *incunabula* can be translated in a literal sense into the old biblical term of 'swaddling-clothes'. In bibliographical terms *incunabula* has come to be accepted as denoting books printed during the infancy of the art, usually any book printed before the arbitrary but convenient date of 1500. The first book printed by Gutenberg's invention of movable metal type was the magnificent '42-line' *Bible,* which was finished in or around 1456. However, we have to wait for well over a hundred years before the appearance of the first book specially published for children and young people, so that the word *incunabula* (its singular form is *incunabulum*) must be allowed a more generous time-scale when applied to works specially produced for a juvenile audience. In *The Collector's Book of Children's Books,* 1971, I suggested the date 1700 as an arbitrary mark before which any book produced for the amusement or instruction of children in particular, or young people in general, could be accorded the distinction of belonging to a select collection of volumes known as juvenile *incunabula*. Most are undoubtedly rarer than their adult predecessors, the 'fifteeners' as the Victorians called them, with a familiarity bred of a frequent meeting with pre-1500 folios and quartos offered for sale in antiquarian booksellers' catalogues. Those days are long since passed, but even then books published for young people before 1700 were extremely rare, and such examples that have survived are treasured by a dwindling band of private collectors. The majority have long since found their ultimate resting place in the archives of museums and national libraries.

In addition to those already discussed, and leaving aside the numerous editions of *Aesop* as not being intended primarily for the amusement or instruction of children, we find hardly enough volumes to fill a sizable shelf. To include some of the borderline titles listed below I have allowed a little latitude in all but dates.

Historia di Lionbruno was a fairy-tale written in the Italian vernacular and published in Venice almost certainly before 1477 by Vindelinus de Spira. The little black-letter volume of some ninety-seven stanzas tells the story of Lionbruno, the youngest son of a fisherman. His father trades his son to the Devil in return for a good catch and some gold; but Lionbruno eventually marries a good fairy who gives him a magic ring. The book is reputed to contain the first mention of seven-league boots. The only copy I know of this extremely rare title is in the Toronto Public Library, Canada, and the details given above are from their catalogue of *The Osborne Collection of Early Children's Books,* 1975, volume 2. There is, of course, no title-page, nor apparently any dated colophon, so the title *History of Lionbruno* is purely conjectural but it exactly fits the tale.

The Mother's Blessing: or, The Godly counsell of a gentlewoman, not long deceased, left behind for her children, 1616, by Mrs Dorothy Leigh, was an exhortatory work whose popularity with parents kept it in print for over a hundred years, while *Milk for babes; or, A mothers catechism for her children,* 1646, by Robert Adam, did its best to expound 'the Chiefe principles of Christian religion'. Perhaps these were read by young people for instruction, but certainly not pleasure in either case.

In 1656 Francis Osborne's *Advice to a Son. Or, Directions for your better conduct, through the various and most important encounters of this life,* made its appearance and, perhaps because of its satirical references to 'Love and Marriage' in the second section, immediately went through five editions that same year. Meanwhile, *A Looking Glass for Children,* 1672, by Abraham Chear, was a pleasant-sounding title from a pleasant-sounding author, but any young hopeful who picked up the book in the expectation of a light-hearted discourse about nature and the world around him was due for a frowning disappointment.

> What a pity such a pretty maid
> As I should go to Hell

muses a little girl, as she gazes at her own reflection in that snare for the unwary — a looking-glass. The book purported to be a narrative 'of God's gracious dealings with some young children', practically all of whom were allowed to die more or less joyous deaths.

Benjamin Keach was next in the fray with his *War with the Devil: or, the Young Mans conflict with the Powers of Darkness,* 1673, in which he told his young readers that he had succeeded in discovering the 'corruption and vanity of youth; the horrible nature of sin, and the deplorable condition of fallen man'. He told his readers that the book was 'worthy the perusal of all, but chiefly intended for the instruction of the younger sort'. The work was still in print in the 1750s. He followed this with his *Instructions for Youth; or, The Child's and Youth's Delight,* 1694, a work which appears calculated to have the opposite effect, but was nevertheless published under a New York imprint the following year.

In America almost the whole of the intellectual activity of the New England colonies was in the hands of puritanical clergy, and all publishing was tinged to greater or lesser degree with religious bias. As A.S.W. Rosenbach pointed out in his introduction to *Early American Children's Books,* 1933, children were brought up on the principle that they were 'not born to live, but born to dye', and any books put into their hands had the definite purpose of instructing them how to die in a befitting manner. *The Rule of the New-Creature To be Practised every Day,* 1644, published anonymously in London, was reprinted in Cambridge, Massachusetts, by Samuel Green in 1668, and then in Boston in 1682, for Mary Avery, New England's first woman publisher. The unknown author tells his young readers that they must be sensible of their original corruption daily, and learn how it inclines them to Evil. 'Groan under it, and bewail under it,' he advises benevolently.

Not to be outdone, John Cotton (1584-1652) produced *Spiritual Milk for Boston Babes,* 1646. At one time vicar of Boston, Lincolnshire, he emigrated to America and, according to some authorities, the city of Boston, Massachusetts, had its name changed from Trimountain on Cotton's arrival there in 1633. First published in London, the work was later reprinted several times in Boston, marked as being for 'either England, and drawn out of the breasts of both Testaments for their Souls nourishment'. Cotton Mather (1663-1728), his grandson, published *A Family Well-Ordered. Or An Essay to render Parents and Children Happy in one another,* 1699, also published in Boston, and even a cursory reading of the work makes it easy to understand why children in those days (and still today) had an almost instinctive fear of the dark. For impious or undutiful children, darkness was used by Mather as a final horror. 'Children,' he warned, 'if by undutifulness to your parents, you incur the Curse of God, it won't be long before you go down into Obscure Darkness, even into Utter Darkness: God has reserved for you the Blackness of Darkness forever.' Cotton Mather's own personal delights and mortifications were never revealed.

Thomas White's *A little book for little children: wherein are set down several directions for little children, and several remarkable stories, (c.* 1670), was not much of a comfort to little minds with its exhortations against singing ballads or reading other than strictly religious works. But another work with the same start to its title, published at the turn of the century, contains an early printing of *A was an Archer, and shot at a Frog,* followed by the rest of the alphabet in rhyme. The version *A was an Apple-pie* was recited by children as early as 1650, although the first printed reference (and that a parody) did not appear until 1671 in John Eachard's pamphlet about the clergy. In America, this nursery rhyme was printed in Boston in 1761.

'Courtesy' books, and works of instruction on how young people ought to behave in polite society, were popular presents, at least with parents, for boys and girls in their late teens. Francis Hawkins' *Youth's Behaviour, or Decency in Conversation amongst Men,* 1636, was followed later by Robert Codrington's *Youth's Behaviour, or Decency in Conversation amongst Women,* 1664; re-issued in 1680 as *The Education of Young Ladies and Gentlewomen.* Such works were commonplace in the late seventeenth century. *A Cap of Gray Hairs, for a Green Head: or, The Fathers Counsel to his Son, An Apprentice in London,* 1671, by 'Caleb Trenchfield, Gent', was one of many similar titles in the field of manners and deportment. All were didactic and of serious intent, and most must have been studied with the same attention given to the grammars and schoolbooks of earlier years. Those wishing to improve their social etiquette were left in no doubt as to the basic rules of courtly conduct, as in this hint to newly-weds, taken from the last-named work:

> Women can with no patience endure to be mew'd up till Mid-night, while you are clubbing it at a Tavern; and you cannot think it a wonder if at such times they sport with your Servants at home . . . How long is Love like to last, where the blundering Husband comes home like a sous'd Hogshead, with a steam of Smoke and Drink, would almost choak a Greenlander who had been fed with Blubber.

The voice of matrimonial experience in the ear of a boy about to make his own way in the world.

A

CAP

OF

Gray Hairs

FOR A

GREEN HEAD:

OR, THE

FATHERS COUNSEL

TO HIS

SON,

An Apprentice in *LONDON*.

Containing wholesome Instructions for the Management of a Mans whole LIFE.

The Fifth Edition.

With Additions of Precepts adapted to each Chapter.

By *CALEB TRENCHFIELD,* Gent.

LONDON:
Printed for *A. Bettesworth,* at the *Red Lyon* on
London-Bridge. 1710.

*First published in 1671, this courtesy book by Caleb Trenchfield was in print almost
to the end of the eighteenth century. It was one of many titles in the field of manners and
deportment. 17 × 10.5cm*

While William Wycherley's restoration comedies were still playing to packed houses at the Drury Lane Theatre, poetry and verse written for the entertainment, much less the amusement, of young people was still almost unknown. The only rhymes composed especially for reciting and singing in the nursery, the true nursery rhymes as opposed to spoken poetry and verse, were the rhyming alphabets, the lullabies, and perhaps the little songs that sometimes accompany children's ritual games. The seventeenth century provided them with a few emblem books in which the morals to be learned were set out in verse, but these were intended for adults and were only commandeered by children because of the attraction of the pictures.

Artificial Versifying or; The School-Boy's Recreation, 1677, was, at first glance, a light-hearted treatise on schoolboy doggerel rhyme. But when the rest of the title-page is read the work turns out to be severely instructional in character and as didactic as any strait-laced schoolmaster of the day could have wished. John Pater, who published the work anonymously, exhibited a quaint wryness of style, or so the composition of the subtitle indicates: *A New Way to make Latin Verses. Whereby Any one of ordinary Capacity, that only knows the A.B.C. and can Count 9 (though he understands not one word of Latin, or what a Verse means) may be plainly taught, (and in as little time as this is Reading over,) how to make Hundreds of Hexameter Verses, which shall be True Latin, True Verse, and good Sense.*

The late-seventeenth-century child could have found few books really to entertain him, and even fewer that contained pictures likely to interest the young. An exception was the edition of *Aesop's Fables* produced by John Ogilby in 1651, 'paraphras'd in Verse.'; but, as was mentioned earlier, the *Aesop's* of the time were not primarily intended for children, and a glance at the majority's close-packed black-letter Latin texts reveals that it would have been a formidable academic exercise for any juvenile to attempt a translation of the fables for his own amusement. Children liked looking at the pictures and knew many of the fables, such as the legend of the fox and the grapes, from oral tradition since their nursery days. But they were starved of interesting books they could read for their own enjoyment, and only slowly did the printers and publishers come to realise the vast potential of the juvenile market. It was to be left to John Newbery in the 1740s to be the first to try to exploit this potential by revolutionising the methods and outworn ideas associated with what the adult world considered to be suitable books for the young. ' . . . 'tis hoped the whole will seem rather an Amusement than a Task,' he wrote in the preface of one of his earliest works for children, and that sentence contained the key by which the gates opened to an extent that was later to flood the juvenile world.

2

CHOICE SCRAPS FROM THE EIGHTEENTH CENTURY

During much of the first half of the eighteenth century young people could have found little to excite their imaginations in the books available to them, scarcely more in fact than their predecessors did in the literature of the century just past. As before, they had almost nothing to read except adult works they had adopted as their own, and if these were personal possessions it would nearly always be in the style of debased, chapbook versions of well known prose tales, or doggerel verses with a moral left dangling beneath.

One form of light relief came with the arrival of versions of the *Arabian Nights,* published in England early in the eighteenth century from a translation made from the French of Antoine Galland. He was the first to introduce them to Europe, having had them from the mouth of a Syrian friend who would himself have heard them from an Arabic professional story-teller. Stories from this collection were soon circulating in the form of chapbooks, as were the fairy tales of Charles Perrault, but these, and other fairy and folk tales, are discussed at length in a following chapter.

The colporteurs, chapmen and pedlars carried what literature there was for children in the form of small pamphlets, usually no more than sixteen pages in length, illustrated with crude little woodcuts and selling at anything from a halfpenny to as much as sixpence a copy. In them young people could read the Arthurian legends, and of the princes and ogres and the brave-hearted knights of the Middle Ages, the *Adventures of Robin Hood, St George and the Dragon, Tom Thumb, Valentine and Orson, Robin the Cobbler, The Knight and the Beggar Wench,* and literally hundreds of other titles. Often advertised as 'Small Merry Books', these chapbook tales were coarsely told, full of strange oaths and the groans of the fallen, the thud of cloth-yard arrows and the clang of swords, stories as violent and earthy as the hawkers who carried them in their packs.

With nothing better for their own amusement, children of towns and isolated villages where the chapmen called read or had read for

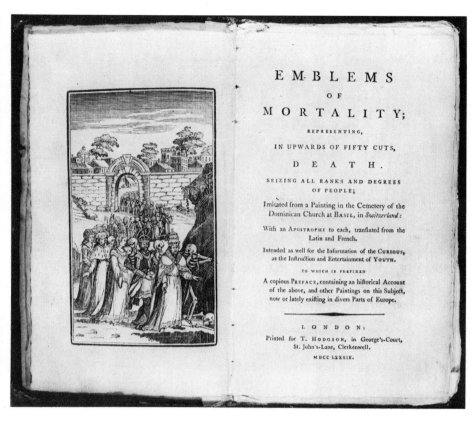

A rare edition of the 'Dance of Death', intended for the 'Instruction and Entertainment of Youth'. Published in 1789, it is one of the finest examples of the woodcut illustrations of Thomas Bewick. Most of the printed edition, and all of the wood blocks, were soon afterwards destroyed at a fire at Hodgson's in London. Size of title-page: 18 × 11cm

them all they could afford to buy, the older members of the family spelling out the adventures of *Guy of Warwick, Springheel Jack, Tom Hickathrift, Friar Bacon, The Chapter of Kings* or *Jane Shore*. In his pack would be bundles of ballad sheets, with such titles as *The Cripple of Cornwall, The Children in the Wood, Lord Thomas and Fair Eleanor, The Yarmouth Tragedy, Cat-Skin*, with scores of others to choose from, to be sung or recited around the winter's fire with the younger children listening in the doorway.

A delightful picture is drawn for us by Sir Richard Steele of children's reading tastes in *The Lucubrations of Isaac Bickerstaff Esq*, appearing in the ninety-fifth issue of *The Tatler* on 15 November 1709. He had been visiting an old school friend and his wife, lately come up to London from the country, when they are interrupted by the children:

31

On a sudden we were alarm'd with the Noise of a Drum, and immediately entered my little God-son to give me a Point of War. His Mother, between Laughing and Chiding, would have put him out of the Room; but I would not part with him so. I found, upon Conversation with him, Tho' he was a little noisy in his Mirth, that the Child had excellent Parts, and was a great Master of all the Learning on T'other Side Eight Years old. I perceived him a very great Historian in *Aesop's Fables;* but he frankly declared to me his Mind, That he did not delight in that Learning, because he did not believe they were true; for which Reason, I found he had very much turned his Studies for about a Twelvemonth past, into the Lives and Adventures of *Don Bellianis of Greece, Guy of Warwick,* the *Seven Champions,* and other Historians of that Age. I could not but observe the Satisfaction the Father took in the Forwardness of his Son; and that these Diversions might turn to some Profit, I found the Boy had made Remarks, which might be of Service to him during the Course of his whole Life. He could tell you the Mismanagements of *John Hickathrift,* find Fault with the passionate Temper in *Bevis of Southampton,* and love *St. George* for being the *Champion of England;* and by this means had his Thoughts insensibly moulded into the Notions of Discretion, Virtue, and Honour.

I was extolling his Accomplishments, when the Mother told me, That the little Girl who led me in this Morning, was in her Way a better Scholar than he. *Betty* (says she) deals chiefly in Fairies and Sprights; and sometimes in a Winter Night, will terrify the Maids with her Accounts, till they are afraid to go up to Bed.

There were a host of other heroes and heroines, both real and mythical, whose exploits were recounted to mute and attentive circles of round young eyes and ears. Long after the pedlar had stridden off to the next village, his pots and pans jangling and his string-tied bundles once more back in his canvas pack, they would continue to be told and retold until the young audience and young readers had all the plots by heart. Chapbooks may have been beneath the dignity of established booksellers, but the youth of the day devoured the stories they told like modern children their comics. They fought their playground battles dubbed with the names of the indigenous heroes from a long-past age of chivalry, all taken from the only form of cheerful literature they were ever likely to own.

It goes without saying that eighteenth-century and early-nineteenth-century chapbooks are now extremely difficult to find. Without the protection of any type of binding, and invariably printed on the cheapest and coarsest of untrimmed paper, most must have been read

THE
HISTORY
OF
TOM WHITE,
THE
POSTILLION.

Sold by S. HAZARD,
(PRINTER to the CHEAP REPOSITORY for Religious and Moral
Tracts,) at BATH;

By J. MARSHALL.
At the CHEAP REPOSITORIES, No. 17, Queen-street Cheapside,
and No. 4, Aldermary Church Yard; and R. WHITE, Piccadilly, LONDON; and by all Bookfellers, Newfmen, and
Hawkers, in Town and Country.

☞ Great allowance to Shopkeepers and Hawkers.

Price 1d. or 4s. 6d. per 100.   2s. 6d. for 50.   1s. 6d. for 25.

[Entered at Stationers Hall.]

A Samuel Hazard chapbook of 1792. 17 × 10cm

RHYMES

FOR THE

NURSERY.

LITTLE
JACK HORNER.

LONDON

THE
Woodman's
HUT,

A Turn-up Book, Price
SIXPENCE
COLOURED.

The following are Turn-up Books, just
published in the same Manner, Price
ONLY SIXPENCE COLOURED.

Blue Beard.

Miller and his Men.

Maid and the Magpie.

Bertram.

Woodman's Hut.

Philip and his Dog.

LONDON:
PUBLISHED BY G. MARTIN, No. 6,
Great St. Thomas Apostle, Bow-Lane, Cheapside.

THE
HISTORY
OF
Valentine and Orson.

Reader, you'll find this little Book contains
Enough to answer thy expense and pains;
And if with caution you will read it through,
'Twill both instruct, and delight thee too.

Printed for the Company of Walking
Stationers.

A
PRESENT
FOR A
LITTLE BOY.

LONDON:
PUBLISHED BY
DARTON, HARVEY, & DARTON,
No. 55, Gracechurch-Street.

[Price One Shilling.]

to death within weeks of their first existence. Their often grubby-fingered owners paid scant attention to the ephemeral nature of their little books, the sheet usually folded roughly into an eight-, sixteen- or even twenty-four-page gathering, the leaves unopened to await the knife or ruler-edge of their first readers. A crude woodcut illustration always headed the text, lurid and dramatic in content and invariably badly drawn and printed, and often with no apparent connection with any event in the story. Any block that was available was pressed into service, although the larger publishers such as John Pitts (1765–1844) and James Catnach (1792–1841) of the Seven Dials area of St Giles-in-the-Fields, London, usually managed to tie the two together. This was the district devoted largely to supplying the needs of The Company of Walking Stationers, as the colporteurs and chapmen liked to style themselves, with ballad sheets, tracts, legends, fairy stories, last-dying-speeches and a host of other unbound and unprotected printed ephemera, left there in bundles of a hundred at a time over the imprint of Pitts, Catnach, William Thackeray, William Dicey, Robert Powell, John Marshall and others.

Songs and nursery stories produced in book form specially for children appeared during the first half of the eighteenth century, though the titles published were very few and could have been available to only a minute percentage of the country's juvenile readership. This was an appreciable advance in format from that of the unbound chapbooks which were printed in their tens of thousands. The little books probably had runs of only a few hundred to a thousand copies, so despite the protection of their bindings few have survived to the present day. *Tommy Thumb's Pretty Song Book* was an early example. It was published in two miniature volumes about 1744, although this date, and even the existence of volume one, is only conjectural, for only an undated copy of volume two is known to have survived. It is now safe in the keeping of the British Library. Measuring only 7.5 × 4.5cm, and still almost certainly in its original binding of Dutch flowered paper over boards, the volume starts on page five with a warming to the ladybird:

> Lady Bird, Lady Bird,
> Fly away home,
> Your house is on fire,
> your children will burn

(Opposite) *Typical of the chapbooks and cheaply printed children's books issued before and during the first quarter of the nineteenth century.* Valentine and Orson *dates from 1785; the rest are all before 1820*

The present author remembers as a child setting the little insect on his fingertip before reciting a similar rhyme and then blowing gently on it. Whether it was his warm breath which the insect found irritating or not, it nearly always dutifully spread its wings and took to flight immediately the words were spoken, which was very gratifying.

Page six of the same tiny book gave the original version of *Little Robin Redbreast,* a version rapidly bowdlerised by removing the pole and erecting a rail:

> Little Robin red breast,
> Sitting on a pole,
> Niddle, Noddle, Went his head,
> And Poop went his Hole.

The pages are printed alternately in red and black, and most have a woodcut picture to accompany the rhyme. Here, for the first time, we find *London Bridge is broken down, Hickere, Dickere, Dock, There was a little man, and he had a little gun, Oranges and Lemons* and many more. If only the first volume could come to light!

The final page is headed 'Advertisement', having a picture of a little boy wearing a three-cornered hat and reading a book on which is written *The Child's Plaything,* 1744. Beneath the cut are the words:

> The Childs Plaything
> I recommend for Cheating
> Children into Learning
> Without any Beating.
>   N. Lovechild.
> Sold by M. Cooper.
> Price one Shilling.

'Nurse Lovechild' was a pseudonym often used at that time and later, and the 'M. Cooper' who published the book may possibly have been Mary Cooper, widow of Thomas Cooper, bookseller. She continued the business after her husband's death, until her own death in 1761. As far as the present writer is aware, no copy of the advertised *The Child's Plaything* has survived.

In the meantime, Thomas Boreman had commenced issuing his series of ten little (about 5.8 × 4.5cm) volumes he entitled *Gigantick Histories,* from his two addresses at the Guildhall, London, or the 'Boot and Crown' on Ludgate Hill. *The gigantick history of the two famous giants, and other curiosities in Guildhall, London,* 1740, was the first to appear, and he continued issuing similar titles until 1743, when he

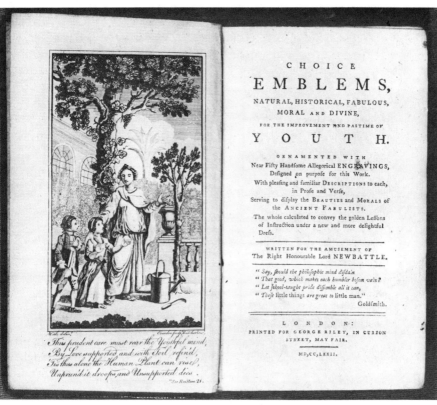

Written by John H. Wynne, the frontispiece of this first edition, dated 1772, is by Samuel Wale, librarian to the Royal Academy. 15.3 × 9cm

Thomas Boreman's little books, each about 5.8 × 4.5cm, were very popular in the 1740s, but few have survived to the present day

advertised whole sets of ten volumes. The preface to the first encouraged children to persuade their parents and relatives to buy the little book:

> Then, very soon I'll print another
> Which, for size, will be its brother.

Curiosities in the Tower of London appeared in two volumes in 1741, some verses in the first volume stating that:

> The author, doubtless, aims aright,
> Who joins instruction with delight,
> Tom Thumb shall now be thrown away,
> And Jack, who did the giants slay;
> Such ill concerted, artless lyes,
> Our British youth shall now despise.

But of course they did no such thing, although many will have learned from and liked such titles, and also his *A Description of three hundred animals, viz beasts, birds, fishes, serpents and insects . . .*, 1730, and *A description of a great variety of animals and vegetables, adapted to the use of all capacities, but more particularly for the entertainment of youth,* 1736. The *History of Cajanus, the Swedish Giant,* 1742, was another of his titles calculated to entertain.

One of the earliest collections of songs and poems specially written for children was published about 1742. *Little Master's Miscellany* also appeared under the Birmingham imprint of Thomas Warren, his second and third editions being dated 1748 and 1750 respectively (see illustration, page 111). It is undoubtedly one of the first, if not *the* first poetical and prose miscellany produced for young people, and as such is of considerable importance as representing another milestone in the history of the genre. Examples of books for the young dating from as early as the reign of George II always command high prices, if and when they come on the market, so that any fragment of any children's book of this period or earlier is well worth keeping. In too many cases titles have completely disappeared, their existence being known only through the advertisements contained in other works.

It was about this time that one of the most important names in the annals of children's books made his appearance. John Newbery (1713-67) was the first to realise what a vast market there must be for specially written and produced volumes to amuse and interest children, with an even greater potential sale if these could be displayed in a format that made them immediately attractive and desirable possessions in the eyes of young people.

Friends and business associates who knew him personally described him as continuously restless, a commercial dynamo whose nervous energy had him darting from one successful enterprise to another with hardly a pause for breath. 'A red-faced, good-natured little man who was always in a hurry,' to quote the words of Oliver Goldsmith in *The Vicar of Wakefield,* 1766. 'He had no sooner alighted, than he was in haste to be gone, for he was ever on business of the utmost importance.'

Newbery had started in business on his own account in Reading, Berkshire, in 1740, moving to London four years later to establish a thriving book publishing business. He soon branched out, widening his commercial activities to include several newspaper and magazine enterprises, and then began to manufacture patent medicines on a large scale, including the famous 'Dr James's Fever Powder'. Newbery is remembered today as the first bookseller (the term at that time synonymous with publisher) to appreciate the desire of young people for books of an amusing and entertaining nature, rather than the didactic and morally uplifting works they had been forced to yawn their way through in the past.

From his newly opened shop at the sign of the 'Bible and Sun', 65 St Paul's Churchyard, London, an address soon famous with the younger members of the reading public, he started to issue the tiny volumes of his *Juvenile Library.* Each was bound in brightly gilt, embossed and coloured paper over boards, designed in a flowered pattern. It came to be called 'Dutch paper', and the secret of its manufacture has long since been lost, but it certainly made an attractive binding and was quite unlike materials used in adult books. Newbery probably imported it in sheets from the Low Countries. He personally designed the format of most of his books and took a special interest in those meant for children, often writing the texts himself.

So it was that, in May 1744, the *Daily Post* carried his advertisement of the first of his books to amuse and interest children, *A Little Pretty Pocket Book, intended for the Instruction and Amusement of little Master Tommy and Pretty Miss Polly,* a work almost certainly entirely written by Newbery himself. The frontispiece showed a governess teaching a boy and girl, and the title expanded to read: *with an agreeable Letter to read from Jack the Giant Killer, as also a Ball and a Pincushion, the use of which will infallibly make Tommy a good Boy, and Polly a good Girl . . . Price of the Book alone, 6d., with a Ball or Pincushion, 8d.*

The work was published from his first London address at the 'Bible and Crown', near Devereaux Court, Temple Bar, from whence he moved the following year to St Paul's Churchyard, the firm remaining there until well into this present century. Most of *A Little Pretty Pocket Book,* whose earliest surviving edition seems to be the seventh, published in 1763, consisted of pictures of children playing games, with rhymes added that often seem to have little relevance to the cuts. Many of the blocks used Newbery had doubtless bought second-hand, for they have been identified as having illustrated various ABCs in the past.

A Little Pretty Pocket Book eventually became one of his longest-selling titles, revised and expanded versions still appearing in the lists of his business successors up to forty years later. In the text Newbery was at pains to include a 'letter on education humbly addressed to all Parents, Guardians, Governesses, &c., wherein rules are laid down for making their children strong, Healthy, Virtuous, wise and happy'.

It was not long before he had invented an exciting string of fictitious characters whose adventures children came to anticipate in much the same manner that the modern child follows the escapes and uncertainties of present-day heroes and heroines: Primrose Prettyface, Toby Ticklepitcher, Nurse Truelove, Woglog the Giant, Giles Gingerbread, Tommy Trip, Peter Puzzlewell and Robin Goodwill, the reputed secretary of the *Lilliputian Magazine*.

Part I of this earliest of all magazines for the amusement of children was advertised in the *Public Advertiser* early in March 1751 as being ready for sale, but no monthly parts have ever been traced, either bound up or loose, and it may not, in fact, have been issued as a periodical. It did, however, appear in volume form in 1752, with the text possibly by Christopher Smart, a poet remembered for the splendid imagery displayed in his *A Song to David*, 1763. The full title is worth quoting: *The Lilliputian Magazine; or the Young Gentleman and Lady's Golden Library, being an Attempt to mend the World, to render the Society of Man more Amiable, and to Establish the Plainness, Simplicity, Virtue and Wisdom of the Golden Age, so much celebrated by the Poets and Historians . . . Printed for the Society, and Published by T. Carnan at Mr Newbery's, the Bible and Sun, in St Paul's Church Yard.* There were twelve engravings for the children to look at, plus an engraved frontispiece and four little woodcuts, and the volume was once again issued in the brightly coloured Dutch paper binding favoured by Newbery. The Thomas Carnan mentioned was Newbery's stepson.

Some of the titles we know the firm published in its early years solely for the use of children were: *A Museum of young Gentlemen and Ladies; or, A Private Tutor for little Masters and Misses* (1750); *Nurse Truelove's Christmas-Box,* 1750, advertised as being given away free to those who visited Newbery's premises, 'only paying one penny for the binding'; *Nurse Truelove's New-Year Gift,* 1753, this time two pence being asked 'for the binding'; *A Pretty Book of Pictures for little Masters and Misses: or, Tommy Trip's history of beasts and birds; to which is prefix'd the History of little Tommy Trip himself, of his dog Jowler, and of Woglog the great Giant,*

40

1752; 'Tommy Trapwit'. Be Merry and Wise: or, The Cream of the Jests and the Marrow of Maxims for the conduct of Life, 1753; John-the-Giant-Killer. Food for the Mind: or, A New riddle book, compiled for the Use of the Great and the Little good Boys and Girls in England, Scotland, and Ireland, 1757; 'Abraham Aesop', Fables in Verse, 1757, the text possibly by John Oakman; A Pretty Play-Thing for Children of All Denominations, 1759; 'Tom Telescope'. The Newtonian System of Philosophy, adapted to the capacaties of young Gentlemen and Ladies, 1761; The Renowned History of Giles Gingerbread, a little Boy who lived upon Learning, 1765; The Easter Gift: or, The way to be very Good, a Book very much Wanted, 1765 (followed by similar titles for Whitsuntide and Valentine's Day); and The Fairing: or, Golden Toy for children, in which they can See all the Fun of the Fair, 1765.

Many of the titles listed above are known today only by editions published much later than the dates I have given, and the first-edition dates themselves are partly conjectural, having been taken from the newspapers and magazines in which Newbery advertised his wares.

Even his most famous title had its first edition date guessed at until just a few years ago, but happily a single (and possibly unique) example was discovered, which now has its final resting place in the British Library. The History of Little Goody Two-Shoes, otherwise called Mrs Margery Two-Shoes; with the means by which she acquired her Learning and Wisdom, 1765 (second edition, dated the following year, was enlarged), is now familiar to modern children only through the name of the heroine, but late in the eighteenth century it was a well loved best-seller amongst the young. Margery Meanwell, alias Goody Two-Shoes, was probably written by Oliver Goldsmith:

> Who from a State of Rags and Care,
> And having Shoes but half a Pair;
> Their Fortune and their Fame would fix,
> And gallop in a Coach and Six.

It was published during a period when Goldsmith was working almost full-time for Newbery, who he described as 'the philanthropic publisher of St Paul's Churchyard'. Goldsmith lived quite close, residing in Islington, and Newbery is known to have paid for his writer's board and lodging and much else besides. It was Charlotte Yonge (1823–1901), herself a prolific writer of tales for children, who first pointed out the similarity of style and content of parts of Goody Two-Shoes and Goldsmith's later The Deserted Village, 1770, but even today we cannot be absolutely sure of the author. If it was Goldsmith, his dry humour is evident in the reference he makes to his employer's patent medicine in the opening paragraph of the story:

Care and Discontent shortened the Days of Margery's father. He was forced from his Family, and seized with a violent fever in a place where Dr James's Powder was not to be had, and where he died miserably.

There were many famous figures who, in their later years, acknowledged their debt to John Newbery, and who looked back with nostalgia on the days when they first learned to decipher the stories and romances in the little books he published. Robert Southey, a future Poet Laureate, had a collection of twenty different titles, which he later described as 'delectable histories, in sixpenny books for children, splendidly bound in the flowered and gilt Dutch paper of former days . . . and [these] laid the foundation of a love of books which grew with the child's growth'. And as late as 1802, Charles Lamb wrote to S. T. Coleridge:

Goody Two Shoes is almost out of print. Mrs Barbauld's stuff has banished all the old classics of the nursery, and the shopman at Newbery's hardly deigned to reached them off an old exploded corner of a shelf, when Mary asked for them. Mrs Barbauld's and Mrs Trimmer's nonsense lay in piles about . . . Science has succeeded to poetry no less in the little walks of children than with men. Is there no possibility of averting this sore evil? Think what you would have been now, if instead of being fed with tales and old wives' fables in childhood, you have been crammed with geography and history!

Goldsmith is the acknowledged author of *An History of England, in a Series of Letters from a Nobleman to his Son*, 1764, published anonymously in two volumes under the Newbery imprint; and, of course, of *Dr Goldsmith's Roman History, Abridged by himself for the Use of Schools*, 1772. *An History of the Earth, and Animated Nature*, 1774, eight volumes (with 'tygers' roaming Canada!) was amongst the last of his works, going through edition after edition, many of which were embellished with series of hand-coloured plates of animals and birds. It remained a favourite with children until late into the second half of the nineteenth century.

For a moment we shall ignore the chronological sequence of this chapter to sketch the somewhat complicated Newbery history, so that the collector of early children's books may identify, with some degree of certainty, the various imprints and initials he will meet with in the period 1745–1810. We return to Berkshire, to what was then the village of Waltham St Lawrence. It was here, in 1713, that Newbery was born, the son of a farmer whose few acres were insufficient to supply the needs of a growing family. John left home before he was sixteen in order to find work in nearby Reading, where he eventually obtained a place in the office of William Carnan, the proprietor and editor of one of the earliest provincial newspapers, the *Reading Mercury*.

The only education Newbery had received was from his village school at Waltham, but his love of reading and of books in general, coupled with a diligent and untiring pursuit of knowledge in every sphere of the arts and sciences, soon made him an invaluable asset to Carnan and his publishing business. Seven years after he joined the firm his employer died, leaving most of his property to his one-time assistant, at that time twenty-four years of age. John, perhaps to consolidate his position still further, promptly proposed to his late employer's widow, some six years his senior. So 1740 saw him established as a book publisher and newspaper proprietor in Reading, but ambition prompted him to move to London in 1744 to the addresses given previously. The troubles of 1745 and the trade depression which followed almost bankrupted him; but after this precarious start the business began to thrive, to an extent that made him one of the most successful men in his profession. He was a friend of almost every leading literary figure of his day, a great many of whom contributed to his newspapers and periodicals. A final picture of John Newbery came from the pen of Samuel Johnson, who had gently satirised the mercurial little publisher in *The Idler*, dubbing him 'Jack Whirler'. Johnson told his readers:

When he enters a house, his first declaration is that he cannot sit down, and so short are his visits that he seldom appears to have come for any other reason but to say he must go.

Newbery died on 22 December 1767 at his house in St Paul's Churchyard, leaving his publishing business to his son, Francis, who promptly entered into what proved to be an uneasy partnership with his stepbrother Thomas Carnan (the son of John Newbery's wife by her first marriage). Carnan had been publishing on his own account since about 1750, sometimes as nominee of his stepfather, and proved himself an enterprising man of business and a pioneer in several aspects of the trade. It was Carnan who first offered his young readers a choice of binding styles. For an extra penny a copy they could have their books bound with vellum spines (frequently stained green) on which paper labels giving the title and volume number were pasted. The boards were usually covered with a glazed blue paper which contrasted vividly with the spines. Children were thus able to have their own library of volumes bound in a style that was tough enough to withstand years of handling (vellum is the longest-lasting of all binding materials), whereas the earlier paper-covered spines usually parted company with their boards after a few months' wear and tear. Young people were seldom able to persuade their parents to go to the expense of rebinding favourite texts, whereas the boarded books bought by adults for their own libraries were usually sent to the binder after their initial reading for clothing in calf or morocco in their owner's favourite style. Examples of Carnan's green spines and blue boards are now sought by collectors of publishers' binding styles, as well as those of early children's books, and therefore command high prices in any edition.

Francis Newbery (1743–1818) remained in partnership with Carnan until the latter's death in 1788, but spent much of his time managing the patent medicine side of the business. He married Mary, the sister of Robert Raikes, the founder of Sunday schools for children. Described by a contemporary as 'a scholar and a poet, and a lover of music', Francis Newbery must be distinguished from his cousin of the same name, with whom he and Carnan quarrelled violently. This Francis Newbery (the nephew of old John Newbery) had been intimately connected with his uncle's publishing business during the latter's lifetime, but seems to have been forced out of the firm soon after his uncle's death, setting up on his own account at 20 St Paul's Churchyard (the rival business was at 65). He died in 1780, and from that time onwards his widow, Elizabeth Newbery (1746–1821), carried on the business, employing as manager Abraham Badcock, who died in 1797, and then a craftsman whose name will always be associated with children's books, John Harris. He succeeded to the business on Elizabeth's retirement in 1802, having bought her share of the company.

I have gone into the details of the Newbery family tree at some length, as the name is one of the most important in the annals of children's books, and the confusion of imprints caused by rival businesses trading under similar names has led to many bibliographical errors in the past. Mysteries still remain, and it is still not clear which of the two Francis Newberys, son or nephew, was designated by his uncle or father to publish the first edition of *The Vicar of Wakefield*, 1766, which was printed in Salisbury, Wiltshire, in two small volumes. Benjamin Collins, bookseller and printer there, and part-purchaser of the title, produced the work for Newbery, Goldsmith having been paid £60 for it some four years earlier, the sum being just sufficient to save him from being sent to a debtor's prison.

The row between the two firms reached such a pitch of intensity after John Newbery's death that Thomas Carnan and Francis Newbery (the son) regularly had printed on their title-pages:

Printed for T. Carnan and F. Newbery, junior at No. 65, in St Paul's Church Yard, (but not for F. Newbery, at the Corner of Ludgate street, who has no share in the late Mr. John Newbery's Books for Children).

Where Newbery led, his rivals were quick to follow, and by the 1790s the trade in books for juveniles had increased to a degree that had at least six other publishing houses specialising in the production of children's books in England alone. Much the same situation existed in other parts of Europe and, to a lesser degree, in America, for traders there, with no language problem, imported the productions of the London booksellers.

On the Continent, a picture was drawn of the situation which had developed by L. F. Gedike, a German schoolmaster, quoted by Percy Muir in his *English Children's Books*, 1954. Gedike was an annual visitor to the Leipzig Book Fair during the second half of the eighteenth century, and wrote in 1787:

No other form of literary manufactory is so active as book-making for young people of all grades and classes. Every Leipzig Summer and Winter Fair throws up a countless number of books of this kind like a flooding tide. And see how young and old rush to buy — there are few pearls and little amber, but much mud, and, at the best, painted snail-shells. They take all kinds of names and forms: almanacks for children, newspapers for children, comedies for children, dramas for children, geography for children, history for children, physics for children, logic for children, catechisms for children, travels for children, morals for children, grammars for children, and reading books for children in all languages without number, poetry for children, sermons for children, letters for children, talks for children, and unlimited variations on the same theme, so that the literary doll-shops are crammed all the year round with them but especially at the time when loving parents and aunts and uncles may be attracted by the appositeness of the notice 'Christmas Gifts for good children'.

Although the Newberys and their business associates were the leading figures in the field of book production for children and young people during the second half of the eighteenth century, they had many rivals in trade and were never able to dominate the market. Even John Newbery, the innovator and pioneer, owed much to his predecessors and to those whose identities are remembered only by their names on the little volumes they sponsored and exhibited in the bow-fronted bull's-eyed glass windows of their bookshops. Newbery we know most about because, by a happy chance, his records and lists were preserved, and this enabled Charles Welsh, the historian of the firm, and a partner in the late nineteenth century, to write so factually in his biography of Newbery: *A Bookseller of the Last Century*, 1885.

A glance at the shelves of any collection of early children's books of the period would reveal a host of forgotten titles and publishers, all dating from the time when John Newbery was doubtless begrudging himself a full night's sleep above his warehouse within the shadow of the dome of St Paul's. The majority would be grammars and school-books, for which there was a constant and increasing demand; but stories and picture books for the amusement and entertainment of children were being published in rapidly expanding numbers as the century entered its final quarter.

As early as 1713, one of the masters of Charterhouse School, Andrew Tooke (1673–1732), a Fellow of the Royal Society, translated and published on behalf of his scholars *The Pantheon, representing the Fabulous Histories of the Heathen Gods*, a work which passed through over thirty editions before the end of the eighteenth century. Looking at a copy of the seventeenth edition, dated 1750, one finds a series of twenty-eight full-page copperplate engravings depicting the more dramatic adventures of the old-time gods and goddesses. As was often the case, the text is posed in a series of questions and answers, the child readers being expected to learn each answer by heart. Typical are the following:

Q. Who are those two handsome, beautiful, young
   Men that ride upon White Horses.
A. They are the Twin-Brothers, the sons of *Jupiter*
   and *Leda*; their Names are *Castor* and *Pollux*.
                    or
Q. What were the Seven Wonders of the World?
A. They are these that follow:
   The Colossus at Rhodes
   The Temple of Diana . . .

In the meantime, many versions of *The Life, and Strange Surprizing Adventures of Robinson Crusoe; of York, Mariner*, by Daniel Defoe, were making their appearance in abbreviated form 'embellished with cuts' for the use of children. Almost immediately, it established itself as a firm favourite with young people of all ages, and it has never ceased to be in print since its original publication in 1719. Two later volumes, entitled *Further Adventures of Robinson Crusoe*, 1719, and *Serious Reflections . . . of Robinson Crusoe*, 1720, followed from the same pen, and

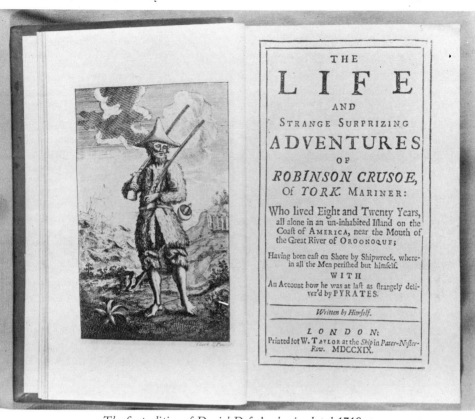

The first edition of Daniel Defoe's classic, dated 1719

eighteenth-century juvenile versions of the tales have been eagerly sought by collectors for many decades.

The first issue of the first edition of *Travels into Several Remote Regions of the World, by Lemuel Gulliver,* appeared on 28 October 1726, and over ten thousand copies of the work are said to have been sold in three weeks. The first edition was issued by Benjamin Motte, London, in two volumes. The author was, of course, Jonathan Swift, and all those who had been captivated by the realism and cliff-hanging expectancy of *Robinson Crusoe* were probably equally fascinated by the sustained logic of his satirical fable of Gulliver, a giant towering high above the Lilliputians, and a minikin crouching amongst the boat-sized feet of the Brobdingnagians. Drastically abbreviated, the tale made an instant appeal to the young. It was a believable story of fantastic travels in far-distant unexplored lands, on a par with the popularity of space exploration and science-fiction stories of modern youth. The first of the many shortened versions for children appears to have been an unauthorised edition of 1727, published by J. Stone and R. King. The later chapbook editions, usually containing only a condensed version of Lilliput, started to appear a few years later.

The themes of these two famous classics have served as plots for a multitude of romances and novels ever since, the majority not in any way intended for the juvenile market. Crusoe's desire to escape from humanity, plus the idealised notion of fending for oneself in a patch of territory safe from the rest of the world, whether it is a warm and benevolent desert island, a clearing in the jungle or a remote cottage in the country, lurks within most of us. Eighteenth-century children delighted in the story of *Robinson Crusoe*, and it was not long before other writers cashed in on the tale's popularity with versions of their own. The first to appear came from the pen of J. H. Campe (1746–1818), a German author, whose *Robinson Crusoe der Jüngere* was issued in two volumes in Hamburg in 1779. He translated it into French the same year and into English in 1781 as *Robinson the Younger*. However, the most

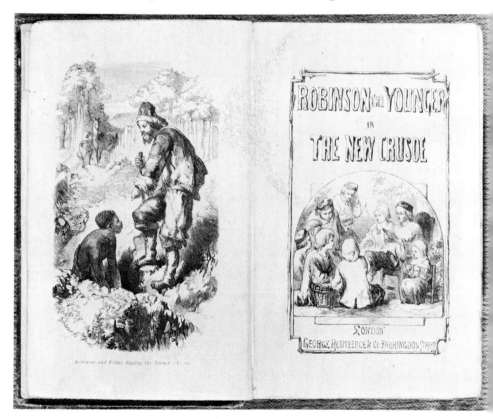

Written by J. H. Campe, this edition of Robinson the Younger *is dated 1856. The translation from the German was by R. Hick*

popular version of Campe's original text was published by John Stockdale in four volumes in 1788, complete with a set of thirty-two woodcut illustrations by John Bewick, the younger brother of the famous Thomas Bewick.

Mention can be made here of *The Swiss Family Robinson*, by Johann David Wyss (1743–1818), a Swiss army chaplain, who wrote the story for his four sons in 1792. The work remained in manuscript until the first edition of the German text appeared in book form in two parts in Zurich, during 1812–13, the author's son, Johann Rudolf Wyss (1781–1830) having prepared the work for the press. The first English edition came out as *The Family Robinson Crusoe: or, Journal of a father shipwrecked with his wife and children, on an uninhabited Island*, 1814, having been translated by William Godwin, whose daughter Mary the poet Shelley married. The little book contains four plates engraved by Springsguth after Henry Corbould. The first edition in French, *Le Robinson Suisse*, 1814, was published in Paris with twelve full-page plates. Any edition, in any language, published before 1830, is a prized collector's piece, as are the various versions of the book which inspired the story.

During the 1770s elaborate picture books for children were being produced on the Continent, with Leipzig and Frankfurt as the main centres for innovation and experiment. One of the most impressive of these was J. D. Basedow's *Elementarwerke für die Jugend und ihre Freunde*, printed and published in Berlin in April 1774 and, although certainly not intended for their amusement, undoubtedly gave the lucky owners hours of enjoyment. Johann Bernhard Basedow (1723–90) was one of the greatest German educational reformers, a strong admirer of Rousseau's *Emile*, 1762, and his own *Elementarwerke* was infused with his hero's theories. *Elementarwerke* was, in essence, an illustrated school-book; in the same year as its publication he was able to open his Philantropin school at Dessau in Germany, with the help of contributions from wealthy patrons and admirers.

To accompany the text a separate volume of copperplate engravings was produced in the form of an oblong quarto containing a hundred full-page illustrations after designs by Daniel Chodowiecki (1726–1801), F. Bang and C. H. Wolke. The first of these was immensely superior in artistic skills, often being referred to as the German Hogarth because of his truthful presentation of middle-class everyday life. The illustrations Basedow commissioned covered almost every aspect of human endeavour, and the few examples given here allow only a glimpse of the breadth and the scope of Basedow's monumental work. The quality of Chodowiecki's finely executed series of copperplate engravings make the work one of the cornerstones of any comprehen-

Daniel Chodowiecki, a Polish painter and engraver, depicted German middle-class life in a fashion unequalled by his contemporaries. This series of children's games is taken from Elementarwerke für die Jugend und ihre Freunde, *1774. Size of total engraved surface: 21.7 × 16.7cm*

sive collection of early children's books. About thirty different child-ren's games are depicted (including, for teenage youth, one of the earliest printed illustrations of a game of billiards in progress, on what appears to be a full-size table with cues, with probably a baize-covered marble bed fitted with cushions of flock and list). The book also contains one of the finest series of pictures depicting circus acts that we know of up to that time, as well as illustrations of the arts, trades and crafts, and all the domestic offices the artist had room to include. The eight full-page maps, some hand-coloured, were amongst the best to be included in a work intended for a juvenile readership up to that time.

In England, the year 1744 saw the publication of the two massive quarto volumes of Chesterfield's *Letters to his Son*, issued on behalf of Eugenia Stanhope from the originals in her possession. Philip Stanhope, fourth Earl of Chesterfield (1694–1773), compiled a volumi-nous correspondence to his son and godson. These private letters, instructional in character, warning the two young men of the perils they might well encounter, make fascinating reading even today. They were quickly discovered by the parents and guardians of the young people of the period and put into the hands of teenage youth as a work they should read, learn from and enjoy. Chesterfield's *Mis-cellaneous Works*, 1777, two volumes, with 'Volume the Third' (really a separate and much rarer work), 1778, are sometimes found bound as a matching set with his *Letters*. The latter well deserve a place in any collection of books devoted to children, giving an intimate glimpse of the dangers which a fond parent thought confronted those about to make their own way in the world of the mid-eighteenth century.

Another great admirer of Rousseau was Thomas Day (1748–89), the author of a classic example of eighteenth-century children's literature— *The History of Sandford and Merton*, published in three volumes and dated variously 1783, 1786 and 1789, having been issued over a period of six years. The first volume is much the rarest of the three to find in first-edition form, and complete sets dated as above are seldom encountered. It was originally Day's intention to write a short story for inclusion in Richard Lovell Edgeworth's *Practical Education: or, the History of Harry and Lucy*, a work which was being prepared for publication as early as 1780. But once having started to write the tale, he became so absorbed that his efforts resulted in a full-length book.

Written with almost no trace of humour (what humour there is seems an unconscious slip on the author's part), *Sandford and Merton* tells the story of a rich young prig, Tommy Merton, who is contrasted with the hard-working and too-good-to-be-true Harry Sandford, the moral being constantly drawn by the Revd Mr Barlow, their tutor. Day apparently wished to emphasise that, in theory, virtue eventually

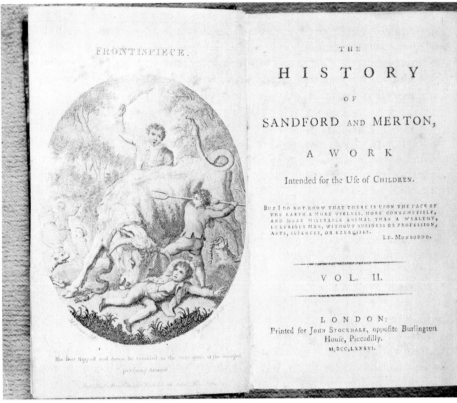

FRONTISPIECE.

THE

HISTORY

OF

SANDFORD AND MERTON,

A WORK

Intended for the Ufe of CHILDREN.

BUT I DO NOT KNOW THAT THERE IS UPON THE FACE OF
THE EARTH A MORE USELESS, MORE CONTEMPTIBLE,
AND MORE MISERABLE ANIMAL THAN A WEALTHY,
LUXURIOUS MAN, WITHOUT BUSINESS OR PROFESSION,
ARTS, SCIENCES, OR EXERCISES.   LD. MONBODDO.

VOL. II.

LONDON:
Printed for JOHN STOCKDALE, oppofite Burlington
Houfe, Piccadilly.
M,DCC,LXXXVI.

His foot flipped and down he tumbled in the very path of the enraged
ferocious Animal.

Written without the slightest trace of humour, The History of Sandford and
Merton, *by Thomas Day, was nevertheless one of the most widely read of the late-
eighteenth-century story books for children. Size of title-page 16.6 × 10cm*

proves superior to vice, and that man can be converted from his evil
ways by an appeal to his humanity and reason. The book quickly
became an eighteenth-century best-seller, and was translated into
several foreign languages. Needless to say, there were parodies, a
typical example being *The New History of Sandford and Merton,* 1872, by
F. C. Barnard, with illustrations in characteristic fashion by Linley
Sambourne. Day also published *The History of Little Jack, who was
suckled by a Goat,* 1788, and in 1798, *The Grateful Turk,* which appeared
as one of the series of *Moral Tales, by Esteemed Writers.* This latter story
had been extracted from the first volume of *Sandford and Merton.*

As early as 1749 we find Sarah Fielding (1710–68), sister of the
novelist Henry Fielding, publishing a book of stories for schoolgirls
and incorporating several fairy-tales in the text. *The Governess; or, little
Female Academy: being the history of Mrs Teachum and her nine Girls*
appeared as a second revised edition the same year, and was paid the

compliment, about three-quarters of a century later, of being revised and rewritten (omitting most of the fairy-tales) by that moral evangelist Mrs Martha Mary Sherwood. It was a work highly praised in its original form by the formidable Mrs Sarah Trimmer, who, writing in *The Guardian of Education* in June 1802, said:

> the desire is irresistable of speaking a word or two in praise of an old acquaintance which certainly deserves a better fate, than to be shoved aside to make way for Books of inferior merit now standing forth in proud array, blazing in scarlet, purple and gold, to tempt the curiosity of childhood and youth — too frequently to the injury of their principles and morals! Nothing of this sort is to be apprehended from the engaging history of Mrs. Teachum's nine young Ladies; we cannot but wish that this little volume . . . may be estimated according to its real merit, as long as the world lasts.

And not one word of criticism against the fairy-tales!

By the 1780s, an increasing number of women writers succeeded in finding publishers, and this despite (or, perhaps, because of!) the fact that many seemed to have the avowed intention of making a puritanical onslaught on the literate youth of the day. Anna Laetitia Barbauld (1743–1825) discusses in the preface to her *Hymns in Prose for Children*, 1781, the necessity of preventing children reading verse:

> It may well be doubted whether poetry ought to be lowered to the capacities of children, or whether they should rather not be kept from reading verse till they are able to relish good verse . . . The Author of these Hymns has therefore chosen to give them in prose. They are intended to be committed to memory, and recited.

Her *Lessons for Children, from two or three Years old*, was published in 1778 (parts two and three following in 1794 and 1803 respectively) because, as she put it, no book adapted to the comprehension of little children, printed in large type and easy to read, could as yet be found. The work was printed on good-quality paper, with generous margins and widely spaced lines, all of which were innovations in juvenile book production. Her *Hymns in Prose* was in similar format, and the works proved to be examples for many imitators who sought to copy the style. Mrs Barbauld was the sister of John Aikin (1747–1822), with whom she wrote *Evenings at Home; or, The Juvenile Budget Opened*, which appeared in a series of six volumes, 1792–6, as a companionable and homely collection of miscellaneous pieces 'designed to provide entertainment for Thirty Evenings'.

THE
TWO GARDENERS.

Sold by J. MARSHALL,
(PRINTER to the CHEAP REPOSITORY for Moral and Religious Tracts) No. 17, Queen-Street, Cheapside, and
No. 4, Aldermary Church-Yard, and R. WHITE, Piccadilly, London.
By S. HAZARD, at Bath; J. Elder, at Edinburgh, and
by all Bookfellers, Newfmen, and Hawkers, in Town
and Country.

Great Allowance will be made to Shopkeepers and Hawkers.

PRICE ONE HALFPENNY,

Or, 2s. 3d. per 100 — 1s. 3d. for 50. — 9d. for 25.

A cheaper Edition for Hawkers.

[*Entered at Stationers Hall.*]

A children's tract of 1796, with the text in verse by Miss Hannah More. 19.5 × 12.8cm

Hannah More (1745–1833) was next in the literary pulpit with her *Sacred Dramas: Chiefly intended for Young Persons*, 1782, brought out by the well known publisher Thomas Cadell. In it, the authoress related in verse the histories of Moses, David and Goliath, Daniel and other assorted saints and sinners. 'A laudable and useful work', as Mrs Trimmer described it, with none of the 'perverted Scripture history' produced by Madame de Genlis in her own version of *Sacred Dramas*. Comtesse de Stéphanie de Genlis (1746–1830) had published her *Théâtre de l'education* in France in 1779–80; followed by *Les veillées du Chateau*, 1784; the two being published in English translation as *Theatre of Education*, 1781, in a set of four volumes; and *Tales of the Castle*, 1785 (five volumes) under London imprints. The Comtesse had been governess to Louis-Philippe, and was credited with being considerably in advance of her time as an educationalist. She was one of the first to illustrate her lessons by means of lantern slides and, an unheard-of thing, often taking her pupils on nature walks to teach them botany. She was introduced to the British public by the Thomas Cadell mentioned above who was himself responsible for the publication of scores of children's books in the period 1780–93, eventually being succeeded by his son, also Thomas Cadell (1773–1836), founder of the famous publishing firm of Cadell & Davis, whose imprint appears on countless works for juveniles.

Lady Eleanor Fenn (1743–1813) wrote most of her books for children under a bewildering set of pseudonyms: 'Solomon Lovechild', 'Mrs Teachwell' and 'Mrs Lovechild' are some which can be associated with her with certainty. She was the wife of the antiquary Sir John Fenn, the first editor of the Paston letters, and fully shared his literary zeal, writing over a score of books for children, although she had none of her own. 'May God preserve you blameless amidst a crooked and perverse generation,' she implored on behalf of her young readers in the dedicatory letter prefacing her *School Dialogues, for Boys* (1783), two volumes. In her preface to *The Rational Dame; or, Hints towards supplying Prattle for Children* (1784), she remarks: 'Curiosity is in children an *appetite* craving perpetually for food; but alas! how often are its cravings disregarded; or, still worse, appeased with trash!' and later: 'In making amusement the vehicle of instruction, consists the grand secret of early education.' *The Rational Dame* is one of the earliest natural history books for children, its series of ten full-page copperplate engravings covering almost every aspect of animal, insect and reptile life likely to be met with on a nature walk, although, strangely, she ignores the birds. Amongst her other works were *School Occurrences: Supposed to have arisen among a set of Young Ladies*, (1782); and *Sketches of Little Girls: The good-natured little girl. The Thoughtless, the Vain, the*

Orderly, the Slovenly, the Forward, the Snappish, the Persevering, the Modest, and, the Awkward little Girl. By Solomon Lovechild (1783); though one of her most successful titles was the attractively named *Cobwebs to Catch Flies* (1783), a book specially written for children, volume one being for those from three to five years, and volume two for those between five and eight.

Dorothy Kilner (1755–1836) was another prolific writer of the period, and can usually be identified by her use of the initials 'M.P.', taken from Maryland Point, the village in Essex in which she lived at one time. Later, at the request of her publisher, she adopted the pseudonym 'Mary Pelham', using the same initials. The illustration below shows one of her most successful titles, *The Life and Perambulation of a Mouse* (1783), volume two appearing the following year with exactly the same title. These two little books of 108 and 100 pages respectively

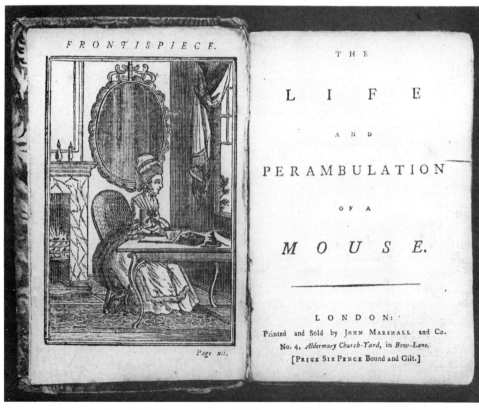

Written by Dorothy Kilner, this first edition was published, undated, in 1783, and is still in its original binding of boards covered with brightly coloured Dutch flowered paper. Size of title-page: 12 × 8cm

were advertised by their publisher John Marshall at one shilling the set, bound in Dutch flowered boards. At the end of volume two there appears a list of fifteen titles by the same author, plus a further five by her sister-in-law mentioned below.

In *The Life and Perambulation of a Mouse*, Dorothy Kilner relates the story of a country house party for children and young people which took place, so she says, at Meadow Hall:

> After the more serious employment of reading each morning was concluded, we danced, we sung, we played blind-man's buff, battledoor and shuttlecock, and many other games equally diverting and innocent. And when we tired of them, we drew our seats round the fire, whilst each in turn told some merry story to divert the company.

Their young hostess set each child the task of relating to the assembled company the story of his or her life, two days being allowed for writing down the facts and incidents of their respective careers. But the young lady who narrates the tale is unable to write a single word of her memoirs:

> The adventures of my life (though deeply interesting to myself) will be insipid and unentertaining to others, especially to my young hearers: I cannot therefore attempt it: nor will I disgrace myself by endeavouring to transcribe my own stupid life. 'Then write mine, which may be more diverting,' said a little squeaking voice that sounded as if close to me.'

And there, of course, sat Nimble, the mouse, who promptly proceeds to tell his own life-story, and that of his three brothers, Longtail, Softdown and Brighteyes. Dorothy Kilner was one of the first authors of children's books to employ the literary device of having an animal, bird or even an inanimate object act as narrator of the tale, and there have been a host of imitators ever since. She herself used the method more than once, notably in *The Rational Brutes: or, Talking Animals*, 1799, published by Vernon & Hood.

Her sister-in-law, who was Mary Ann Maze (1753-1831) until she married Dorothy's brother in 1774, used the same device in *The Adventures of a Pincushion, designed chiefly for the use of Young Ladies* (1780), published in two volumes; and in *Memoirs of a Peg-Top: an entertaining History* (1782). Other titles by her were *Jemima Placid; or, The Advantage of good nature* (1785), *Familiar Dialogues for the Instruction and Amusement of Children four and five years old* (1782) and *William Sedley; or, The evil day deferred* (1783). Her works were issued by John Marshall (1755?–1828), a rival-in-trade of Elizabeth Newbery, who had been quick to copy the Newbery binding style for his children's books, having apparently procured a close imitation of their flowered and gilt Dutch paper. He dated few, if any, of his juvenile titles at this period of his career, thus causing generations of bibliographers a deal of exasperation and many hours of sometimes fruitless research. Most can, however, be dated with a degree of accuracy by a time-consuming process of elimination. By cataloguing the many dated inscriptions made by the earliest owners, the comparison of dated advertisements in newspapers and periodicals and from the lists often found in the books themselves, and by comparing the dates (hopefully!) found in dedications and prefaces, one can be reasonably certain that a particular title must have been published before or after a given date. Once the first few are isolated the rest fall more easily into place, and this is a task with the works of certain publishers and authors the seasoned collector is well aware of. *Anecdotes of a Boarding-School; or, an Antidote to the Vices of those Useful Seminaries* (*c.*1781) was an early work of Dorothy Kilner's which appeared in two volumes; while *A Course of Lectures for Sunday Evenings*, which appeared in a series of four volumes during the period 1783–90, was written by her sister-in-law, who commonly used the pseudonym 'S.S.' taken from her address in Spital Square, Spitalfields, London, and more rarely 'Sarah Slinn'.

Little is known of the life of that enterprising young lady Miss Lucy Peacock, who, after writing several books at her private address in Lambeth, set herself up in business as a bookseller in Oxford Street, London. Her first work, written when she was still in her early teens, is notable for the fact that she stood in attendance at Mr A. Perfetti's shop at 91 Wimpole Street, and personally signed all the copies sold there. *The Adventures of the Six Princesses of Babylon, in their Travels to the Temple of Virtue*, 1785 (second edition, also usually bearing the signature of the authoress, dated 1786), is unusual in a book presumably meant for young people in that it was issued in quarto size (approximately 25 × 19cm in uncut copies) as well as having a most impressive sixteen-page list of aristocratic and wealthy-sounding subscribers amounting in all to over 1,250 names. The work is dedicated, by gracious permission, to HRH the Princess Mary, and seems to have been something of a literary best-seller in its day, despite the fact that it sold for 3s 6d (17½p) a copy. The usual price for children's books of the period issued by E. Newbery, John Marshall and other publishers was 6d (2½p) a copy, 'bound and gilt'. Lucy Peacock's allegorical romance of the six princesses is modelled, as the young authoress freely admitted in her preface, on Edmund Spenser's *The Faerie Queene*.

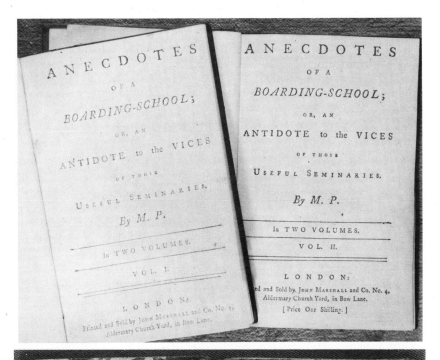

(Top) *The initials 'M.P.' stand for 'Mary Pelham', itself a pseudonym for the writer Dorothy Kilner, and this two-volume work was issued about 1781. Size of title-page: 15 × 9.5cm.* (Above) *One of the frightening illustrations in the first edition of* The Holyday Present *(1783), by Dorothy Kilner. The running title was changed to 'The Holiday Present'. 11.8 × 7.8cm*

Amongst her other works for children were *The Rambles of Fancy*, 1786, two volumes, *The Knight of the Rose*, 1793, *The Visit for a Week; or, Hints for the Improvement of Time*, 1794, and *The Little Emigrant*, 1799. She also translated from the French F. G. Ducray-Dumenil's *Lolotte et Fanfan*, 1788, as *Ambrose and Eleanor; or, The Adventures of two Children deserted on an uninhabited Island* in 1796, shortening and abridging it to make it more suitable for children. She is also remembered as the editor of one of the first periodicals ever produced for children, *The Juvenile Magazine*, which appeared in a series of twelve monthly parts during 1788, and was later published in book form as a two-volume work. Both Dorothy and Mary Kilner were contributors.

Literature for the instruction and amusement of children, with the emphasis very much on the former, was dominated for a period of almost twenty years by a solid phalanx of didactic females. This heavy brigade of formidable matrons seemed determined to root out any tendency on the part of the young to read solely for their own entertainment and amusement, especially such frivolous fiction as fairy-tales and other pernicious rubbish. The superiority of virtue over vice, 'however dignified by birth or fortune', was their reiterated theme; and vice was usually designated by these belligerent moralists as the type of conduct we should today class merely as youthful naughtiness or boisterous high spirits.

In the vanguard of this 'Monstrous Regiment of Women', as the late Percy Muir dubbed them, no doubt with a backward glance over his shoulder at John Knox, were several named above, reinforced by their contemporaries listed below. Lady Sarah Pennington contributed *An Unfortunate Mother's advice to her absent Daughters; in a Letter to Miss Pennington*, 1761, which passed through three editions within a twelve-month. In it she condemned all novels, retracting slightly in a later edition by making one exception in favour of *The Vicar of Wakefield*. Mrs Elizabeth Pinchard was one of Elizabeth Newbery's authors, and through her in 1791 she published *The Blind Child, or Anecdotes of the Wyndham Family*, stating in her preface:

> My principal aim, it will be seen, is to repress that excessive softness of heart, which too frequently involves its possessor in a train of evils, and which is by no means true *sensibility*, that exquisite gift of heaven which no one can esteem more highly than myself, though its abuse every day serves more and more to convince me, it can never be sufficiently discouraged and contemned.

Her *Dramatic Dialogues, for the use of Young Persons*, 1792, appeared in two volumes, and two years later Elizabeth Newbery issued *The Two*

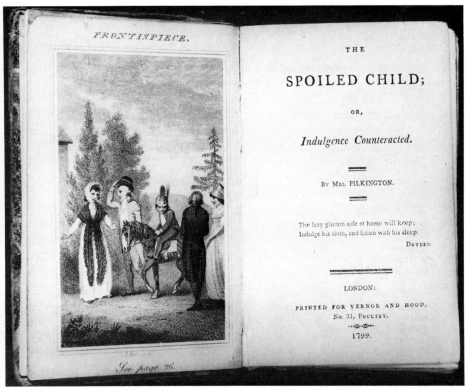

FRONTISPIECE.

THE

SPOILED CHILD;

OR,

Indulgence Counteracted.

By Mrs. PILKINGTON.

The lazy glutton safe at home will keep;
Indulge his sloth, and fatten with his sleep.

DRYDEN.

LONDON:

PRINTED FOR VERNOR AND HOOD,
No. 31, POULTRY.
1799.

See page 26.

Mrs Mary Pilkington wrote over sixty books for children, and, despite the forbidding title, this particular tale is quick-moving and full of unconscious humour. 13.3 × 8.8cm

Cousins, a Moral Story, in which she had the narrator of the tale strongly condemning the growing practice of teaching servants to read and write, 'especially women servants'.

Mrs Mary Pilkington (1766–1839), the wife of a naval surgeon, wrote over sixty books for children, with *Tales of the Hermitage; Written for the Instruction and Amusement of the Rising Generation*, 1798, being amongst the most successful. *Obedience Rewarded and Prejudice Conquered: or, The History of Mortimer Lascells*, 1797, *Edward Barnard: or, Merit Exalted*, 1797, *Tales of the Cottage: or, Stories Moral and Amusing, for Young Persons*, 1798, *The Spoiled Child; or, Indulgence Counteracted*, 1799, *The Asiatic Princess*, 1800 (2 vols), *Marvellous Adventure; or, The Vicissitudes of a Cat*, 1802, *Violet Vale*, 1806, and *The disgraceful effects of Falsehood, and the Fruits of early Indulgence*, 1807, were amongst her other titles, nearly all of which were published by Vernon & Hood, 31 Poultry, London.

Priscilla Wakefield (1751–1832) started her career with *Mental Improvements: or, The Beauties and Wonders of Nature and Art*, 1794

(2 vols); soon turning her attention to nature and travel books for the young, in which she came to specialise. *Juvenile Anecdotes, founded on Facts*, appeared as a single volume in 1795, the second volume to complete the set not being issued until 1798, in which the author has the mother of the children in the tale carefully examine their story books before taking her scissors and 'freely cutting out as many leaves as contained passages likely to give them false ideas or to corrupt their innocence'. All the best bits excised! *An introduction to Botany, in a Series of familiar Letters*, 1796, and *The Juvenile Travellers*, 1801, were followed by *A Family Tour through the British Empire*, 1804, *Excursions in North America*, 1806, *Perambulations in London and its Environs*, 1809, *The Traveller in Africa*, 1814, and *The Traveller in Asia*, 1817.

Elizabeth Helme, who died in 1806, had written in much the same vein, and her *Instructive Rambles in London, and the adjacent villages*, 1798 (2 vols), was followed by a sequel entitled *Instructive Rambles extended in London, and the adjacent villages*, 1800 (2 vols).

The century drew to its close with the appearance of *The Parent's Assistant; or, Stories for Children*, 1795 (3 vols), published anonymously. This first edition of the first work for children by Maria Edgeworth (1767–1849) is of the utmost rarity, and may not have survived, while copies of the second edition of 1796, also published by J. Johnson, London, as Parts I & II in three volumes, is also so rare as to be known by only single-figure examples. This famous collection of short stories for young people was written to exemplify the principles expounded in *Practical Education*, 1798 (2 vols), written in conjunction with her father, Richard Lovell Edgeworth. *The Parent's Assistant* contains the stories of *The Little Dog Trusty, The Orange Man, Tarlton, The False Key, The Purple Jar, The Bracelets, The Birthday Present* and several others, including *The Barring-out*, not appearing until the second enlarged edition. The work was re-issued in six volumes in 1800, and again in 1804, with Maria Edgeworth's name on the title-pages. To these editions she added eight new stories and omitted three, transferring these to *Early Lessons*, which was first issued under the title *Harry and Lucy*, 1801. Most of the stories in this latter work were by her father and Mrs Honora Edgeworth.

The critical works of the redoubtable Mrs Sarah Trimmer (1741–1810) are discussed in a later chapter; but no treatise on eighteenth-century books written for children can ignore her most famous work, a book that has continued in print almost to the present day. *Fabulous Histories. Designed for the Instruction of children, respecting their treatment of animals*, 1786 (second edition the same year), was a landmark in the annals of children's literature. Under its later title, *The History of the Robins*, numerous generations of children have delighted in the adventures and hair's-breadth escapes of the daring little birds Robin,

FABULOUS

HISTORIES.

DESIGNED FOR THE

INSTRUCTION

OF

CHILDREN,

RESPECTING THEIR

TREATMENT OF ANIMALS.

By Mrs. TRIMMER.

SECOND EDITION.

LONDON.

PRINTED FOR T. LONGMAN, AND G. G. J.
AND J. ROBINSON, PATER-NOSTER-
ROW; AND J. JOHNSON, ST.
PAUL'S CHURCH-YARD.

M DCC LXXXVI.

The first edition of this famous work appeared the same year as the second (shown here), and Mrs Sarah Trimmer later changed the title to read The History of the Robins. *13.3 × 8.8cm*

*Eat there, said Claribell to him, it is all that
I have left to give you. You are the Father
of this Child, and if you do not devour him
Famine and Misery shortly will.*

THE

CHILDREN's FRIEND.

BEING

A SELECTION

FROM THE

WORKS OF M. BERQUIN.

CITO NEQUITIA SUBREPIT; VIRTUS DIFFICILIS INVENTU EST;
RECTOREM DUCEMQUE DESIDERAT. ETIAM SINE MAGISTRO
VITIA DISCUNTUR.
SEN.

A NEW EDITION.

LONDON:
PRINTED FOR A. MILLAR, W. LAW, AND R. CATER,
AND WILSON, SPENCE, AND MAWMAN, YORK.

M,DCC,XCVI.

THE

HISTORY

OF

TOMMY PLAYLOVE

AND

JACKY LOVEBOOK.

WHEREIN IS SHEWN

THE SUPERIORITY OF VIRTUE OVER VICE,

HOWEVER DIGNIFIED BY

BIRTH OR FORTUNE.

WRITTEN BY A FRIEND.

Adorned with Cuts.

LONDON:
PRINTED FOR E. NEWBERY, THE CORNER
OF ST. PAUL'S CHURCH-YARD.

M,DCC,LXXXVIII.

Dicky, Flapsy and Pecksy, whose names she seems to have culled from the works of John Newbery. Between writing her many religious tracts and educational works, Mrs Trimmer found time to have no less than twelve children of her own. She was a tireless advocate of the necessity of establishing Sunday schools throughout Britain.

Arnaud Berquin (1747–91) published his *L'Ami des Enfans* in Paris in a series of twenty-four monthly parts beginning on 1 January 1782. The French Academy later awarded him 'a Prize for usefulness', and his work was acclaimed as the finest book for children of the period. As *The Children's Friend* it quickly established itself as a firm favourite with the youth of Britain, appearing in five volumes during 1783–4, and thereafter in a variety of formats and selections. Another popular translation in the latter half of the eighteenth century (other than fairy stories, discussed separately) was *Paul et Virginie*, 1788, by Jacques Henri Bernardin de Saint-Pierre, issued in England as *Paul and Mary, an Indian Story*, 1789, in two volumes. A later translation by Helen Maria Williams was entitled *Paul and Virginia*, 1795, and it is under this heading that the work is usually found.

One final title known to every child and annexed by the youth of the day within a few months of its first appearance was *The Diverting History of John Gilpin*, by William Cowper, first printed in *The Public Advertiser*, 14 November 1782, and later in book form as the final item in *The Task, A Poem in Six Books*, 1785, issued as a companion volume to his *Poems*, 1782. Children of the late eighteenth century learned many of the sixty-three verses by heart, and the fact that prose, illustrated, abridged, parodied, chapbook, movable and innumerable imitative versions have since appeared aimed at the juvenile market gives it a place in this present work. The final stanza has been shouted in chorus in schools and nurseries through the length and breadth of the English-speaking world for close on two hundred years:

> Now let us sing, long live the king,
> And Gilpin long live he,
> And when he next doth ride abroad,
> May I be there to see!

(Opposite above) *First published in Paris in 1782, under the title* L'ami des Enfans, *this translation by Lucas Williams contains thirty-three of Arnaud Berquin's stories and first appeared in 1788. 17 × 10cm.* (Below) *A story by Stephen Jones (1763-1827), first published in 1783, the copy shown being the second edition of 1788. 11 × 7.2cm*

3

FAIRY- AND FOLK-TALES

Children have never ceased to enjoy hearing and reading fairy-tales since long before the first collection of them appeared in print early in the seventeenth century. As such, they became the first literature for children unmoralised and unashamed, naked of the usual stifling swaddle of didacticism and religious instruction, and therefore immediately attacked and condemned by puritanical critics. The battle between the strait-laced juvenile tract and the fairy stories young people delighted to read extended until well into the 1830s; but by the time Victoria came to the throne they had been grudgingly accepted by most parents, guardians and governesses of even the most strictly regulated children. Well-thumbed collections of the best-known tales were to be found on nursery shelves throughout the land.

Stories about fairies and supernatural beings exist in the mythology and folklore of all nations, in the majority of cases a continuous prose narrative centring around the fortunes and misfortunes of a hero or heroine who finally wins through to a happy-ever-after ending. The first collection to appear in print was fifty stories, all of peasant origin with a long oral tradition, set down as he heard them in the Neopolitan dialect by the Italian poet and short-story writer Giovanni Battista Basile (known also as Giambattista Basile, and under the anagrammatic pseudonym of Gian Alesio Abbattutis) (1575–1632). They were published in Naples in five volumes of ten stories each as *Lo Cunto de li Cunti*, during the period 1634–36, and as a single-volume work in 1637, from the manuscript left by Basile after his death. The Italian edition of 1674 was published as *Il Pentamerone*, the name by which the collection is now known, translated as *The Story of Stories*. It first appeared in English as a direct translation from the Neapolitan by John Edward Taylor, who had been helped in his task by Gabriele Rossetti, the Italian poet and father of Dante Gabriel, Christina and William Michael Rossetti. Gabriele was at that time Professor of Italian at King's College, London. Taylor's translation, dated 1848, contained a delightful series of copperplate engravings after illustrations by George Cruikshank, some of which were considered to be equal to the best of this artist's work.

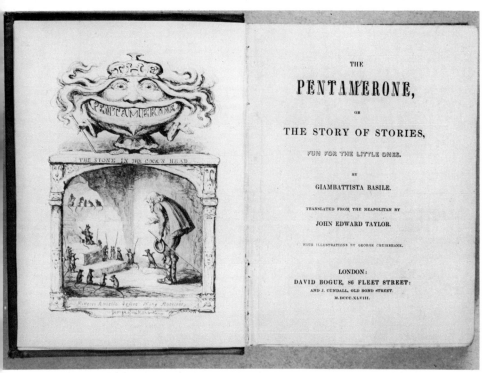

The first English edition, dated 1848, of the earliest collection of European folk-tales. It was illustrated by George Cruikshank

In his preface to *The Pentamerone* Taylor admitted that he had given only thirty of the original fifty stories:

> The gross license in which Basile allowed his humour to indulge is wholly inadmissable at the present day in a work intended for the general reader . . . the moral sense of our age is happily too refined and elevated to tolerate indelicacy.

Nevertheless, his translation was robust and earthy enough to bring criticism in its day, with tales such as *Peruonto*, in which the mother of the hero describes her son as not being worth 'a dog's mess', and in which princesses are made magically pregnant by peasant boys, and phrases such as 'Better to have a pig for a husband than an emperor for a lover' appear. These, and much more, made other nineteenth-century publishers pause, and it was not until 1893 that T. Fisher Unwin issued a new and revised edition of the classic in his 'Children's Library' series, bound in the usual blue pinafore cloth. It was edited by Helen Zimmern and contained only eighteen stories, but even in these, as she stated

giants, who could not defend themselves; and, drawing his own sword, he slew them both, and so delivered himself from their intended cruelty. Then taking the bunch of keys, he entered the castle, where he found three ladies tied up by the hair of their heads, and almost starved to death, who told Jack that their husbands had been slain by the giant, and who had been kept many days without food, in order to force

The more horrific the fairy story the better children seemed to like it, and this late-eighteenth-century chapbook version left little to the imagination

in her preface, she had been forced into 'omitting offensive words and expressions and adapting the stories to juvenile ears'. This, then, was the second English version of Basile's original collection issued for children, twice censored and doubly emasculated.

The Pentamerone is a key book in the annals of folklore and a milestone in the history of fairy stories, the first English edition of 1848 being one of the most difficult children's books of the nineteenth century to find in acceptable condition in its original cloth binding, blocked pictorially in gold. It is a heavy, almost square octavo, of some 404

pages, plus the bulk of six full-page engravings printed on thick paper·
It it were dropped, or handled and read frequently, it would be enough
to strain the hinges of the cloth binding and eventually to spring the
text. After that it is not long before the interior of the book parts
company with its covers.

The collection in its original form is considered a priceless asset to
folklorists, retaining as it does all the freshness of the oral tales as
Basile heard them from the lips of Italian and Cretan peasants. The
best of the editions in the original format is that by G. Croce, *Giambattista Basile ed il Cunto de li Cunti*, 1891, of which English translations
exist. Thomas Keighley (1789–1872) wrote *The Fairy Mythology*, 1828
(2 vols), and *Tales and Popular Fictions: their Resemblance and Trans-
mission*, 1834, both of which contain extracts from Basile's collection
of tales, but these works were intended for literary historians rather
than children. *Stories from the Pentamerone*, 1911, edited by Edward F.
Strange, and with thirty-two coloured plates by Warwick Goble
mounted on art paper, is a handsome volume for the specialist collector
of de luxe editions.

Comtesse Marie Catherine d'Aulnoy (1650–1705) was a French
authoress who wrote several romances now all but forgotten, but her
collection of fairy-tales has endured, with stories which are still
favourites such as *The Blue Bird* and *The Yellow Dwarf*. First issued in 1698,
Contes des fées was followed immediately by *Les contes nouveaux ou les fées à
la mode*, the first part of which appeared the same year and with two other
volumes by 1711. *Tales of the Fairies* was published in English translation in London as early as 1699; then as *Tales of the Fairies in three parts
compleat*, 1707, with the same translation appearing as an illustrated
work in 1715. Next came *A Collection of novels and tales of the Fairies,
written by that celebrated wit of France, the Countess D'Anois*, 1728, in three
volumes, later to have a fresh title as *The Court of Queen Mab*, 1752,
published by Mrs Mary Cooper. Variations on the same themes continued to appear until at least the end of the nineteenth century, some
reprinting the stanza found on some of the early title-pages:

> The monarchy of fairies once was great,
> As good old Wives, and nurses do relate;
> Then was the golden age from whence did spring,
> A race of fairies dancing round a ring.

France contributed much to the spread of interest in fairy-tales,
notably with the appearance of the delightful *contes* of Charles Perrault
(1628–1703), a collection first translated into English by Robert
Samber in 1729. Perrault, a member of the *Académie Française*, is

believed to have received some assistance from his son, who himself might have first heard some of the tales from the lips of his old nurse. Perrault senior entitled his collection of stories *Histoires ou Contes du temps passé*, translated as *The Histories of Passed Times* (*sic*) in some early editions; the work first appearing in Paris in January 1697 under the imprint of Claude Barbin. All the very early editions had little morals appended in verse form at the conclusion of each tale. The frontispiece had the legend *Contes de ma Mere l'Oye*, and from this legend grew the familiar name of *Tales from Mother Goose*.

Many stories from this famous collection of fairy-tales were probably invented by unrelated individuals, to be gradually collected as groups in the memories of children who grew up to tell their own children the stories. In Britain, from the 1730s onwards, children took to their hearts the adventures of *Red Riding Hood, Cinderella, Blue-beard, The Sleeping Beauty, Puss-in-Boots* and the rest of the tales told by Mother Goose. Robert Samber used as his text for the English translation the 1721 Amsterdam edition illustrated here, the first to recognise the authorship of Charles Perrault, and with the dedication leaf bearing the name of his son Pierre Perrault-Darmancour as 'P. Darmancour'. It is illustrated with frontispiece and head-pieces to each story, as in the first edition.

Samber's original English edition was re-issued in 1736, then in 1764 as *Tales of Passed Times, by Mother Goose*, and again in 1785, this time in two volumes, and has never been out of print in some form for nearly two hundred and fifty years, right up to the present day. All eighteenth-century editions are very rare and would be extremely costly to acquire even in comparatively poor condition.

Jacob Ludwig Karl Grimm (1785–1863) and his brother, Wilhelm Karl Grimm (1786–1859), were born at Hanau, Germany, and both eventually became professors of linguistic studies, first at Göttingen and later at Berlin University. Together they spent years collecting from the mouths of country folk and from literary sources as many of the old folk and fairy stories as they could find, finally publishing them in three separate volumes as *Kinder- und Haus-Märchen*. This scholarly collection appeared as volume one in 1812, volume two in 1815 and volume three in 1822. Before this final volume was issued the publisher, G. Reimer, realised the appeal that the work would have for children, so a two-volume edition made its appearance in 1819, this time specially designed for young people, with frontispieces and added pictorial title-pages by L. Haas after original designs by Ludwig Emil Grimm. It was this series that became affectionately known throughout the English-speaking world as *Grimms' Fairy Tales*.

Translated by Edgar Taylor, the work appeared as *German Popular*

Stories, Translated from the Kinder und Haus Marchen, 1823, with the umlaut marks missing from 'Märchen'. This first volume was issued under the imprint of C. Baldwyn, in a binding of pictorially printed paper-covered boards with uncut leaf-edges, as being by 'M. M. Grimm'. Then in 1825 James Robins & Co., London, published the second edition of this volume, this time in a binding of pink paper-covered boards with uncut leaf-edges, with a second volume of stories coming out the following year and dated 1826, both again being attributed to 'M. M. Grimm'. George Cruikshank supplied a series of twenty-two full-page engravings to illustrate the work, and it has been a favourite subject with artists and book illustrators ever since.

This, possibly the most popular collection of fairy-tales ever published, has been translated into the vast majority of languages. The first French edition, *Vieux Contes pour l'Amusement des Grands et des Petits Enfans* (1824), was published in Paris by Auguste Boulland, George Cruikshank's illustrations being re-engraved by Ambroise Tardieu from the 1823 English edition. The printing of extracts, individual stories or short collections has continued without interruption since the early 1830s. *Hans in Luck, The Fisherman and his Wife, Tom Thumb, The Adventures of Chantileer and Partlet, Snow Drop* (since doubly immortalised on film and television as 'Snow White and the Seven Dwarfs'), *The Elves and the Shoemaker, The Golden Goose, Hansel and Grettel, The Frog Prince, Rumpel-Stilts-Kin, The Goose Girl, Hans in Love, Cat-Skin, The Juniper Tree* and a dozen or more other stories whose titles have since become household words all appeared in this collection of German fairy stories, folk-tales and legends that the brothers Grimm preserved for posterity by establishing texts in the early years of the nineteenth century.

It was after reading the first edition of *Kinder- und Haus-Märchen* that Thomas Crofton Croker (1798–1854) determined to make a collection of *Fairy Legends and Traditions of the South of Ireland*, later published by John Murray, London, dated 1825, and illustrated by a series of vignettes from designs made by W. H. Brooke. The work was highly complimented by the Grimm brothers and was translated into German by them under the title *Irische Elfenmärchen*. Two further volumes of Croker's *Fairy Legends* appeared in 1828, the last of which was dedicated to Wilhelm Grimm. A collected edition, edited by T. Wright, was published in 1882.

Brief mention must be made here of a few early collections of fairy-tales that perhaps lack many of the best-loved stories in original form, but were nevertheless the forerunners of the well known selections which followed. *The Fairy Spectator; or, the Invisible Monitor*, 1789, by Mrs Teachwell (ie Lady Eleanor Fenn), was published by J. Marshall

The Giant Ogre. discovers Hop'o my Thumb & his Brothers whom his wife had endeavoured to conceal from him

A George Cruikshank illustration for Hop-O'My-Thumb and the Seven-League Boots, *1853, the first of four booklets he edited in the series* George Cruikshank's Fairy Library, *published by David Bogue*

& Co., London. A more important early collection was the anonymous *Temple of the Fairies*, 1804, two volumes, revised in 1823 as *The Court of Oberon: or, Temple of the Fairies*, and again, this time under a Glasgow imprint as *Fairy Tales, or The Court of Oberon* (1824). Most of the stories had been culled from Charles Perrault's *contes*, although, strangely, *Cinderella* is missing, being replaced by *Jack and the Beanstalk*. This latter tale has origins lost in the mists of time, first appearing in print in chapbook form, although the tale, in almost exactly similar form, appears to have been known to the North American Indians and to some of the native tribes of South Africa long before the coming of the white man. Amongst other stories included in this collection of thirteen tales were *The White Cat, Prince Fatal and Prince Fortune, The Invisible Prince* and *The Fair One with The Golden Locks*.

The last title mentioned has no connection with the favourite nursery tale of *Goldilocks and the Three Bears*, although the name of the heroine may well have appealed to later publishers of the story. Goldilocks in fact started life as a disagreeable old woman in the earliest printed versions, only being converted to a pretty little girl many editions later. *The Story of the Three Bears* started life as an English nursery story apparently well before the 1830s, the first manuscript giving the text that we know of being accurately dated to September 1831, the work of Eleanor Mure. She was already describing the story as 'The celebrated nursery tale of the Three Bears'. The work first appeared in print in volume four of *The Doctor,* 1837, by Robert Southey. *The Three Bears and their Stories*, with a dedication signed and dated 'G. N.', July 1837, appeared in time for Christmas that year, and was subsequently re-issued by Wright & Co. in 1841. Any text of the story dated before 1850 is a rare and desirable possession.

The publisher John Harris celebrated his succession to the business of Elizabeth Newbery in 1801 by publishing under his own imprint such works as a ten-volume edition of *The Book-Case of Knowledge* and *The Nursery Garland* by W. F. Mavor, amongst a collection of other titles for children. He was soon off the mark with fairy-tales by issuing *Mother Bunch's Fairy Tales*, 1802, taken from Countess d'Alnoy's volume of stories. During the succeeding years her *The Renowned History of Prince Chery and Princess Fair-Star* and *The Renowned History of the White Cat* (both 1803), and Perrault's *Histories, or Tales of Past Times*, 1803, appeared under the Harris imprint, while by 1807 a new title for children was being issued every week. Harris was one of the first to try out the technique described in *A Complete Course of Lithography*, 1819, by Alois Senefelder, by issuing *The Renowned Tales of Mother Goose as Originally Related* (1820), complete with a lithographed frontispiece of the 'Discreet Princess'. This title appeared in the binding style he established as his own: marbled paper-covered boards with a spine of red roan crossed horizontally by gold lines. Literally hundreds, perhaps thousands, of his titles appeared in this identical clothing, the variation in later years being not in the leather spine, but in the paper-covered boards having printed titles and pictures on the front, while the back board had one of Harris's circular emblems bearing the house name.

All the early editions of *Tales of Mother Goose* and variations of this title seem to have been read to death by the generations of children who first possessed them, for examples dating from the first few decades of the nineteenth century are scarcely ever met with, while the eighteenth-century texts seem to have disappeared completely.

Children have known the story of *Punch and Judy* since its original appearance in England in 1662, the drama of Mr Punch and his wife Joan (later Judy) having been watched by Samuel Pepys in the theatre at Covent Garden soon after the Restoration. The name of Punch derives from the *Commedia dell'arte* character Pulcinella, stemming from the traditions of the Italian peasantry as portrayed by highly trained professional actors. The first printed text in English of *Punch and Judy* is, surprisingly enough, dated as late as 1828. John Payne Collier (1789–1833), remembered unhappily for his falsifications of ancient documents and his forgeries of marginal corrections of the text of Shakespeare in the 'Perkins folio', had to his credit the distinction of being the first to record the text of a puppet show which my own and earlier generations delighted in during our seaside holidays. Today's performances seem to take place mostly indoors.

At the instigation of Samuel Prowett of Pall Mall, Collier accompanied George Cruikshank to a Punch and Judy show. As the artist sketched his series of drawings, Collier busied himself with taking extensive notes for the text. By this means, as the editor tells his readers in the preface, the publisher was able 'to fill up a *hiatus* in theatrical history'. Of the 1828 first edition, a small number of large-paper copies were issued with the plates hand-coloured, a second edition appearing the same year. Within months abridged versions of the text Collier had taken down verbatim, accompanied by fresh sets of illustrations, were being issued for children under the imprints of many of the leading publishing houses of the day, the work seldom being out of print until the 1930s.

Wonderful Stories for Children, 1846, was the first translation into English of the 'modern' fairy-tales of Hans Christian Andersen (1805–75), although his stories had been appearing in his native Denmark since 1835. Further collections of his own creations and remoulded folk tales (differing in this respect from the brothers Grimm) were issued at regular intervals until, after 1848, he abandoned his other literary

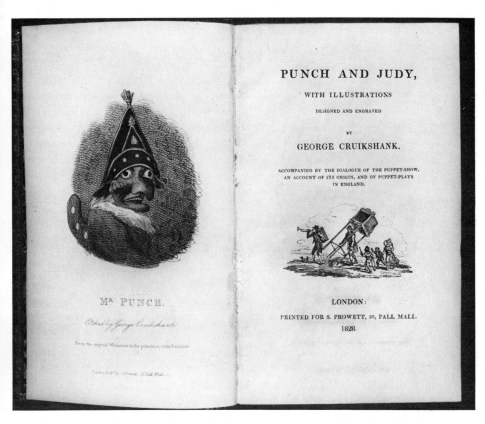

Frontispiece and title-page of one of the few large-paper copies of Punch and Judy—
the first appearance of the text in English. The twenty-four full-page copperplate engravings were hand-coloured

activities and concentrated solely on the children's stories which would soon make his name known throughout the civilised world. *The Ugly Duckling, The Tinder Box, The Emperor's New Clothes, The Snow Queen* and many others soon came to be known and loved by children of all ages.

During an early visit to Britain he met Charles Dickens and later befriended Mary Howitt (1799–1888), the author of a number of natural history books for young people and a prolific contributor to the annuals of the period. She was the wife of William Howitt (1792–1879), author of *The Boy's Country Book*, 1839, and many other works. Due to her meeting Andersen she conceived the idea of translating his stories, then almost totally unknown in Britain, actually learning Danish to enable her to do this. *Wonderful Stories for Children* was published in a straight-grained full-cloth binding, blocked in blind and gold, and with a complement of four full-page hand-coloured plates. Mrs Howitt was grief-stricken when she discovered that she had spelled the author's name incorrectly on the title-page of the 1846 first English edition (it was printed 'Anderson'), taking this as a particularly bad omen. Her fears proved right, for the work did not repay the cost of publication, possibly because two other rival translations appeared later that year, just in time to capture the Christmas trade in books for the young. The publisher William Pickering issued a translation by Caroline Peachey, and a similar selection of Andersen's children's stories entitled *A Danish Story-Book*, 1846, was issued by Joseph Cundall as a translation from a German edition by Charles Boner.

The following year, 1847, saw the publication of *A Picture-Book without Pictures*, translated by Meta Taylor from a German version of Andersen's stories of de la Motte Fouque. *The Ice-Maiden*, 1863, was translated from the Danish by a Mrs Bushby, the original story having been published in Copenhagen in 1862. From that time onwards, English editions of Andersen's tales and of individual stories appeared every few years, many of them lavishly illustrated by the foremost artists and engravers of the day. *Ole Lukoie*, *The Daisy*, *The Naughty Boy*, *Tommelise*, *The Rose-Elf*, *The Garden of Paradise*, *A Night in the Kitchen*, *Little Ida's Flowers*, *The Constant Tin Soldier* and *The Storks* all appeared in the first English edition of 1846, and the rest of the stories at short intervals after their original appearance in Danish.

By the 1840s, collections of fairy stories were becoming commonplace. One of the most important events of the period was the appearance of *The Home Treasury of Books,* by Sir Henry Cole (1808–82), issued under his pseudonym of 'Felix Summerly'. The first title in the series to make its appearance was *Bible Events*, 1843, but he then turned his attention to such popular and saleable extravagances as *Little Red Riding Hood*, *Reynard the Fox*, *Beauty and the Beast*, *Traditional Nursery Songs* and *Sir Hornbook*. Cole had long been dissatisfied with the quality of books available to young people and be became determined to design and produce well printed and illustrated volumes for children himself. His new venture was advertised as *The Home Treasury of Books, Pictures, Toys, etc., purposed to cultivate the Affections, Fancy, Imagination, and Taste of Children*. In the prospectus, he told his would-be readers that 'Little Red Riding Hood and other fairy tales hallowed to children's use, are now turned into ribaldry as satires for men . . . this is hurtful to children.' When they finally made their appearance, the books set a new standard of quality in works for young people. Their format, although expensive, was influential in moulding the taste of the public, and this eventually led to a demand for finely produced, illustrated books in the decades which followed.

The Home Treasury was published under the imprint of Joseph

Cundall, *Bible Events. First Series*, 1843, being offered at 2s 6d (12½p) plain, or 4s 6d (22½p) coloured; the second and third series of this title were issued the following year. *The Pleasant History of Reynard the Fox*, 1843, was a more ambitious venture, appearing with no less than forty coloured plates by Everdingen, and priced as high as 6s 6d (32½p). Titles continued to appear until 1847, in which year the fourth (and final!) series of *Bible Events* made its appearance, being available singly, or four parts in 'one volume handsomely bound, 10s 6d (52½p), or splendidly bound, with the plates coloured at 21s' (£1.05).

In 1846, Joseph Cundall started advertising a new series of titles, selling under the name of *Gammer Gurton's Pleasant Stories*, 'newly revised and amended, for the Amusement and Delight of all good little Masters and Misses, by Ambrose Merton, Gent, F.S.A.' This was the pseudonym of W. J. Thoms, and under his editorship Cundall issued *Gammer Gurton's Garland*, *The Famous History of Sir Guy of Warwick*, *A True Tale of Robin Hood*, *The Gallant History of Sir Bevis of Hampton*, to a total of thirteen titles, all with a full-page illustration 'by an

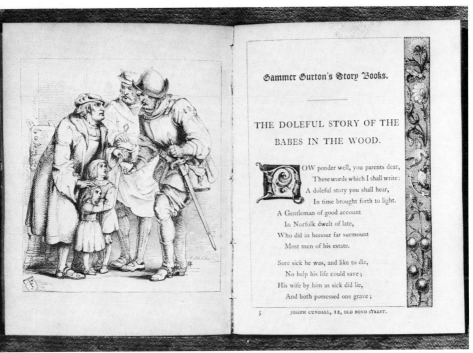

The first in the series of Gammer Gurton's Pleasant Stories, *1845, printed at the Chiswick Press by Charles Whittingham, and edited by 'Ambrose Merton, Gent.', the pseudonym of William John Thoms (1803-85). John Franklin and John Absolon supplied the illustrations. Size of page: 16 × 12.2cm*

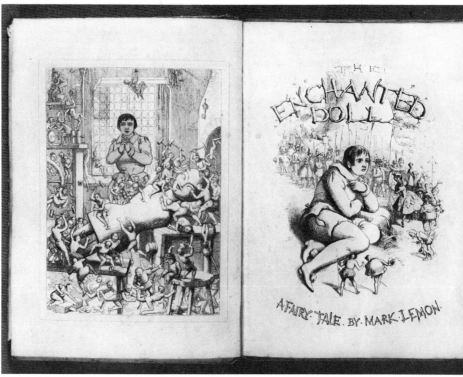

The first book written by Mark Lemon, one of the founders, and later the sole editor, of Punch. *It was published in 1849. Size of title-page: 17.7 × 12.5cm*

eminent artist'. Once again it was possible to purchase each work in differing formats: in gilt paper covers at 6d (2½p) or with the picture coloured at 9d (4p approx.). Present-day collectors will discover that none of the 'Felix Summerly' titles is easy to find, and that all command quite high prices when offered at auction or in the catalogues of antiquarian booksellers. All were finely printed by Charles Whittingham at the Chiswick Press, and are therefore probably collected as much by those whose interest lies in the history of typography and publishers' binding styles as those seeking examples of early children's books.

The difficulty of finding new and unused plots for fairy stories presented obstacles that few writers of the day were able to surmount with any degree of success. One who tried was Mark Lemon (1809–70), remembered as one of the founders, and later as sole editor, of the magazine *Punch*. He produced *The Enchanted Doll. A Fairy Tale for Little People*, 1849, a work which was illustrated in characteristic style by Richard Doyle (1824–83), the famous 'Dicky' Doyle, whose elaborately designed front cover for *Punch* contained a gross obscenity which apparently passed unnoticed by generations of Victorians. *The Enchanted Doll* is a most difficult first edition to find in acceptable condition, due to the fact that it was issued in a fragile binding of glazed, pink paper-covered boards, pictorially printed on both front and back covers.

Today, Doyle's most sought-after book is *In Fairyland — A Series of Pictures from the Elf-World*, 1870, (second edition 1875), acknowledged as a masterpiece of book illustration and an outstanding example of colour printing by Edmund Evans, a craftsman whose work for Walter Crane, Randolph Caldecott, Kate Greenaway and other writers and illustrators was to put him at the top of his profession. *In Fairyland* was published by Longmans, Green, Reader & Dyer, the text being supplied by a poem by William Allingham (1824–89), the Irish poet who became a friend of Leigh Hunt and was introduced to the Pre-Raphaelite Brotherhood by Coventry Patmore. His poem, *The Fairies*, first published in *Poems*, 1850 (which he withdrew from circulation), and later in his most famous work *The Music Master*, 1855, has been recited by several generations of children:

> Up the airy mountain,
> Down the rushy glen,
> We daren't go a-hunting,
> For fear of little men;
> Wee folk, good folk,
> Trooping all together;
> Green jacket, red cap,
> And white owl's feather!

A late edition of *The Fairies* (1883), with illustrations by E. Gertrude Thomson, was published by Thomas de la Rue & Co., London. The following year, Andrew Lang (1844–1912) wrote a new story to accompany Richard Doyle's original pictures used for *In Fairyland*, and the book was issued, undated, by Longmans, Green & Co., London, as *The Princess Nobody, a Tale of Fairy Land*.

Original stories inspired by folk-tales and fairy legends continued to appear throughout the latter half of the nineteenth century. John Ruskin (1819–1900) contributed *The King of the Golden River*, 1851, three editions appearing the same year. Published anonymously, the story was written some ten years before at the request of twelve-year-old Euphemia ('Effie') Chalmers Gray, the girl Ruskin married in 1848. She later obtained a divorce and married John Millais. In 1932 a new edition of *The King of the Golden River* was issued, this time with illustrations by Arthur Rackham, of which the limited edition, bound in

Japon vellum and signed by the artist, has risen steeply in price. The ordinary trade edition of the same year, bound in pictorial cloth, was unsigned.

William Makepeace Thackeray (1811–63) was remembered briefly by children for *The Rose and the Ring; or, The History of Prince Giglio and Prince Bulbo*, 1855, written under his pseudonym of 'M. A. Titmarch'. A book of more enduring quality, this time with a moral to preach, was *The Water Babies: A Fairy Tale for a Land Baby*, 1863, illustrated by J. Noel Paton. The author, Charles Kingsley (1819–75), had first published the tale serially from August 1862 to March 1863 in *Macmillan's Magazine*. The first issue of the first edition in book form is distinguished by a leaf with the poem *L'Envoi*, which the author suppressed during the printing run because it was thought to be anti-Semitic. One can understand why:

> Hence, unbelieving Sadducees,
> And less-believing Pharisees,
> With dull conventionalities;
> And leave a country muse at ease
> To play at leap-frog, if she please,
> With children and realities.

Only a few hundred copies had escaped the press before the leaf was removed. Meanwhile, *The Water Babies* has become a classic in children's literature, and new editions, lavishly illustrated by scores of artists at different periods, have been appearing ever since. None of these, in either artistic or financial terms, approaches the sumptuous edition of 1909, issued in limited form and bound in vellum with silk ties, which Warwick Goble illustrated; but the 1915 version with illustrations by Heath Robinson is also much sought after.

Kingsley's other works for children never achieved the same success, although two which young people quickly adopted as their own proved to be best-sellers in their day: *Westward Ho! or, The Voyages and Adventures of Sir Amyas Leigh*, 1856 (3 vols), and *Hereward the Wake, 'Last of the English'*, 1866 (2 vols). His fairy-tales include *The Heroes; or, Greek Fairy Tales for my Children*, 1856, with eight full-page illustrations by the author; but his other works, *Glaucus; or, Wonders of the Shore*, 1855, and *Madam How and Lady Why*, 1870, could more properly be classed under the heading of natural history.

Fairy-tale and fantasy reached perhaps their highest point of achievement with the publication of *Alice's Adventures in Wonderland*, 1865, and *Through the Looking-Glass, and what Alice found there*, 1872. Both works were written with a dream-like blend of logic and fantasy, and both were in many senses 'children's books for grown-ups', some children loving the stories while others remain totally unimpressed. The author, the Revd C. L. Dodgson (1832–98) is known to young and old by his pseudonym 'Lewis Carroll', a title derived from Dodgson's first two names, Charles Lutwidge: Lutwidge equates with Ludwig, of which Lewis is the Anglicised version, and Carroll is another form of the name Charles.

Dodgson delighted in amusing demure little girls of a certain age, seeking their company and assiduously photographing them in various poses with his pioneer equipment of the 1860s. His motives seem obviously to stem from the sexual fantasies he indulged in, but neither he nor his young companions were other than outwardly correct in their social behaviour. No breath of scandal wafted and, had he not conjured his mental *fantoccini,* we might well have been deprived of two classic and world-famous juvenile novels of English literature.

He had met Alice, the daughter of Dean Liddell of Christ Church, Oxford, in 1856, and it was for her that he wrote his masterpiece. By the time his book was published his pretty little girl had just entered her teens, and with the advent of puberty his interest in her waned. He complained in a letter that she had 'changed a good deal, and hardly for the better'. So the model for the illustrations had to be a new child-friend of the same age as his heroine Alice Liddell was when he penned the manuscript.

A review of *Alice's Adventures in Wonderland* appeared in the Christmas annual volume of *Aunt Judy's Magazine*, 1866, from the pen of the editor Mrs Alfred Gatty, a writer of children's stories, whose *The Fairy Godmother and Other Tales*, 1851, had been published by George Bell, London. She was enthusiastic, and began:

> Forty-two illustrations by Tenniel! Why there needs nothing else to sell this book, one would think. But our young friends may rest assured that the exquisite illustrations do but justice to the exquisitely wild, fantastic, impossible, yet most natural history of Alice in Wonderland.

Sir John Tenniel (1820–1914) was knighted in 1893, during a long career as joint cartoonist with John Leech of the magazine *Punch*, in which he gained fame for the originality and wit of his political satires. It was the harmony Dodgson's text displayed with Tenniel's inimitable series of illustrations (or the other way round) that combined to produced a work the world soon knew, in almost any language one cares to mention, as *Alice in Wonderland*. This one book immortalised the names of 'Lewis Carroll' and John Tenniel, for never before had any illustrator caught the mood and atmosphere of a story in so intimate a fashion. The characters imagined in the mind's eye seem to equate almost exactly with the pictures seen as the leaves are turned and the adventure unfolds.

The story of the book's first appearance and subsequent withdrawal has been told many times. Dodgson commissioned Macmillan & Company to publish the book, paying the expenses of production out of his own pocket, these to be set later against the income from the sale of the work. He was an irascible and extremely fussy eccentric, meticulous in his attention to detail and almost hysterically anxious that the work should appear without blemish of any sort, real or imagined. Dodgson admitted later that he had 'inflicted on that most patient and painstaking firm about as much wear and worry as ever publishers have lived through', and one imagines that Macmillan's editors must have heaved sighs of relief when the final proofs were grudgingly approved by the author. The book was printed by the Oxford University Press and they delivered 2,000 sets of sheets to his rooms at the university on 30 June 1865. These Dodgson despatched to Macmillan & Company, asking for fifty to be bound up as soon as possible, plus a few special copies in white vellum, one of which he presented to Alice Liddell.

Having sent out his presentation copies in their bindings of red cloth and with their title-pages dated '1865', Dodgson began to fret and worry. From the first he had qualms about the quality of the printing, especially that of the illustrations. Now, after days of increasing anxiety, he finally persuaded himself that the whole work must be reprinted and the fifty copies already in circulation must somehow be retrieved and replaced. Most of the friends and relations to whom he had given copies of the first edition returned the volumes as he requested and, as soon as the new edition was bound and ready, they were sent replacement copies, freshly printed, and dated '1866'. This edition, now known as the first published edition, was in the bookshops in December 1865, just in time for the Christmas rush. Dodgson found himself some £350 out of pocket on the whole exercise; but Macmillan managed to dispose of the balance of the first 2,000 sets of sheets of the 1865 dated edition to Appleton & Company, New York, and sent him a cheque for £120 in payment. In the meantime *Alice's Adventures in Wonderland* began selling in a fashion which far exceeded its author's fondest hopes and a new edition marked 'Fifth Thousand' and dated 1867 was needed to supply the demand. From that time onwards success was assured, the 1868 edition, issued in February, being marked 'Twelfth Thousand', and by October that year a set of electrotype plates had been taken so that more and more copies could be run off. Throughout all these editions, and

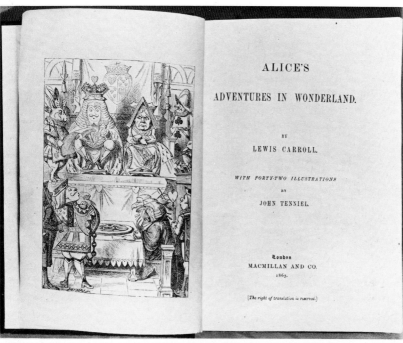

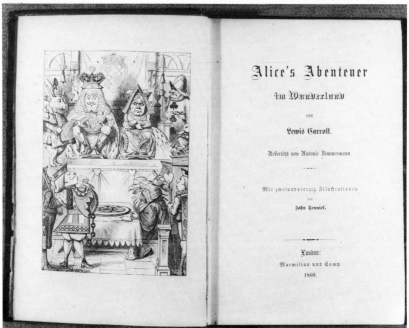

(Top) *The extremely rare first edition of* Alice's Adventures in Wonderland. *Few copies have survived for reasons given in the text.* (Above) *The first German edition of Dodgson's classic fantasy. Size of title-page: 18.5 × 12.2cm*

the scores which followed, the format of the book remained the same. The red cloth was retained, blocked in gold on the front cover with a picture of Alice holding the pig, and on the back with the smiling head of the Cheshire cat, and with the leaf edges gilded. Foreign translations soon appeared, the first being the French edition, *Adventures d'Alice au Pays des Merveilles*, 1869; the first German edition, shown in the illustration on page 83, was published in the same year. Both were available in London, as well as Paris and Berlin, at the shop of P. Rolandi, 20 Berners Street, a bookseller whose extensive circulating library was devoted to foreign books. By the 1880s *Alice* had been translated into most European languages, the first Italian edition, *L'Avventure d'Alice nel paese delle merviglie*, 1872, being followed by the first Russian edition, *Sonya v tsarstve diva* (a literal translation of the title reading 'Sonya in the Kingdom of Wonder'), published in Moscow, dated 1879.

The success of *Through the Looking-Glass* was hardly less marked, and Dodgson wrote several other stories for children in the intervals between producing mathematical treatises of varying degrees of complexity. *The Hunting of the Snark — an Agony in Eight Fits*, 1876, a book of nonsense rhymes, had a delightful series of grotesque illustrations by Henry Holiday, and to find a copy of the first edition in its rather fragile pictorial cloth binding is now a rare event.

> 'Just the place for a Snark!' the Bellman cried,
>   As he landed the crew with care:
> Supporting each man on the top of the tide
>   By a finger entwined in his hair.

Once read, the jingles stay in the memory for ever. *Sylvie and Bruno*, 1889, and *Sylvie and Bruno Concluded*, 1893, the latter written five years before the author's death, never achieved much success and today are largely forgotten.

It is obvious from the details I have given that the first edition of *Alice*, dated 1865, is exceedingly rare, and any copy which appears at auction, even in poor condition, invariably fetches well over £1,000. Dodgson did not destroy or throw away the copies he managed to retrieve; instead he sent them to the Great Ormond Street Hospital for Sick Children where most must have been read to death within a few years. A few escaped, presumably when children took copies home with them. The present writer has carefully compared copies of the 1865 edition with that dated 1866 but, excepting that it is somewhat lighter in the inking of the type and illustrations, no fault in the printing could be detected in the 1865 edition.

We therefore give the copies dated 1865 first-issue priority, while those purchased in sheets by Appleton & Co. and published with a cancel (American imprint) title-page, dated 1866, are the second issue of the first edition. The 1866 Macmillan edition is the second edition, but this itself commands a high price at auction and elsewhere.

Collections of fairy-tales continued to appear during the period when the works of 'Lewis Carroll' were selling by the thousand. Joseph Jacobs (1854–1916), an eminent Jewish historian and the editor of the magazine *Folk-lore*, supplied an original collection of five volumes of fairy-tales for children. At the end of each volume were several pages of scholarly notes and references, preceded by a leaf which warned his juvenile readers that: 'The fairy tales are now closed — little boys and girls must not read any further.' The series was illustrated by John D. Batten, and consisted of *English Fairy Tales*, 1890, *Celtic Fairy Tales*, 1892, *Indian Fairy Tales*, 1892, *More English Fairy Tales*, 1894, and *More Celtic Fairy Tales*, 1894. A particularly attractive, limited edition of large-paper copies of the series was issued, printed on Japon vellum paper, and signed by the publisher David Nutt. In this large-paper edition the full-page plates appear in two states, one being printed in sepia and the other in black.

In contrast, the twelve-volume collection of 'coloured' fairy books made by Andrew Lang (1844–1912) looks best in the brightly gilt and coloured cloth-bound issue, rather than the soberly clad, large-paper limited edition which appears drab and uninteresting by the side of its gaily-coloured shelf-mates. First-edition dates of Lang's most eagerly sought-after collection of volumes are *Blue*, 1889, *Red*, 1890, *Green*, 1892, *Yellow*, 1894, *Pink*, 1897, *Grey*, 1900, *Violet*, 1901, *Crimson*, 1903, *Brown*, 1904, *Orange*, 1906, *Olive*, 1907, and *Lilac*, 1910. All were re-printed many times. Amongst the compiler's other collections of folk-tales and fairy-tales for children, published in similar style and format, were *The Arabian Nights Entertainments*, 1898, *The Book of Romance*, 1902, *The Red Romance Book*, 1905, *The Book of Princes and Princesses*, 1908, and *The All Sorts of Stories Book*, 1911, the last two titles having been compiled by his wife and edited by Andrew Lang. To range with these were a series of six other titles which collectors commonly keep on the same set of shelves, although most are stories taken from real life with only the occasional folk- or fairy-tale. H. J. Ford, who supplied most of the illustrations to the fairy books, was again commissioned, with other artists, to create the pictures to illustrate the texts, the titles being *The Blue Poetry Book*, 1891, *The True Story Book*, 1893, *The Red True Story Book*, 1895, *The Animal Story Book*, 1896, *The Red Book of Animal Stories*, 1899, and (by Mrs Lang) *The Red Book of Heroes*, 1909.

The sometimes voiced belief that fairy-tales and fantasies present little difficulty in composition and execution and are an easily won literary achievement, even by writers endowed with only modest talents, is, of course, nonsense. It might appear deceptively simple to create a plot and then to magic away any doubts, difficulties and unwanted or played-out characters and situations the author might encounter as the tale unfolds 'as from the stroke of the enchanter's wand'. In practice, the original folk stories and traditional fairy-tales between them have utilised such an infinite variety of basic plots that to discover a refreshingly new one is all but impossible without being possessed of the inventive genius of a Hans Andersen or a Lewis Carroll. The two *Alice* books are fantasy rather than fairy stories, but the distinction between the two genres is sufficiently blurred by the similarity of magical ingredients contained in each for both fairy-tales and fantasy to be embraced by a single chapter heading. As the nineteenth century advanced, more and more writers for children interwove the dream-like logic of fantasy with supernatural powers, exemplified by the granting of three wishes, or the magical help or hindrance accorded to humans by benevolent or spiteful beings. One of the most gifted of the Victorian writers of fairy stories in this vein was George MacDonald (1824–1905), a poet and novelist, whose *Phantastes: a Faerie Romance for Men and Women*, 1858, was followed later by *Dealings with the Fairies*, 1867. He is remembered today for his children's books, especially *At the Back of the North Wind*, 1871, which first appeared in the magazine *Good Words for the Young*, with illustrations by Arthur Hughes (1832–1915), a member of the Pre-Raphaelite Brotherhood, which exactly fitted the mood of the book. MacDonald's tale is a religious allegory (he was at one time a Congregational minister), telling how little Diamond, the son of a poor coachman, lives out his harsh and deprived life in the heart of working-class London, while dissolving into a dream-world in which he travels with the North Wind in the shape of a beautiful woman with streaming long black hair. In this fantasy, Diamond shelters and finally dies, to find peace at last 'at the back of the North Wind'. *The Princess and the Goblin*, 1872, *Gutta Percha Willie: the Working Genius*, 1873, *The Princess and Curdie*, 1883, and *The Light Princess, and other Fairy Stories*, 1890, are amongst his best-known tales, none of which is easy to find in first-edition form. This same observation applies to the stories of Jean Ingelow (1820–97), with such titles as *Tales of Orris*, 1860, published at Bath, republished as *Stories told to a Child*, 1865, London (omitting one story), *Mopsa the Fairy*, 1869, and *Wonder-Horn*, 1872; all are extremely difficult to find.

Turning to this present century we find that children have delighted in the whimsical fantasies of writers such as J. M. Barrie (1860–1937), whose book *The Little White Bird*, 1902, contained chapters which first introduced the world to 'Peter Pan'. Barrie's play *Peter Pan, or the Boy who wouldn't grow up*, opened at the Duke of York's Theatre, London, on 27 December 1904, with Nina Boucicault playing the name part. It has been in almost continual production in theatres throughout the world ever since.

In book form, the title first appeared as *Peter Pan in Kensington Gardens*, 1906, accompanied by a series of fifty coloured plates by Arthur Rackham, each guarded by tissues with descriptive letterpress. This is a much-sought-after volume by the many collectors of the work of Arthur Rackham, especially in the form of the signed limited edition with vellum spine. The story of the play was published as *Peter and Wendy* (1911), illustrated by F. D. Bedford; but the play itself was not printed in book form until seventeen years later, being issued by Hodder & Stoughton, London, as *Peter Pan, or the Boy who would not grow up*, 1928, in their series *The Plays of J. M. Barrie*. The author created several vivid and unforgettable characters, including the fearsome Captain Hook, with his steel hook in place of his missing hand; the ticking crocodile; Tinker Bell, the jealous little fairy; Peter Pan himself; and, of course, Wendy, whose name, invented by Barrie, has since been bestowed on generations of little girls.

Three other established classics of children's literature in this field were produced by Rudyard Kipling (1865–1936). *Just So Stories for Little Children*, 1902, was illustrated by the author, and the best of the many later editions is that of 1913, containing a series of coloured plates by J. M. Gleeson. The other two works are *Puck of Pook's Hill*, 1906, and *Rewards and Fairies*, 1910. Neither *The Jungle Book*, 1894, nor *The Second Jungle Book*, 1895, can properly find a place in this chapter, but this most desirable pair of classical series of tales in the field of animal stories will always fill an honourable place in any library of children's books. The first of the two titles is much the most difficult to acquire, and much the most expensive.

The fairy-tale, though falsely attractive to a seemingly endless stream of hack writers with little fresh to say, still lures poets and scholars the highest calibre. Walter de la Mare (1873–1956) wrote many poems and stories in which dreams and reality, fairies and animals, are delight fully blended; while J. R. R. Tolkien (1892–1974), the fantasist and Oxford academic, one-time Merton Professor of English Literature, published a succession of tales based on a mythology of his own. *The Hobbit*, 1937, and the three-volume *The Lord of the Rings*, 1954–5, became the subject of a cult, although it is perhaps a little hard to describe his readers, as Edmund Wilson did, as being those 'with a lifelong appetite for juvenile trash'.

One of the illustrations from The Island of Nose, *1977, discussed in the text*

To choose a favourite from amongst the hundreds of contemporary titles is an invidious task, so my own young children can make the selection for me from the modern, still in print, titles they have on their own shelves. The family unanimously agrees on *The Island of Nose*, 1977, startlingly illustrated by Jan Marinus Verburg, with the text by Annie M. G. Schmidt. Published in Britain by Methuen, and translated by Lance Salway, the work first appeared in Holland under the title *Tom Tippelaar*, and one of the illustrations is shown here.

4

INDUCEMENTS
TO LEARNING

Up to about the middle of the eighteenth century, almost every book produced for children had as its primary aim the instruction of youth in the paths of virtue, the morals and correct manners of the day, or in the basic rules of grammar, mathematics or classical history. As has already been stated, an exception could be made for the chapbooks and ballad-sheets which children often read and enjoyed; but these were intended for an adult market and were annexed by young people as reading matter which afforded a little light relief from the puritanical tracts and devotional manuals the pious thrust upon them.

School textbooks were always assured of a large and ready sale and grammars, ABCs and mathematical primers were being issued as far back as the latter half of the sixteenth century, at a time when hornbooks were in common use. Alphabets were available in English for the use of young people or adults trying to learn to read soon after the turn of the century, though very few have survived. One that we know of is the strangely named *The B.A.C.* [*sic*] *booke in latyn and in Englysshe* issued, undated, in 1538 by Thomas Petyt, and this by a single copy in Emmanuel College Library, Cambridge. *The A.B.C. set forth by the Kynges majestie* (*c.*1545) is also unique, the one and only survivor being in the British Library, while the one copy of *A.B.C. for children* (1561) we know of is in the library of Queen's College, Oxford. There are other similar titles of the same period, known by only a few examples.

Grammars were represented by such titles as *A Booke at Large for the Amendment of orthographie for English speech*, 1580, by William Bullokar, and *Bref grammar for English*, 1586, by the same author, probably meant for children's use, as *The Petie Schole of spelling and writing in English*, 1587, by F. Clement, most certainly was.

A lytel booke of good manners for children, 1532, by that prolific compiler of grammars and schoolbooks Robert Whittinton, was a loose translation of *De civilitate morum puerilium*, 1526, by Erasmus, a work consulted by parents and schoolmasters from the time of Henry VIII to that of James I. Some of the earliest books on mathematics, such as *The Mathematical Jewel*, 1585, by John Dansie, were more for use in universities than in school classrooms, but *Arithmeticke abreviated,*

1634, by William Barton, some fifty years later, had been simplified for the use of children. The far earlier *The groud of artes teachyng the worke and practise of arithmetike*, 1543, by Robert Record, now known by only two copies, was so popular in its day that it passed through dozens of editions and was still in print, with additions and modifications, as late as 1680. During the whole period under review, Latin textbooks were commonplace, but other foreign languages were seldom, if ever, taught in schools. Parents must, therefore, have had special reasons for wishing their children to study *An Introduction for to lerne Frenche* (*c.* 1534), by Giles Duwes, or *A Worlde of Wordes, Italian and English*, 1598, by John Florio.

The pace quickened in the next few decades, and after the Restoration a series of popular works made their appearance, some of which remained in print in modified and corrected form for over sixty years. *Cocker's Arithmetic, a plain and familiar method suitable to the meanest capacity*, 1678, by John Hawkins, used the international reputation of Edward Cocker (1631–76), a writing master and educationalist, as an advertisement for his books on mathematics for the young. It was followed by *Cocker's Morals, or the Muses spring-garden . . . for all public and private grammar and writing-schools*, 1685.

The British Youth's Instructor, 1754, by Daniel Fenning, preceded his very successful *A New Grammar of the English Language*, 1771, which

An early grammar by John Ward, dated 1771, with a Tree of Knowledge as its frontispiece. Size of title-page: 14.5 × 9.5cm

passed through six editions in less than twenty years, but long before this the famous John Newbery had entered the field with his *An Easy Introduction to the English Language*, 1745, published as the second volume in his series *The Circle of the Sciences*. It appeared the same year as the first volume of the set: *Grammar made familiar and easy to Young Gentlemen, Ladies, and foreigners* and within months of his *An Easy Spelling Dictionary*, 1745, later known as *Newbery's Spelling Dictionary of the English Language on a new Plan*.

English Grammar, adapted to the different classes of Learners, 1795, by Lindley Murray, published at York, had a phenomenal sale and became the standard textbook on the subject for the use of schools. Well over one hundred editions of the work appeared, and it was still in print as late as 1871. An abridgement of the text was issued in 1797.

Gradually, even books of instruction took on a sophistication which showed itself not only in their contents but in their binding styles. The solid fare of learning was being sweetened for younger minds by the addition of stories and anecdotes, or was given in the form of question and answer while the supposed narrator and his or her pupils were on nature walks or studying the heavens through telescopes. Typical of the didactic works of the period was *The Rational Dame; or, Hints towards supplying Prattle for Children* (1783), by Lady Eleanor Fenn, some of whose works have been noted in a previous chapter. In her preface to *The Rational Dame* she explains her ideas:

> Children frequently receive their first notions from the most illiterate persons: hence it is the business of some years to make them unlearn what they acquired in the nursery . . . What employment could be more delightful to a mother, than thus, 'Dispensing knowledge from the lips of love?' Curiosity is in children an *appetite* craving perpetually for food; but alas! how often are its cravings disregarded; or, worse still, appeased with trash! . . . In making amusement the vehicle of instruction, consists the grand secret of early education . . . Early impressions are, perhaps, never totally erased — who forgets the nonsense of the nursery? . . . Children listen with avidity to tales — let us give them none but rational information — amuse them with real wonders — entertain them with agreeable suprises — but no deceit; tell them plain, simple truth — there is no need for invention; the world is full of wonders. It is my ambition to have my little volume be the pocket companion of young mothers when they walk abroad with their children; it is my wish to assist them in the delightful task of forming in those children an habit of amusing themselves in a rational manner during their hours of leisure.

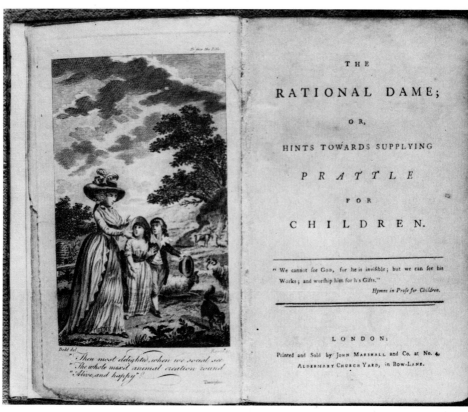

By Lady Eleanor Fenn, who sometimes used the pseudonym 'Mrs Teachwell'. This undated first edition was published in 1783, and carries nine full-page copperplate engravings of animals, insects, etc. 16.7 × 10.3cm

The engraved frontispiece to her book is followed by six full-page copperplate illustrations, divided into compartments, each containing a species of animal or insect and, although the preface points to the work being intended primarily for parents as an instructional manual for the children in their care, the text is couched in simple language easily understood by quite young children. The text is full of pertinent observations on the behaviour of animals both domestic and wild, that on the cat being typical of the rest: 'Cats have much less sense than dogs, and less attachment; their affection is more to the house, than to the persons who inhabit it.'

Her advice to make amusement the vehicle of instruction was by no means a new idea and had been employed from before the time of John Newbery, yet Lady Fenn was an influential figure in her day. The fluency with which children could read her books and absorb the half-hidden truths, due more to her use of simple language than to the extent of her scientific knowledge, had its effect on other writers of the period and on those who followed after. *Rational Sports. In dialogues passing among the Children of a Family* (1783), also published by John Marshall, was a companion volume to that quoted above, and was once again 'designed as a hint to mothers how they may inform the minds of their little people respecting the objects with which they are surrounded'.

Books dealing with natural history, written specially for children, had appeared during the last quarter of the eighteenth century. *The Natural History of Birds; intended for the Amusement and Instruction of Children*, 1791, by Samuel Galton, was published in three volumes with a fine series of hand-coloured copperplate engravings. His *Natural History of Quadrupeds for the Instruction of Young Persons* followed in two volumes in 1801, both works being published anonymously. Natural history books, especially those dealing with birds and animals, have always been best-sellers in the juvenile market, and publishers were not slow to exploit the interest of children in furred and feathered creatures. There is space here to mention only a representative handful of titles, some of them favourites of mine in their own particular fields, such as *A Natural History of Birds. Intended Chiefly for Young Persons*, 1807 (2 vols), by Charlotte Smith (1749–1806), issued in plain, paper-covered boards with leather spines by John Sharpe, from his Juvenile Library, London Museum, Piccadilly. There are twenty-four engravings of birds, hand-coloured in some copies. New editions appeared in 1815 and 1819. Mrs Smith, who wrote to help support her eight young children, was the sister of Mrs Catherine Ann Dorset, author of *The Peacock 'at home'*, a work discussed later, whose help she received when compiling her earlier *Conversations introducing poetry: chiefly on the subject of Natural History*, 1804 (2 vols).

Natural History for Children, 1819, was published in five volumes by Baldwin, Cradock and Joy, London, at the equivalent of 57p for the set but the author's name remains a mystery. Each volume was devoted to a different aspect of natural history; quadrupeds, birds, insects, fishes and reptiles, and trees and plants, with full-page engraved frontispieces and numerous woodcuts in the text. Maria Elizabeth Jackson published her *Botanical dialogues, between Hortensia and her four children*, 1797, anonymously, with eleven full-page plates and a letter of recommendation from Erasmus Darwin and his friend Sir Brooke Boothby; while my copy of *The Natural History of the Bible*, by T. M. Harris, describes itself as 'A new edition, with plates', though I have never seen an earlier. This thick twelvemo of some four hundred pages and twelve full-page plates of animals, birds and plants is unusual in not having its pages numbered, which, in a book of this size, must have led to considerable confusion. It was issued in drab paper-covered boards, and was obviously aimed at both the adult and juvenile markets.

In 1828, John Harris conceived the idea of issuing *The Little Library*, which he described as being 'a familiar introduction to the various branches of useful knowledge for older children'. It was an ambitious venture in which he employed many of the leading writers, scientists and artists of the day, the series finally extending to eighteen volumes. Each was published in a distinctive square octavo, lavishly illustrated with full-page engravings and woodcuts, the binding being a choice between full smooth cloth, with paper-labelled spine and front cover, or the more familiar full morocco-grained cloth, with red leather spine, titled in gold. The series extended over seven years, and the first title to appear was *The Mine*, 1829 (fifth edition, 1834), by Revd Isaac Taylor.

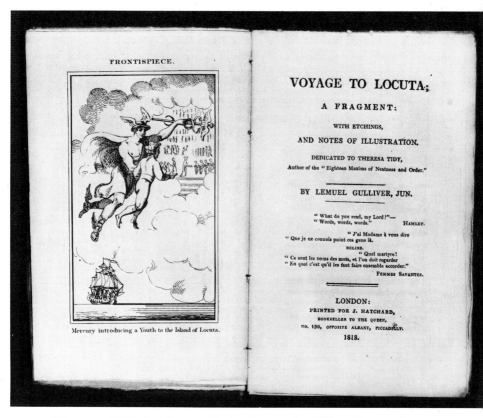

The rarest of Elizabeth Susanna Graham's works for children. She used the pen-name 'Lemuel Gulliver' and (more frequently) 'Theresa Tidy'. Despite its title, the work is an instructional book of grammar. Size of title-page: 17.5 × 11cm

It seems possible that Harris intended Taylor to be the general editor of the entire series, but he died in 1829, soon after finishing the second of the *Little Library* volumes, *The Ship*, 1830. The rest of the series, in order of publication, are: *The Forest*, 1831, by Jeffreys Taylor; *The Public Buildings of Westminster*, 1831, by Christian Isobel Johnstone, published anonymously; *The Public Buildings of the City of London*, 1831, by the same author; *The Garden*, 1831; *Bible Illustrations*, 1831, by Revd Bourne Hall Draper; *The Farm*, 1832, by Jefferys Taylor; *Ancient Customs, Sports and Pastimes of the English*, 1832, by Jehoshaphat Aspin (a work originally issued by Harris in 1825 under the title *A Picture of the Manners, Customs, Sports, and Pastimes of the Inhabitants of England*); *The British Story Briefly Told*, 1832; *The French History Briefly Told*, 1833; *The Ocean*, 1833; *Natural History of Quadrupeds*, 1834 (2 vols), by Frederick Shoberl, with illustrations by Thomas Landseer; *Francis Lever, the Young Mechanic*, 1835; *The Little Botanist*, 1835 (2 vols), by Caroline A. Halstead; and *The Natural History of Birds*, 1836, by Frederick Shoberl, with the illustrations again supplied by Thomas Landseer. The sixteen various titles (in a total of eighteen volumes), dated as shown above, make up a complete set of first editions, and it must be all but impossible today to acquire in this format. There is always difficulty in making up a set of 'firsts' in a series extending over many years; readers bought part of the set, or individual volumes, but few completed a collection as they were issued new by the bookseller. Sets have therefore to be made up by present-day collectors from various sources, and often one or more titles can elude the search for many years. *The Little Library* deservedly passed through many editions. During the course of reprinting the text of some of the volumes was altered or extended, new plates were added or appeared hand-coloured, and the bindings underwent various changes, mostly of a minor nature. Coloured frontispieces were standard, with such titles as *The Little Botanist*, and when *The Ship* made its re-appearance as a fourth edition, dated 1835, its series of sixteen full-page illustrations had been extended to twenty by the addition of four plates of hand-coloured national flags and pendants.

One of the most comprehensive early works on travel and exploration written for children was the *Historical Account of the most celebrated Voyages, Travels, and Discoveries, from the Time of Columbus to the Present Period*, issued in ten volumes, 1796 (last three volumes dated 1797), by William Mavor (1758–1837). Each volume had three full-page copperplate engravings, with volume seven having a folding plate of the death of Captain Cook (which is sometimes missing). The series was issued by Elizabeth Newbery, and proved so successful that a further ten volumes, all dated 1797, were published at the end of that year. Once

Spar Ornaments.

52

Pottery Ware.

53

Salt Refiner.

54

Published Jan.º 1.1823. by Harris & Son, Corner of S.ᵗ Pauls

(Above) *Three of the eighty-four copperplate engravings in* Scenes of British Wealth, *1823, which were designed by Revd I. Taylor, of Ongar, Essex. The title-page and folding map frontispiece are also shown (opposite top). Size of page 17.6 × 10.5cm*

(Opposite below) *The first appearance (1823) of a tale which passed through numerous editions. The story was apparently founded on fact and tells of the adventures of a slave whose kindhearted master lived in Philadelphia. The author was William Gardiner, headmaster of Lydney Academy*

A MAP OF GREAT BRITAIN AND IRELAND.

SCENES
OF
BRITISH WEALTH,
IN
PRODUCE, MANUFACTURES, AND
COMMERCE,
FOR THE
Amusement and Instruction
OF
LITTLE TARRY AT-HOME TRAVELLERS.

BY THE REV. I. TAYLOR,
AUTHOR OF SCENES IN ENGLAND, EUROPE, ASIA, AFRICA,
AND AMERICA.

LONDON:
PRINTED FOR HARRIS AND SON,
ST. PAUL'S CHURCH-YARD.
1823.

Congo.

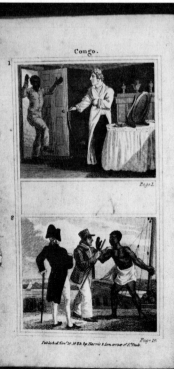

Page 1.

Page 19.

THE
ADVENTURES OF CONGO
IN
SEARCH OF HIS MASTER;
AN
American Tale.
CONTAINING A
TRUE ACCOUNT OF A SHIPWRECK,
AND
Interspersed with Anecdotes founded on Facts.

ILLUSTRATED WITH ENGRAVINGS.

LONDON:
HARRIS AND SON, ST. PAUL'S CHURCH-YARD.

again the final volume of the ten finished with a general index; but in 1801 a further five volumes were published, bringing the series up to date with the latest voyages and discoveries. A full set therefore amounts to twenty-five volumes, and a later, enlarged edition, still under Mavor's editorship, appeared in twenty-eight volumes, dated 1809 and 1810, under the title *A General Collection of Voyages and Travels*.

Another favourite with children of the day must have been the dramatically illustrated *The Mariner's Chronicle* (1810), by Archibald Duncan. Issued in six volumes, the work dealt exclusively with ship-wrecks and other disasters, each tale of death and destruction being accompanied by a copperplate engraving (some of which were folding) vividly portraying the scene. A few years before this *The Juvenile Travellers*, 1801, by Priscilla Wakefield (1751–1832) had made its appearance, complete with large folding hand-coloured map of the world. It was a companion volume to her *Excursions in North America*, 1806, which was similarly embellished.

One of John Harris's most attractive publications was *Cosmorama; A View of the Costumes and Peculiarities of All Nations* (1827), by Jehos-haphat Aspin, issued in the firm's standard binding of pictorially printed paper-covered boards with red leather spine. There are eighteen hand-coloured copperplate engravings, each divided into four com-partments, showing the manners, dress and customs of the inhabitants of the lands described. Aspin was gifted with an unconscious humour which was accentuated by his forthright opinions on the unfortunate members of the human race not lucky enough to have been born British. The Dutch he describes as:

> generally below middle statute, inclined to corpulency, and remark-able for a heavy awkward mien . . . The love of money is their ruling passion, and the spring of all their actions. They never lose a moment in the gratification of malice, the indulgence of envy, or the assump-tion of those petty triumphs, which, in other countries, fill life with much unnecessary misery.

The American nation fares just as badly:

> In the towns, no very striking difference exists among the inhabitants: the same tall, stout, well-dressed men every where appear, much at their ease, shrewd, and intelligent; but indolent; and, though boast-ing of freedom, generally slaves to idleness . . . The use of tobacco pervades the whole frame of society, from the President of the United States to the meanest pauper; neither the chair of state, the senate, the pulpit, the bar, nor the drawing-room, is exempt from

this annoyance and its loathsome consequence, the marks of which are witnessed upon the floors and walls even of the best apartments. Another prevailing vice is excessive drinking, and the pernicious practice of swallowing ardent spirits in large quantities is indulged in by all classes.

More and more books written solely for the amusement and entertainment of children were being published in London and the provinces until, by mid-century, stimulated by the increase in literacy amongst the young, what had been a mere trickle of entertainments swelled into a flood. Authors who leavened their stories too heavily with moral platitudes and pious sermons directed at saving the souls of their young readers from an eternity of hell-fire and damnation did not sell as well as those who produced straightforward romance in which the young heroes of the tale acted in a credible (but, of course, still strictly Christian) way. Commercial considerations were gradually shouldering righteous bigotry aside to give place to more forthright rivals-in-trade who nevertheless had themselves to conform in some degree to social, God-fearing attitudes.

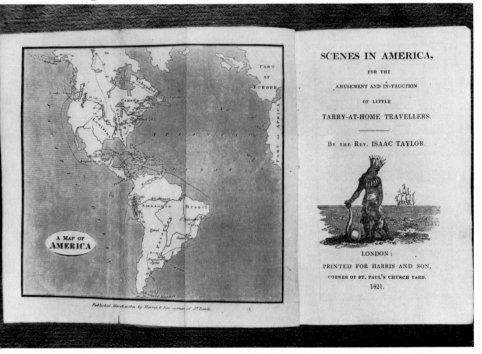

Each of Isaac Taylor's series of Scenes *contained eighty-four engravings and a folding map. They were issued at 4s plain or 6s coloured (20p or 30p). 16.5 × 10cm*

Mexicans is very dark. Those who dwell in the country possess only miserable huts. Maize, or Indian corn, serves them as bread: their favourite beverage is chocolate.

CALIFORNIA.

A large peninsula on the western coast of North America, extends from the tropic of Cancer to the 45th degree of N. latitude, called California.

The natural history of the country is yet very little known.

The authority of the Spaniards is precarious: the Indians here preserve their independence, and are unwilling to unfold the natural advantages of their country, fearful of the settlement of Europeans among them.

A great quantity of dew falls here every morning. which, settling on the rose-leaves, candies, and becomes hard like manna, having all the sweetness of refined sugar without its whiteness. Another singular production is plains of salt, quite firm, and clear as crystal. The coasts of California are noted for the pearl fishery.

Inhabitants of California.

THE

PLAYBOOK OF METALS:

INCLUDING

PERSONAL NARRATIVES OF VISITS TO COAL, LEAD, COPPER, AND TIN MINES;

WITH

A Large Number of Interesting Experiments

RELATING TO ALCHEMY AND THE CHEMISTRY OF THE FIFTY METALLIC ELEMENTS.

BY

JOHN HENRY PEPPER,

F.C.S., &. INST. C.E., LATE PROFESSOR OF CHEMISTRY AT THE ROYAL POLYTECHNIC, AUTHOR OF "THE PLAYBOOK OF SCIENCE."

Illustrated with nearly 300 Engravings.

LONDON:
ROUTLEDGE, WARNE, AND ROUTLEDGE,
FARRINGDON STREET.
NEW YORK; 56, WALKER STREET.
1861.

[The Author reserves the right of translation.]

MALLET'S MORTAR.

(Top) *One of the fifty-nine hand-coloured plates from* A Geographical Present, *1817, by Mary Anne Venning.* 14.7 × 8.8cm. *(Above)* A profusely illustrated work of 504 pages, written as a companion volume to the author's Boy's Playbook of Science. *Size of title-page* 18 × 12cm

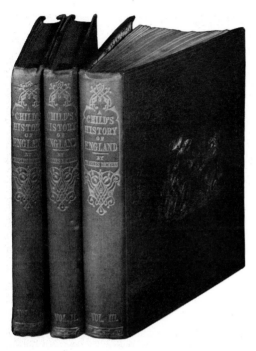

A Child's History of England, *by Charles Dickens, was illustrated by F. W. Topham. Issued in three volumes, dated 1852-3-4, it is a most difficult first edition to find in complete state, the first volume being nearly always a reprint. Height: 16cm*

There was also an expanding market for educational and instructional works for the young, so that two distinctive types of books emerged, the one instructive, the other entertaining, but there was now no necessity to apologise for not doing both. This division did not happen overnight, but by the 1850s a story book was usually a story book and not a religious catechism in disguise, or a thinly veiled didactic work on deportment and manners. By the time that Charles Dickens (1812–70) came to write *A Child's History of England*, 1852–3–4 (3 vols), a minor revolution in publishing practice had been accomplished. Books of instruction for children now had to evolve more obvious attractions, both in their binding styles and in the general format of their texts and illustrations. *The Playbook of Metals*, 1861, is an example of a serious work of instruction that had been specifically designed to be attractive and interesting to young readers. Issued, like its companion volume *The Playbook of Science*, 1860, in a bead-grain full-cloth binding, pictorially blocked on the front cover and spine in gold and blind, and with leaf-edges cut and gilded, it contained on its 504 pages a total of nearly three hundred woodcut illustrations by Edmund Evans and others. The *Playbook* was an encyclopaedia of knowledge that any child would have been proud to own. It contained some of the very latest scientific information and theories of the day, including those expounded by Charles Darwin in *On the Origin of Species*, 1859, published only two years before, and, more surprisingly perhaps, the first illustrated and detailed explanation in English of the now popularly accepted theory of Continental Drift. This theory had been propounded by A. Snider-Pellegrini in 1858, in his work entitled *La Création et ses Mystères dévoilés*. The editor of *The Playbook of Metals* and its companion volume was John Pepper (1821–1900), one-time Professor of Chemistry at the Royal Polytechnic, London, and both he and Routledge, Warne and Routledge the publishers are to be congratulated for issuing the best two works of elementary science of their day. Pepper took a delight in amusing young people by conducting a series of popular experiments, illusions and magic-lantern shows in halls throughout London. And it was in the same year, 1861, that Michael Faraday published for children his ever popular *A Course of Six Lectures on the Chemical History of a Candle*. The lectures themselves actually took place before a juvenile audience at the Royal Institution during the Christmas holiday break in December 1860 and January 1861, the book, with numerous woodcut illustrations, being published later that year. It passed through numerous editions.

In the USA, one of the most active writers in the field of children's literature in general, and school textbooks and primers in particular, was Samuel Griswold Goodrich (1793–1860), universally known by his pseudonym 'Peter Parley'. This name was shamelessly appropriated by publishers in Britain and used for the works of ghost writers whose sales were boosted by the Peter Parley label. Goodrich's first book was *Peter Parley's Tales of America*, 1827, published in Boston. It was here that the legendary figure first introduced himself to children:

Here I am! My name is Peter Parley: I am an old man. I am very gray and lame. But I have seen a great many things, and had a great many adventures, and I love to talk about them. I love to tell stories to children, and very often they come to my house, and they get around me and I tell them stories of what I have seen and of what I have heard. I live in Boston.

Goodrich probably coined the name from a character created by Hannah More (1745–1833), whom she had named 'Old Parley the Porter'. It is known that he had read and admired her works, and the fact that Miss More had described Parley as 'always talking about his experiences and adventures' may well have prompted Goodrich to borrow the name when he was seeking a pseudonym. However, according to his biographer Daniel Rosell, whose *Samuel Griswold Goodrich, Creator of Peter Parley*, 1968 (State University of New York Press, New York), contains much new information and bibliographical details, the name Peter Parley was fortuitous:

According to his daughter, one day when Goodrich was deliberating on the selection of a suitable pseudonym, he absent-mindedly started conjugating the French verb *parler*. Suddenly, either by the grace of Heaven or by the luck of a chance mispronunciation, he discovered the fascinating word *Parley*. It took Goodrich but a moment to realize the strong connection between Peter the Talker and Peter Parley, and his long sought *nom de plume* was born.

Whichever story is correct, the name was an instant success. The contents of his *Tales of America*, as with his other books of history and travel, were 'designed to give the child the first ideas of Geography and History', for which reason he was careful to research thoroughly, and to present what was then considered to be a factual background, although today his bias is obvious.

The secret of his success was once again the use of simple language coupled with an interesting text, full of action, and a real-life atmosphere in which the heroes occasionally actually ended up dead and the wicked occasionally escaped from justice. At the foot of many pages were series of simple questions relevant to the text immediately above, which children could ask themselves or each other as they read the book. Typical of Goodrich's prose style is this extract from his first book for children, taken from near the end of his *Tales of America*:

> In the year 1607, some English people, about one hundred in number, came to Virginia, and made a settlement on James River. The first town they built they called Jamestown. I need not tell you, that no people but Indians lived in this part of North America at that time. The great towns, such as Boston, New York, Philadelphia, and others, did not exist then. Vast forests extended over the whole country, and in those forests lived numerous tribes of Indians. These Indians were generally unfriendly to the white people, and would often kill them if they could.
>
> One day, Captain Smith, who was one of the people of Jamestown, had been up a river in a boat. He was discovered by the Indians, seized by them, and carried before Powhattan, who was their king. Powhattan and his counsellors decided that he should be put to death. Accordingly, he was brought forward and his head laid upon a stone. Powhattan then took a club, and raised it in the air to strike the fatal blow. What was his astonishment to see his daughter, a beautiful Indian girl, run shrieking between him and Smith, and place herself in a situation to shelter him from the club of her father!

The solid fare of fact sugared with the instant drama and excitement of a real-life (or backwoods fiction) hair's breadth escape from death at the hands of the Redskins. Youthful attention had seldom time to flag.

By the mid-1830s the name of Peter Parley was a household word with the juvenile reading public of the United States of America, but it was 1835 before the first of his collections of tales appeared in Britain. *Tales About Europe, Asia, Africa, and America*, 1835, was published by Thomas Tegg & Son, London, and printed by C. Whittingham at the Chiswick Press. This unauthorised version was issued in the same format as Peter Parley's American editions, a square octavo, in this case containing five hundred pages, with a total of 137 woodcut illustrations in the text. The four tales were originally published separately in Boston, but were here collected into a single volume. *Tales of Animals, comprising Quadrupeds, Birds, Fishes, Reptiles and Insects*, 1835, followed almost immediately, once again published by Thomas Tegg, who had obviously managed to acquire a set of the texts of the American editions.

Once Goodrich realised he had discovered a magic formula, he started churning out titles at a speed which led William Howe, writing later in *The Cambridge History of American Literature*, to describe him as 'the most prodigious literary hack of his day'. His first Peter Parley tale was followed by over a hundred others, and that number can be at least doubled by the titles which appeared over the same signature, but were in fact written by other authors in both Britain and the United States. Tegg in London dutifully republished all the titles he could lay his hands on, and *Tales About the Sun, Moon and Stars*, 1837, was followed by numerous others. But well before he issued *Tales about Rome and Modern Italy*, 1839, other London publishers were on the scent. *Peter Parley's Visit to London during the Coronation of Queen Victoria*, 1838, was issued by Charles Tilt and was almost certainly written by him. Another bookseller, Edward Lacy, had earned for himself the title of 'remainder man' due to his habit of making a substantial business out of buying up the printed sheets left unsold with other publishers, casing them up in flashy cloth bindings, and then issuing them with newly tipped-in title-pages, always undated, bearing his own imprint. Often he went so far as to change the title of a work, especially some of the annuals he issued. With his list of Peter Parley titles, he simply bought up sheets containing stories by other authors, tore out the original and correct titles and then inserted new and false ones. Such a one was his *Grandfather's Tales*, allegedly by Peter Parley.

Goodrich eventually found out what was going on in England and, to put it mildly, was extremely displeased, as he tells his readers in his autobiographical *Recollections of a Lifetime*, 1857 (2 vols, New York). The demand for Peter Parley titles grew to such an extent that Tegg was obliged to commission a hack writer, George Mogridge (1787–

1854), whose many pseudonyms included 'Old Humphrey' and 'Ephraim Holding', besides his later assumed title of 'Peter Parley'. His task was to compose a series of tales in the style of those originally compiled by Goodrich. *Peter Parley's Tales about Christmas*, 1839, and *Peter Parley's Shipwrecks and Disasters at Sea*, 1840, were two of the many titles from his pen. Tegg was eventually obliged to make a furious Samuel Goodrich an *ex gratia* payment of £400 in reluctant acknowledgement of his debt to the author, but books of instruction disguised in the Peter Parley manner were by this time available in quantity from several London publishing houses, including the well known Darton & Clark. In fact, John Maw Darton, and his business associates Samuel Clark and William Martin, systematically pirated every Peter Parley title they could lay their hands on. Within a few months of the first titles being issued, Samuel Clark, who was Darton's brother-in-law, began turning out fictitious Peter Parley books under the pseudonym of 'Revd. T. Wilson', a name he used with much success on a long series of *Popular School Catechisms* (1845–8), which embraced subjects as diverse as geography, music, natural philosphy, astronomy, Bible history and botany, among others. A number of the Peter Parley books contained a letter, apparently from Goodrich (although the initials are incorrect), stating:

Gentlemen:

I think it is now understood between us that I am to prepare a series of books, of which you are to be the Publishers. I undertake this task with pleasure, because it is my wish to be judged in England by what I do write, and not by what has been written for me.

I have been much vexed, since my arrival in this country, to see the name of Peter Parley attached to a number of books published in London, which I never saw or heard of, and which contain much of which I wholly disapprove, and consider to be contrary to good morals. I have also seen my books mutilated and altered so that I could scarcely recognize anything in them as my own, except the title and some disfigured fragments.

It is therefore a real satisfaction to me, that my future works are to make their appearance in England in genuine form . . .

S. E. Goodrich.

London; Aug. 1842.

Whether this letter was genuine or not, the activities of Darton & Clark finally led to Goodrich issuing writs for damages against the firm in the Supreme Court of New York State, where he obtained judgement in his favour in the sums of $7,816.40 damages, plus $138.76 costs. It is unlikely that the London firm ever paid him anything in settlement of this action. Acts of literacy piracy were not, however, confined to England, and publishers in the USA were equally guilty. Goodrich himself was as blameworthy as those he sued, for in 1819 he had published an eight-volume edition of the works of Walter Scott without obtaining the author's consent or paying him a penny in royalties.

Before leaving the subject of Goodrich's almost painless method of imparting facts, figures and a wealth of miscellaneous information to the young, mention must be made of the long series of annuals which appeared in England using his well known pseudonym. Issued as a magazine in monthly parts during 1839, the first *Peter Parley's Annual: A Christmas and New Year's Present for Young People* was published at the end of that year, dated forward to 1840. It was issued in a binding of straight-grained green cloth, blocked on the front cover and spine in gold and blind, with yellow end-papers and with the leaf-edges trimmed. The publishers were Simkin, Marshall & Co., London, and the unknown editor of the first volume told his young readers:

> I have had only one end in view; that is, your improvement. I do not think that you will complain of these pages ever being dry or tedious; but your *instruction* has been my *first aim*.

From the first issue a high standard was set; each volume had a series of full-page steel engravings finely executed by leading artists and engravers, and the numerous woodcuts in the text were above the average quality found in children's books of that period. The issue for 1843 had the frontispiece and engraved title-page printed by a two-colour patent chromographic process invented by Griffith, a combination of steel engraving and lithography. In the meantime, Darton & Clark had purchased an interest in the enterprise and their advertisements were tipped in the back of the volumes from 1842 onwards. In 1845 they took over the series completely from Simkin, Marshall & Company, and substituted a bright red cloth binding, blocked in gold and blind, in place of the drab green, brown or plum-coloured cloths used previously. Their issue dated 1846 contained some startling innovations and was a milestone in the annals of book production for children. Darton had never been afraid to experiment with new processes and his books were printed on the newly installed steam presses of D. A. Doudney, Long Lane, London, from the mid–1840s onwards. He was the first publisher to have colour-printed illustrations inserted in children's books, a more expensive process at that time than hand-colouring, especially for comparatively short runs. When the

1846 *Peter Parley's Annual* appeared in the bookshops, there was a brightly coloured frontispiece and title-page, both taken from designs by the young and as yet unknown artist Harrison Weir (1824–1906), who had been apprenticed to the famous George Baxter. These illustrations had been printed in about ten colours from woodblocks by Gregory, Collins & Reynolds of Charterhouse Square, and from that time onwards each new annual contained plates colour printed by various processes. The enterprise well deserved the success that attended it, and for a total of fifty-five years, until 1894, Peter Parley annuals were on sale in the bookshops in time for Christmas.

In later years, Samuel Goodrich even came to resemble the fictitious character he had created — gouty foot, silver hair, stout wooden cane and all. He deserves a niche in the annals of American literary history as the author of some of the most popular and widely read books produced for the instruction, amusement and education of nineteenth-century children, books they apparently read with a great deal of pleasure and by means of which they were introduced to a world of interests they would not otherwise have known. His books are on my shelves here in my isolated home on the cliffs of far west Cornwall, their spines blocked in gold pictorially in a rainbow of coloured cloth bindings, side by side with the imitators who recognised the value of his approach to young people.

5

VERSE AND RHYMES

Most of the early verse aimed at juveniles seemed intended to chill them into righteous submission. Nathaniel Crouch (1632?–1725), the author of many books attributed on the title-pages to 'R.B.' or 'Robert (or Richard) Burton', published *Youth's Divine Pastimes*, 1691, consisting of thirty-six Bible stories in verse, each illustrated with a crude woodcut, and each calculated to instil fear of the wrath of a vengeful God into the hearts of youth:

> When Men by Sin and Violence
> Did stain the Earth with Blood,
> God did resolve to wash them thence
> By Waters of a Flood.
>
> Yet did he warn before he struck,
> *Noah* was sent to tell
> They by their Sins would God provoke
> To cast them down to Hell.

Some of the first printed verse recited with at least a modicum of amusement by children, for many of the rhymes jingle in the memory long after the book is read, were contained in *Divine Songs, Attempted in Easy Language; for the Use of Schools*, 1745, by the Nonconformist schoolmaster and hymnologist Isaac Watts (1674–1748). The work was an immediate and lasting success, and at least twenty editions in book and chapbook form were called for in less than seven years. Watts, unlike many of his contemporaries, had realised that the power to understand complex religious argument is not given to the very young, so he sugared his moral propaganda with catch-phrases in tramping rhymes and jingles. He gave his young readers easily remembered pictures of the comedy and tragedy of everyday life, as well as glimpses of the thunderous religious dramas being played by well-meaning theologians who were constantly at each other's throats. His versatility enabled him to move from the gentleness of a *A Cradle Hymn*, with its lullaby of words:

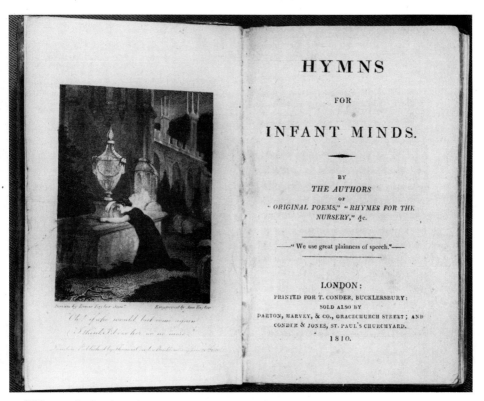

HYMNS

FOR

INFANT MINDS.

BY
THE AUTHORS
OF
"ORIGINAL POEMS," "RHYMES FOR THE
NURSERY," &c.

——"We use great plainness of speech."——

LONDON:
PRINTED FOR T. CONDER, BUCKLERSBURY:
SOLD ALSO BY
DARTON, HARVEY, & CO., GRACECHURCH STREET; AND
CONDER & JONES, ST. PAUL'S CHURCHYARD.
1810.

This was the first book to be written entirely by Jane and Ann Taylor, daughters of the Revd Isaac Taylor. Size of title-page: 14 × 8.6cm

Hush! my dear, lie still and slumber,
   Holy Angels guard thy Bed!
Heavenly Blessings without Number
   Gently falling on thy Head.

Sleep, my Babe; thy Food and Raiment,
   House and Home thy Friends provide;
All without thy Care or Payment,
   All thy Wants are well supply'd

to the grim Janeway warnings and the dark threats of his verses *Against Lying*:

The Lord delights in them that speak
   The Words of Truth; but ev'ry Lyar
Must have his Portion in the Lake
   That burns with Brimstone, and with Fire.

109

Then let me always watch my Lips,
Lest I be struck to Death and Hell,
Since God a Book of Reck'ning keeps
For ev'ry Lie that Children tell.

Many of Watts' verses are only remembered today in the form in which Lewis Carroll parodied them, but children in the early eighteenth century read the words as he wrote them. They were a task set at school and repeated in front of the class of other young hopefuls awaiting their turn; most of whom no doubt had their revenge when they had children of their own:

Let Children that would fear the Lord
Hear what their Teachers say:
With Rev'rence meet their Parents Word,
And with Delight obey.

Have you not heard what dreadful Plagues
Are threaten'd by the Lord,
To him that breaks his Father's Law,
Or mocks his Mother's Word?

Any eighteenth-century copy of Watts' *Divine Songs*, whether in the authorised versions or in one of the many piracies that appeared throughout the succeeding decades, is a prize which deserves a prominent place in any collection of early children's books. Despite the large number of editions which appeared before the end of the century, all are difficult to find, a tribute to the number of times the little books were handled and read, mothers handing sons and daughters their own childhood copies to peruse, and fathers solemnly presenting what had been their favourite book of verse to their offspring to enjoy. Disbound and unstitched, the leaves would be collected as they fell, until finally the fire or the dustbin claimed what was left. Reprints, extended to the present day, are legion, one of the most attractive of the earlier ones being *Songs, Divine and Moral*, 1826, published by W. Simkin, R. Marshall and J. Johnson, London, issued in a binding of pictorially printed paper-covered boards, the leaf-edges being left uncut. This edition had sixty fine-quality woodcut illustrations, the text being enclosed in ruled borders; the whole book being designed, edited and printed by J. Johnson, whose *Typographia; or, Printer's Instructor*, 1824 (2 vols), was the definitive work of its day.

Little Master's Miscellany, 1742, has been mentioned in a previous chapter, the compiler being unknown, but most of the verse printed in

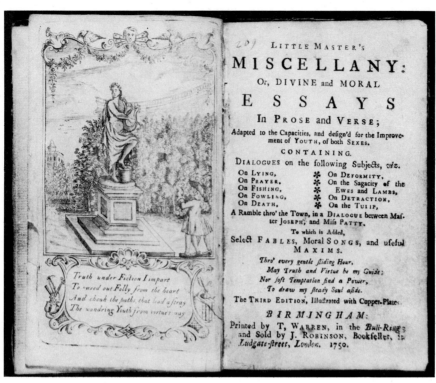

One of the earliest books of children's verse to have survived, shown here in the third edition, 1750. The poems and songs were specially written for the work, but the editor has not been identified. Size of title-page: 15 × 9cm

it appears to be original, some, as usual, being directed to improving the minds and morals of the young:

> Their Parent's hopes they'll not defeat,
>   By passion for a tinsel Dress,
> Appearing modest, plain, and neat,
>   Nor laws of decency transgress.

> Such are the little Trifflers gay,
>   Sweet objects of our Hopes and Fear
> That sooth our Thoughts, by Night and Day,
>   Our Joy, or Sorrow centers here.

Children lucky enough to be given a copy of this first juvenile miscellany of prose and verse had a wide choice of reading, with a selection of poems on the tulip, the woodlark, fishing, hunting and wild fowling; or, if they preferred it, on death, deformity, lying and

111

detraction, as well as stories, dialogues and a succession of fables in verse. Of particular interest to literary historians and the students or collectors of the works of the great Cham of literature is the printing of a supposed conversation between a brother and his young sister in a bookshop:

> Here's a Poem just now from the Printer come in;
> 'Twas Puff'd I presume in the last *Magazine*!
> My Master Sir! never descended so low,
> Mr. Cave, I believe, knows the Author, — or so!
> Here's *London* Sir! wrote in an elegant Style,
> That would make the old Satyrist Juvenal smile . . .

This reference to Samuel Johnson's *London: A Poem, in Imitation of the Third Satire of Juvenal*, 1738, and to Edward Cave (1691–1754), the printer and publisher who founded *The Gentleman's Magazine*, on which he employed Johnson in a journalistic capacity for many years, is surprising in a book intended for young children.

The Top Book of All, for Little Masters and Misses (c.1760) contains eight well known nursery rhymes, including 'Jack Nory' and 'The Three Jovial Welshmen'. *A Little Pretty Pocket Book*, 1744, has already been mentioned as the first book for children published by John Newbery on his arrival in London to set up business. In its verses, it describes a number of children's games, including the familiar 'Boys and Girls come out to Play', as well as a rhyming alphabet, giving the version commencing 'Great A, B, and C'. The earliest known example of this device for teaching children the alphabet is that contained in *A Little Book for Little Children* (c. 1710), by 'T.W.', and sold at the Ring in Little Britain, a district of central London where many booksellers had their stalls. This version commences:

> A was an Archer, and shot at a Frog;
> B was a Blind-man, and led by a Dog;
> C was a Cutpurse, and liv'd in disgrace;
> D was a Drunkard, and had a red Face:
> E was an Eater, a Glutton was he;
> F was a Fighter, and fought with a Flea:
> G was a Gyant, and pul'd down a House;
> H was a Hunter, and hunted a Mouse:

and so on, to the end of the alphabet. The same rhyme was printed at Boston, USA, as early as 1761.

Many of the later versions had a second line couplet for each letter:

112

A was an Archer and shot at a frog,
But missing his mark shot into a bog;
B was a Butcher and had a great dog,
Who always went round the streets with a clog.

Visions in Verse, for the Entertainment and Instruction of Younger Minds,
1751, published anonymously by Nathaniel Cotton (1705–88), claims
a place in a library of children's books chiefly by virtue of its title.
Cotton was a physician who had studied at Leyden before settling at
St Albans, where he established a general practice and a private mad-
house which later housed the poet William Cowper. *Visions in Verse* was
popular in its day (the tenth edition appeared in 1782) and consisted
of nine allegories, including slander, pleasure, health, marriage,
life and death. But the book was aimed, one would have thought, at
parents and guardians rather than at the children in their care. Political
and social satire was freely used, and in so oblique and obtuse a form
that no young person under the age of eighteen could possibly have
understood the author's allusions. Despite this, he tells his readers that:

Childhood and Youth engage my Pen,
'Tis Labour lost to talk to Men.
Youth may, perhaps, reform, when wrong,
Age will not listen to my Song.
He who at Fifty is a Fool,
Is far too stubborn grown for School.

On quite another level, and one that could be comprehended by any
intelligent child over the age of, say, twelve, was John Newbery's
Circle of the Sciences mentioned earlier. The first three volumes of the
series were advertised in *The Penny London Post* on 18 January 1745;
but it is the fourth volume which concerns us here. *Poetry made familiar
and easy to Young Gentlemen and Ladies*, 1746, is represented in my own
collection only by the third edition of 1769, published by Newbery &
Carnan. However, the little volume is still in its original binding of blue
paper-covered boards with a spine of green vellum, on which is
Carnan's printed label giving the title and the volume number, and even
individual copies of this important juvenile production are now so rare
as always to command very high prices. The only complete set of the
first edition of all twelve volumes I know of is that in the British
Library. *Poetry made familiar and easy* is almost certainly by Newbery
himself (the dedication is signed by him) and sets out rules enabling
young people to recognise metre and the differing styles of versifying,
although most of the examples quoted had been culled from other pens.

His successor in the business, Elizabeth Newbery, published several books of verse, including a number by John Huddlestone Wynne (1743–88), an eccentric whose promise to his mother on her deathbed that he would 'shun horses, and never go into a boat or a belfry' led him, when drunk, to step backwards under the wheels of a hackney carriage when avoiding an approaching horse. He survived with a badly crippled leg for another ten years. *Choice Emblems . . . for the Improvement and Pastime of Youth*, 1772, was the first of several poetical works he published, while *Tales for Youth; in thirty poems*, 1794, contained a delightful series of woodcuts by Thomas Bewick which rank with the best of the artist's work. Probably the most sought after of Wynne's books for children are issues of the first edition of *Fables of Flowers, for the Female Sex*, 1773, containing fifteen engraved plates, each divided into two scenes. The work was issued with and without the plates, the latter edition being at a reduced price. The first issue of the first edition may be recognised by the Latin date being misprinted 'MDDCLXXIII'.

As the eighteenth century drew to its close, poetry books for children were issued in increasing numbers by provincial as well as London booksellers (the term being synonymous with publisher in those days). *Pretty Little Poems for Pretty Little Children* (*c*.1790) appeared under a Gainsborough imprint, while *The Twelfth Cake. A Juvenile Amusement consisting of little Ballads, to be Sung by the following characters viz King, Queen, Sailors wife, Match girl, Simon Pure, Ballad singer, and Harlequin*, by Reginald Spofforth (*c*. 1798), was illustrated with eight charming vignettes and issued in paper covers.

My own copy of *The Bee, a Selection of Poetry from the best Authors*, 1793, proclaims itself to be a 'New Edition' on its engraved title-page. It was a collection of poetry for children which sold extremely well. Published by Darton & Harvey, London, new editions continued to appear until well into the first quarter of the nineteenth century.

Poetry for Children, by Lucy Aikin (1781–1864), made its appearance in 1801, the book being composed for the most part of selections from the works of such diverse authors in both quality and time as John Dryden and Mrs Barbauld, although the young compiler included several original poems of her own. The title was a success, five editions being published in the space of the ensuing seven years and the work continued in print until the 1850s. This may well have been the collection used by Lewis Carroll when he selected the poems he parodied so successfully in the *Alice* books. The Isaac Watts verses he converted were in Miss Aikin's book, and also 'The Old Man's Comforts and how he Gained them', by Robert Southey, starting with the well known line ' "You are old, father William," the young man cried,' also used by

114

Carroll. Lucy Aikin was the daughter of John Aikin, man of letters and physician, who was himself joint author with his sister Mrs Anna Laetitia Barbauld (1743–1825), of *Evenings at Home; or, The Juvenile Budget Opened*, 1792–6 (6 vols), already mentioned, a collection of stories, poems, etc, that had been warmly praised by Maria Edgeworth.

It was in June 1803 that the publishers William Darton and Joseph Harvey hit upon the idea of compiling a poetical miscellany especially for children, with the result that they finally produced one of the most popular books of verse for juveniles of the nineteenth century. They started by writing to likely correspondents asking them to submit 'something in the way of moral songs (though not songs) or short tales turned into verse'. The work was published as *Original Poems, for Infant Minds, by Several young persons*, (1804–5), in two volumes. Jane Taylor (1783–1824) and her sister Ann Gilbert, née Taylor (1782–1866), were the principal contributors, although Isaac Taylor, their brother, and possibly their father Isaac Taylor of Ongar also provided verses. Others were Bernard Barton and Adelaide O'Keeffe, the last named having a total of thirty-four poems accepted, although neither of them at that time was known to any of the Taylor family. In her autobiography, published in 1874, Ann Gilbert complained that having 'written to order we had no control over the getting out of the volumes and should have been better pleased if contributions from other hands had been omitted'. Her sister Jane wrote, for the most part, about nature and the countryside, while Ann's poems were centred more on town life and the domestic scene. The first poem in the book is from her hand and is almost certainly drawn from a scene she remembered from early childhood:

> Little Ann and her mother were walking one day,
> Through London's wide city so fair;
> And bus'ness oblig'd them to go by the way
> That led them through Cavendish Square.

> And as they pass'd by the great house of a lord,
> A beautiful chariot there came,
> To take some most elegant ladies abroad,
> Who straightway got into the same.

> The ladies in feathers and jewels were seen,
> The chariot was painted all o'er,
> The footmen behind were in silver and green,
> The horses were prancing before.

Little Ann, by her mother walk'd silent and sad,
A tear trickled down from her eye;
Till her mother said, 'Ann, I should be very glad,
To know what it is makes you cry.'

'Mamma,' said the child, 'see that carriage so fair,
All cover'd with varnish and gold,
Those ladies are riding so charmingly there,
While we have to walk in the cold:

You say God is kind to the folks that are good,
But surely it cannot be true;
Or else I am certain, almost, that he wou'd
Give such a fine carriage to you.'

Inevitably, by the end of the poem her mother had drawn the expected moral. However, the work saw the first appearance of some established favourites, including the oft-quoted *My Mother*. Adelaide was the daughter of the famous dramatist John O'Keeffe, and in her verses she attempted to draw her young readers' attention to many of the domestic dramas and tragedies about the home by poems headed 'Never Play with Fire', 'False Alarms', 'The Truant Boys', etc, with 'George and the Chimney-Sweeper' commencing:

His petticoats now George cast off,
For he was four years old;
His trousers were nankeen so fine,
His buttons bright as gold.
'May I,' said little George, 'go out
My pretty clothes to show?
May I, papa? may I, mamma?'
The answer was — 'No, no.'

Five editions of *Original Poems for Infant Minds* were called for in a space of less than twelve months and the work was never out of print for the rest of the nineteenth century. In 1875, a complete edition, finally revised by Mrs Gilbert, was published. Many selections of the poems, under a succession of differing titles, were issued, illustrated by the leading artists and engravers of the day, of which *Little Ann and Other Poems* (1883), by Kate Greenaway, is possibly the best known. Ann and Jane Taylor produced several other books of verse. *Rhymes for the Nursery*, 1806, containing the famous *Twinkle, twinkle, little Star*, reached its twenty-seventh edition in 1835, while *Hymns for Infant*

Minds, 1810, went through no less than sixty editions before 1890. Many literary historians consider that *Poetry for Children* and its successors had a most important influence in the development of the genre, subsequent 'moral songs', with their characteristic combination of pedestrian rhymes and sweet sentiment, having a notable effect on Victorian versifiers almost to the Edwardian era.

The appearance of *The Butterfly's Ball and the Grasshopper's Feast* in 1807 ushered in an era where children could sometimes be permitted to be amused without having to pay the penalty of admonition. Almost every tale or poem until then was finger-shaking in their direction: they must say their prayers, wash their faces, take care of their clothes, respect their parents, salute the vicar, and be loving and kind to the brat next door. However, the appearance of this little book, with its fourteen copperplate engravings in a binding of bright yellow pictorially printed wrappers, was a landmark in the annals of children's literature. The verses had first appeared in *The Gentleman's Magazine* in November 1806, before being issued in book form in January 1807, with plain or coloured engravings by William Mulready. Their author, William Roscoe (1753–1831), had left school before the age of twelve to help in his father's market garden, where he shouldered sacks of potatoes until the age of sixteen. With the help of friends he studied the classics and foreign languages, and in 1774 he was admitted as an attorney in the King's Bench. By 1796 he was a rich man, and retired from business to live in his mansion some six miles from Liverpool. It was here that he wrote what was to become a classic of the nursery for his young son Robert, and *The Butterfly's Ball* became assured of even greater success when the work attracted the attention of the King George III and Queen Charlotte, who requested that it should be set to music by Sir George Smart to amuse the little princesses. It proved immensely popular with several generations of children and soon led to a host of imitators. The best known of these was *The Peacock 'at home'*, 1807, by Mrs Catherine Dorset (1750?–1817?), published, as was Roscoe's title, by John Harris. It appeared in September 1807 in a format that matched Roscoe's original work, with a blue binding and pictorially printed covers containing an advertisement for *The Butterfly's Ball* on the back. The six copperplate engravings after William Mulready were once again available in either plain or coloured form.

Roscoe followed his success by producing *The Butterfly's Birth-Day* in 1809, again issued by John Harris, but this time in conjunction with Longman, Hurst, Rees and Orme, who must have paid well for their share of the copyright. On the back cover Harris had written: 'A better proof cannot be given of the estimation in which these little works have been held by the public, than the assurance of the publisher, that, together, nearly forty thousand copies!!! have been sold in twelve months.' Whether *The Butterfly's Birth-Day* did as well as its two predecessors we don't know, but presumably it did, for at least twenty unauthorised sequels under various titles, such as *The Elephant's Ball*, 1807, by an unidentified 'W.B.', *The Lion's Parliament*, 1808, *The Horse's Levee*, 1808, *Flora's Gala*, 1808, and *The Lobster's Voyage*, 1808 — most of which were published anonymously — were quickly in the bookshops. Similar titles continued to appear, and even some fifty years later a version, this time in quarto size, but with verses akin to Roscoe's, came out as *The Butterfly's Ball and the Grasshopper's Feast*, 1857, by 'Comus' (ie R.M. Ballantyne), under the imprint of Thomas Nelson & Sons.

> On the smooth-shaven grass by the side of the wood,
> Beneath a broad oak that for ages has stood,
> See the children of earth, and the tenants of air,
> For an evening's amusement together repair.
>
> And there came the Beetle, so blind, and so black,
> Who carried the Emmet, his friend, on his back;
> And there came the Gnat, and the Dragonfly too,
> And all their relations, green, orange, and blue.
>
> And there came the Moth, with her plumage of down,
> And the Hornet, with jacket of yellow and brown,
> Who with him, the Wasp, his companion did bring;
> They promised that evening to lay by their sting.
>
> Then the sly little Dormouse peep'd out of his hole,
> And led to the feast his blind cousin the Mole;
> And the Snail, with her horns peeping out from her shell,
> Came fatigued with the distance, the length of an ell.

And so on, verse after verse under the original heading:

> Come, take up your hats, and a-way let us haste,
> To the Butterfly's Ball, and the Grasshopper's Feast:
> For the trumpeter Gadfly has summon'd his crew,
> And the revels are now only waiting for you

which acted as the repeated chorus.

The year before this, Ballantyne had published, in similar format, the now well known poem of *The Three Little Kittens,* the verses having made their first British appearance in *The Charm Almanack* of 1853, published by Addey & Co., Old Bond Street, London, having originally appeared in the USA in both *New Nursery Songs for all Good Children* (1843), by Eliza Follen (1787–1860), and in *Only True Mother Goose Melodies* (1843). However, in both cases they are assumed to have been culled from traditional sources.

The 1807 appearance of *The Butterfly's Ball* paved the way for the appearance of the illustrated limerick books, the first printing of this jingling metrical form being that of *The History of Sixteen Wonderful Old Women*, 1820, which was Number 15 in *Harris's Cabinet of Amusement and Instruction*. Engravings, hand-coloured in some copies, were printed above the limericks, the first of which reads:

> There was an Old Woman named Towl,
> Who went out to Sea with her Owl,
> > But the Owl was Sea-sick,
> > And screamed for Physic;
> Which sadly annoy'd Mistress Towl.

Anecdotes and Adventures of Fifteen Gentlemen (*c*.1822), published by John Marshall, with verses attributed to R. S. Sharpe, was described as embellished with 'fifteen laughable engravings' (probably by Robert Cruikshank) and takes its place as the second limerick book, once again originally published for the amusement of children. The limerick form of verse is always associated with the name of Edward Lear (1812–88); but he certainly did not invent it and acknowledged that he modelled his verses on those found in the book quoted immediately above. His *Book of Nonsense*, 1846 (2 vols), was published by Thomas McLean, London, in pictorially printed paper-covered boards, lettered in white, with the spines of a distinctive bright red linen. Each volume had an illustrated title-page, but, needless to say, complete and unsullied copies are seldom (if ever!) found.

> There was an old Derry down Derry
> Who loved to see little folks merry:
> > So he made them a book,
> > And with laughter they shook,
> At the fun of that Derry down Derry!

was the first of the little verses that were to make his name famous, and which he continued to produce in works such as *A Book of Nonsense and more Nonsense*, 1862, *More Nonsense, pictures, rhymes, botany, etc*, 1872, and *Laughable lyrics: a fresh book of nonsense poems*, 1877.

119

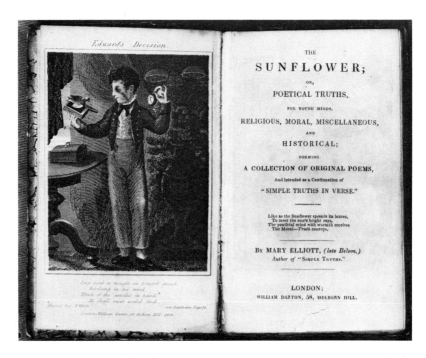

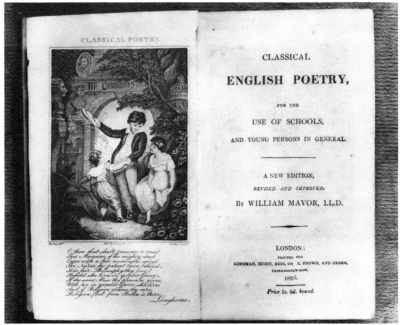

(Top) *Mary Elliott, a Quaker by birth and persuasion, published her first book of children's verse,* Simple Truths, *in 1816, followed by this continuation of her moral theme in 1822. 14.3 × 8.8cm.* (Above) *First published in 1823, this second edition of collected poems runs to 480 pages. The author was headmaster of Woodstock Grammar School, Oxford. 17.5 × 10cm*

Amongst the shelves devoted to poetry and verse for children I see a handful of works by Mrs Mary Elliott (née Belson), such as *Simple Truths in Verse*, 1812, *The Sunflower; or, Poetical Truths* (1822), *The Baby's Holiday*, 1812, *The progress of the Quartern-Loaf* (1820) and *The Rose, containing original poems for Young People* (1824), several of which have hand-coloured engravings to accompany the text.

Classical English Poetry, for the Use of Schools, and Young Persons in General, 1823, was edited by William Mavor (1758–1837), the second edition of which, dated 1825, is described in inserted advertisements as being 'closely printed in Duodecimo'. With a total of 480 pages, they advised that it was good value at 5s 6d (27½p). *Selections from the Poems of William Wordsworth, Esq. Chiefly for the Use of Schools and Young Persons*, 1831, published by Edward Moxon, London, is now a scarce and expensive book, especially if still in its original binding of drab paper-covered boards, with paper-labelled spine and uncut leaf-edges. A work even more desirable and of far greater rarity is the slim little volume published by William Pickering in July 1839 of *Songs of Innocence and of Experience, shewing the Two Contrary states of the Human Soul*, by William Blake (1757–1827), the poet and painter. The first issue, in its blind-stamped binding of plum-coloured cloth, is now an extremely expensive volume to acquire, one of the poems included having given great offence to the Establishment of that time, so that when the volume was re-issued the leaf containing 'The Little Vagabond' was excised.

> Dear mother! Dear mother! the church is cold,
> But the ale-house is healthy, and pleasant, and warm;
> Besides I can tell when I am used well;
> Such usage in heaven will never do well.
>
> But if at the church they would give us some ale,
> And a pleasant fire our souls regale,
> We'd sing and we'd pray all the live-long day,
> Nor ever once wish from the church to stray.
>
> Then the parson might preach, and drink, and sing,
> And we'd be as happy as birds in the spring,
> And modest dame Lurch, who is always at church,
> Would not have bandy children, nor fasting, nor birch.
>
> And God, like a father, rejoicing to see
> His children as pleasant and happy as He,
> Would have no more quarrel with the devil or the barrel,
> But kiss him and give him both drink and apparel.

121

Blake's verses were originally published as *Poetical Sketches*, 1783, by 'W.B.', and it is a fortunate collector who can boast of having that volume on his shelves. Even the second issue of the 1839 edition, both being the first typographical issues of Blake's *Songs*, containing as it does all the well known and admired poems, such as 'Piping down the valleys wild', 'When the voices of children are heard on the green, and laughing is heard on the hill', 'Little lamb, who made thee?', 'Tiger! Tiger! burning bright, In the forests of the night', 'I was angry with my friend, I told my wrath, my wrath did end' and the enigmatic 'O Rose! thou art sick!', to quote first lines, is itself a delightful book to own, though one wonders if any but highly perceptive teenagers would have grasped all his subtleties of meaning. The 1839 edition had been edited by J. J. G. Wilkinson (1812–99), a mystic and leading member of the Swedenborgian Society, and a friend of Henry James and Emerson. One of the poems he printed in this collection had made its appearance some fifteen years before in *The Chimney-Sweeper's Friend, and Climbing-Boy's Album*, 1824, edited by James Montgomery (see illustration, page 144), an important collection of tales, essays and poems aimed at putting pressure on legislators to have the laws changed to prevent the manifest cruelty of thrusting little boys up chimneys as human brushes. Sir Walter Scott had written to Montgomery stating that he was a sincere friend of the cause:

and in building my house at this place [Abbotsford] I have taken particular care, by the construction of vents, that no such cruelty shall be practised within its precincts. I have made them circular, about fourteen inches in diameter, and lined them with a succession of earthen pots, about one and a half inch thick, (like the common chimney-tops) which are built round by the masonry, and form the tunnel for the passage of smoke. The advantage is, that the interior being entirely smooth, and presenting no inequality or angle where soot could be deposited, there is, in fact, very little formed; and that which may adhere is removed by the use of a simple machine.

Scott was in many ways an innovator, Abbotsford being one of the first houses in Scotland to be illuminated by gas. No doubt the chimneys still contain their pot linings to this day.

Blake's poem had been sent to Montgomery by Charles Lamb, who had apparently discovered it in the beautifully engraved 1789 edition of *Songs of Innocence*:

When my mother died I was very young,
And my father sold me, while yet my tongue

122

Could scarcely cry, 'Weep! weep! weep!'
So your chimneys I sweep, and in soot I sleep.

There's little Tom Toddy, who cried when his head,
That curled like a lamb's back, was shaved, so I said,
'Hush, Tom, never mind it, for when your head's bare,
You know that the soot cannot spoil your white hair'

followed by four more stanzas in similar vein.

In 1842, Robert Browning published *Dramatic Lyrics*, this being the third part of his eight-part collection entitled *Bells and Pomegranates*. It contained one poem that has fascinated children ever since: 'The Pied Piper of Hamelin', taken from a legendary source, possibly the enthusiastic 'Children's Crusade' of 1212, when a child named Nicolas of Cologne roused into religious fervour some twenty thousand youngsters, a great many of whom subsequently perished. However, in Browning's version the piper's name was Bunting.

In 1888 Kate Greenaway published (undated) an illustrated version of the tale which John Ruskin considered marked the pinnacle of her success as an artist. She had met Browning in 1882, having been introduced by her friend Frederick Locker-Lampson, himself a poet and book collector. Greenaway's version of *The Pied Piper of Hamelin* had thirty-five illustrations engraved and colour printed by Edmund Evans, and is a delightful book to read and handle, being bound in glazed pictorially printed boards showing a picture of the piper holding out his hand for payment. An almost square quarto, with the leaf-edges stained blue, it is now a most difficult volume to find in anything like acceptable condition. It was published under the George Routledge imprint as a first edition, later editions being issued by Frederick Warne & Co.

In the second half of the nineteenth century poetry for children frequently occupied the talents of writers of the highest quality. Other, less distinguished, names wrote perhaps a verse or two that are still remembered, though the author or authoress cannot now be recalled without aid of *The Oxford Dictionary of Quotations*, having sunk into the mists of oblivion. One name of enduring fame was Christina Georgina Rossetti (1830–94), the sister of Dante Gabriel Rossetti (1828–82). She contributed her earliest writings to *The Germ*, a periodical that made its first appearance on 1 January 1850 as the journal of the Pre-Raphaelite Brotherhood. Her first regularly published work was *Goblin Market and other Poems*, 1862; although *Verses*, 1847, a small book of poems dedicated to her mother, had been privately printed by G. Polidori, who, in 1842, when Christina was only twelve years of

123

age, had printed one of her poems as a single sheet. *Goblin Market* is also sought by connoisseurs of binding styles, having been issued in an avant-garde format of straight-ribbed blue cloth, blocked in gilt on the front cover with a motif of lines and roundels designed by her brother. The frontispiece and title-page were also designed by D. G. Rossetti, himself a poet and artist of high repute. As a pioneering book design in complete contrast to the general styles of the period in which it appeared, the format is some thirty or more years ahead of its time.

Despite the book's title, the verses could only have appealed to young people in their late teens, whereas *Sing-Song. A Nursery Rhyme Book*, 1872, with its series of 120 delightful woodcut illustrations by Arthur Hughes, engraved by the brothers Dalziel, would have brought

Randolph Caldecott (1846–86), is remembered today for the sixteen picture books he designed and executed for children, as well as for his other illustrative work. This set was issued separately from 1878 to 1885. The one shown here is from A Farmer went trotting upon his Grey Mare, *which formed the second of the stories in verse in the* Ride-A-Cock Horse to Banbury Cross *issue. Size across each page: 23.5 × 20cm*

The mischievous Raven flew laughing away;
Bumpety, bumpety, bump!
And vowed he would serve them the same the next day;
Lumpety, lumpety, lump!

22

pleasure to children of all ages. The first issue of the first edition is blocked pictorially in gold on the front cover and spine, while later issues have the same design blocked in gold and black. Macmillan & Co. issued a 'new and enlarged edition', dated 1893, in a moiré, fine-ribbed cloth binding lettered only on the spine. *Speaking Likenesses*, 1874, again with illustrations by Arthur Hughes, is a fairy story in prose, a fantasy that exhibits many points of similarity with Lewis Carroll's *Alice's Adventures in Wonderland*. The work deserves a special place in any collection of children's books, not only for the text, but for the series of dream-like images which Arthur Hughes drew, no doubt under the influence of Tenniel, in a style which exactly captured the atmosphere of the story.

Pleasant Rhymes for Little Readers or Jottings for Juveniles, 1864, by 'Josephine', is a work by an unknown author which is sought more for the attractiveness of its gold-blocked cloth binding and fine coloured frontispiece by Kronheim than for the quality of its verse. The work first appeared in 1862, under the title *Jottings for Juveniles in Simple Verse*, but in an entirely different format.

A Child's Garden of Verses, 1885, by Robert Louis Stevenson (1850–94), was an instant and enduring success and has seldom, if ever, been out of print since its original appearance. Of the sixty-four poems, thirty-nine had been privately printed in 1883 under the title *Penny Whistles*, but I have never seen a copy of this rarity offered for sale. *A Child's Garden of Verses* was issued in a binding of blue cloth over bevelled boards, the top edges of the leaves gilded and the others left uncut, the text printed on stiff paper surrounded by meadows of margin. The second edition, almost identical in format, appeared dated the same year as the first, and the fourth came out in 1890. The first poem, 'Bed in Summer', displays the deceptively simple style Stevenson employed throughout the work, making it easy for children to recite and memorise each verse:

> In winter I get up at night
> And dress by yellow candle-light.
> In summer, quite the other way,
> I have to go to bed by day.
>
> I have to go to bed and see
> The birds still hopping on the tree,
> Or hear the grown-up people's feet
> Still going past me in the street.
>
> And does it not seem hard to you,
> When all the sky is clear and blue,
> And I should like so much to play,
> To have to go to bed by day?

Nonsense verse was still being written during the closing years of the century. *A Bad Child's Book of Beasts* (1896), *More Beasts for Worse Children* (1897) and *The Moral Alphabet* (1899) were all by Hilaire Belloc (1870–1953), a Catholic controversialist whose main canon of work was historical. His *Cautionary Tales for Children* (1908) had a sequel over twenty years later in *New Cautionary Tales* (1930). His first publication, *Verses and Sonnets*, 1896, contained 'The Justice of the Peace', a left-wing poem he apparently later regretted. He withdrew the volume from publication and destroyed all the copies he could get his hands on, with the result that the work is now extremely rare.

Ruthless Rhymes — for Heartless Homes (1899) by Col D. Streamer (ie Harry J. C. Graham — 1874–1936), issued in red-printed pictorial boards, contained, as stated, some ruthless rhymes:

126

Sam had spirits naught could check,
  And today, at breakfast, he
Broke his baby-sister's neck,
  So he shan't have jam for tea!

In quite different vein were the series of ten volumes in matching format by Juliana Horatia Ewing (née Gatty) (1841–85), with titles such as *Little Boys and Wooden Horses, Touch him if you Dare, Mother's Birthday Review, The Doll's Wash*, etc, published about 1884, and collected as much for their pictorial boards and other illustrations by R. André (see illustration, page 163). They were originally sold at 1s (5p) each, and still make a colourful display that attracts present-day children, just as it once did their grandmothers.

Walter de la Mare (1873–1956) wrote his first book under the pseudonym 'Walter Ramal' — *Songs of Childhood*, 1902. Then there was silence except for *Poems*, 1906, intended for adults, until in 1910 he produced *The Three Mulla-Mulgars* (the title was later changed to *The Three Royal Monkeys*), a work which, after a slow start, established itself as a favourite volume with children of all ages. *A Child's Day*, 1912, a book of rhymes, was followed by *Peacock Pie*, 1913; but he then turned his attention away from children's literature until the 1920s. *Crossings*, 1921, was described as a fairy play with music by C. A. Gibbs; and the following year saw the publication of *Down-adown-Derry: a book of Fairy Poems*, 1922. He continued at intervals to produce books of verse and prose stories for young people until well into the 1950s, but, except for his earliest titles, few command high prices. Several of his works were produced in limited and signed editions.

A. A. Milne (1882–1956) contributed four unforgettable books of stories and verse for children which later generations of adults seem never to tire of reading to their own small offspring: *When we were very young*, 1924; *Winnie-the-Pooh*, 1926; *Now we are Six*, 1927; and *The House at Pooh Corner*, 1928; the first title quoted being much the rarest of the quartet. They contain verse which is only incidental to the stories of the 'Christopher Robin books', the whole series being illustrated in unforgettable form by E. H. Shepard. Milne's verses and songs for Christopher Robin and his animal friends jingle on, and have long since found a niche in *The Oxford Dictionary of Quotations* and similar works of reference. A set of the four titles in first-edition form, especially if still in their original dust-jackets, would be a cherished possession by any collector in the field, who could then proceed to track down the same four books in their strictly limited, signed large-paper form, printed on Japon vellum, and issued at the same time. But he would need a long pocket.

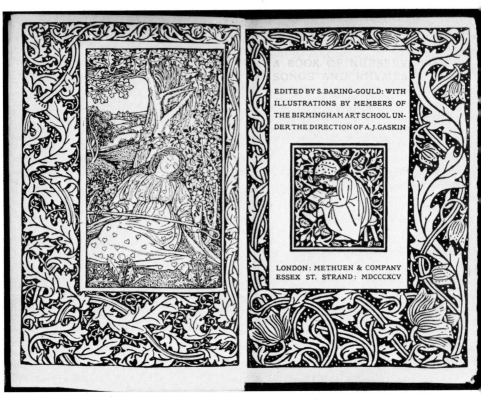

In the tradition of William Morris, the frontispiece and title-page of A Book of Nursery Songs and Rhymes, *1895, were ornamented with woodcut borders and Kelmscott Press type illustrations. 20 × 12.2cm*

In 1929, the publishers of the series, Methuen & Company, London, issued *Fourteen Songs, The King's Breakfast, Teddy Bear and Other Songs, Songs from 'Now we are Six', More Very Young Songs* and *The Hums of Pooh*, a set of folio-sized books in pictorially printed paper-covered boards, in which the words of Milne's songs had been set to music by H. Fraser-Simpson, again with illustrations by E. H. Shepard. All are now hard to find.

Considerations of space prevent me naming the more modern titles on the shelves before me, but one slim quarto lies open in first-edition form. *Old Possum's Book of Practical Cats*, 1939, was published by Faber & Faber, London, in a binding of bright yellow cloth, blocked pictorially in red, priced at 3s 6d (17½p), with a yellow dust-jacket included. The author, T. S. Eliot (1888–1965), had been one of the most important figures in the literary history of the English-speaking world since the 1920s, and his work is too well known to need quoting here. Yet *Old Possum's Book of Practical Cats* would have earned a place in this chapter even if its author was completely unknown, for with it Eliot produced a minor masterpiece that has now earned a classical reputation amongst books for children. The tale of 'Bustopher Jones: The Cat about Town', like the other titles in the book, caricatures its human counterpart while introducing us to the cat:

> Bustopher Jones is *not* skin and bones —
> In fact, he's remarkably fat.
> He doesn't haunt pubs — he has eight or nine clubs,
> For he's the St. James's Street Cat!
> He's the Cat we all greet as he walks down the street
> In his coat of fastidious black;
> No commonplace mousers have such well-cut trousers
> Or such an impeccable back.
> In the whole of St. James's the smartest of names is
> The name of this Brummell of Cats;
> And we're all of us proud to be nodded or bowed to
> By Bustopher Jones in white spats!

6

TALES FOR YOUTH

In May 1802 there appeared the first monthly issue of *The Guardian of Education*, the first publication of any kind, anywhere in the world, which systematically reviewed and criticised children's books. It was edited and largely written by that eminently 'good' woman Mrs Sarah Trimmer, a forthright exponent of the strictly moral tale, whose cautionary figure cast a shadow over the publishing houses of both London and the provinces.

Her *Fabulous Histories*, 1786, or *The History of the Robins*, as it came to be called, has already been discussed, but in addition she had produced a welter of educational books and pamphlets. One of the most successful was *A Series of Prints of Scripture History* (1786), thirty-two copperplate engravings with separate text entitled *A Description of a set of Prints of Scripture History* (1786), both published by John Marshall, London, who invariably left his titles undated. These Old Testament stories achieved a very wide circulation, and even today are not too difficult to find in early editions, thus pointing to large original printings. Thus encouraged, she quickly turned out *A Series of Prints of Ancient History* (text 1786; illustrations, in two parts, 1786-8), *A Series of Prints of Roman History* (1789) and *A Series of Prints of English History* (1792). She continued to alter and expand these titles well into the nineteenth century. *A New Series of Prints, accompanied by Easy Lessons; containing a general outline of Antient History*, 1803, was followed by other revised editions, and the series was still in print in the 1840s. *Sacred Histories*, as the series came to be called, was in fact her public expurgation of the Bible itself, purifying it to make it fit for innocent youth, although no such acknowledgement was ever made. At least one of her contemporaries recognised what she had done: the Revd James Plumptre (1770-1832). He later issued a cleaned-up version of *Robinson Crusoe*, to the delight of the Society for the Promotion of Christian Knowledge, under whose imprint the work continued to be issued some sixty years later; in 1812 they published his *The English Drama Purified* in three fat volumes. He lamented that there were many passages in the Bible 'translated in terms not now generally made use of in polished society', and then went on to rejoice that there was now

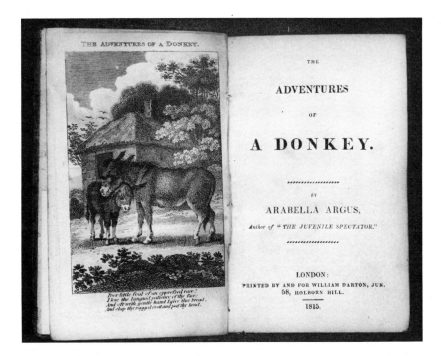

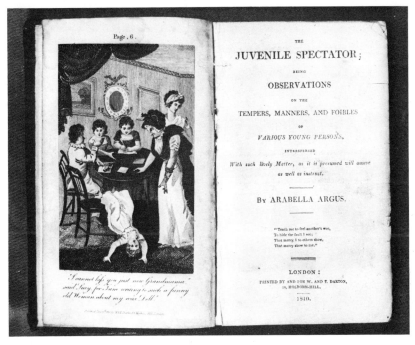

(Top) *The first edition of the most famous of the works of 'Arabella Argus'. 13.5 ×
8.5cm. Nothing is known of this author beyond the fact that she was an elderly lady
living in London and in the preface to* The Juvenile Spectator (above) *she admitted
that she wrote under a pseudonym. 17 × 10.5cm*

Mrs Trimmer's version, where 'these passages are either omitted or the expressions altered'. The Good Book purified.

Mrs Trimmer dominated the juvenile literary scene for over twenty years and long after she had received her heavenly reward her books were still being recommended to parents and governesses. Young Victorian children were made to read them in their classrooms and nurseries, before turning to gaze at the prints of *Sacred History* which John Marshall had sold in thousands, 'glued to boards for hanging— price 10/6d' (52½p). If merely sheets of the pictures were required, they were priced at 8d (3½p) a sheet.

In her *Guardian of Education* Sarah Trimmer acted as a self-appointed censor, champion of virtue in its purest form, and the ruthless exposer of the monster Vice, which 'to be hated needs but to be seen!' The work started as a monthly periodical, but the editor's name did not make its appearance on the title-page until issue No 9 in January 1803. A total of twenty-eight numbers of the magazine appeared at gradually lengthening intervals, and it finished as a quarterly publication at the end of its fifth volume, in September 1806. The first children's book published by the firm of Newbery which she reviewed was *Youthful Recreations; containing the Amusement of a Day*, 1799. Her advice to parents on how to make it suitable reading for the young lacks the thunder of some of her later denunciations, but strikes a chill into the heart of any true bibliophile:

> This little volume has no tincture of the *new School* in its composition, but is well calculated to amuse and instruct young readers. In one particular only we find ourselves at a loss to form a decided judgment —we mean in respect to the account which is introduced of a supposed *haunted house* . . if a child never had heard of *haunted houses*, &c, such a story would certainly do harm, by putting him upon inquiries, which would probably lead to his taking up a painful idea he might not easily get rid of; but a pair of scissors will easily rectify this error.

A pair of scissors! What a delightfully simple solution! And one that could surely be counted on to endear her to another of the regiment, Henrietta Maria Bowdler (1754-1830), commonly called Harriet, and perhaps even prompted her to turn her attention to the task of expurgating the plays of William Shakespeare (for which her brother Thomas wrongly claimed most of the credit). She was determined to make them 'fit for family reading', but few knew that Harriet was the innovator. Spurred on by his sister's success, Dr Thomas Bowdler spent months castrating Gibbon's *History of the Decline and Fall of the Roman Empire*,

THE

GUARDIAN OF EDUCATION:

CONTAINING

MEMOIRS OF MODERN PHILOSOPHERS,

BOTH

CHRISTIAN AND INFIDEL,

AND

EXTRACTS FROM THEIR RESPECTIVE WRITINGS;

ALSO

ABSTRACTS OF SERMONS

ON SOME OF THE MOST IMPORTANT POINTS OF

Christian Doctrine;

TOGETHER WITH

EXTRACTS FROM OTHER WORKS OF ESTABLISHED REPUTATION,

RELIGIOUS AND MORAL,

AND

A COPIOUS REVIEW

OF

Modern BOOKS *for* CHILDREN *and* YOUNG PERSONS.

" The Religious Principle, if strongly inculcated, will secure the well-formed heart from every sudden inroad of passion; will inspire the mind with that unshaken, consistent, and universal virtue, which naturally results from a just and extended view of God's moral government: from this exalting reflection, that we are placed here by our Creator to act a part; and that if we promote the end of his creation, the happiness of mankind, we shall assuredly obtain still higher degrees of virtue and perfection."

DR. BROWN'S SERMONS.

VOL. I.

From MAY *to* DECEMBER *inclusive,* 1802.

LONDON:

PUBLISHED BY J HATCHARD, BOOKSELLER TO HER MAJESTY, OPPOSITE YORK HOUSE, PICCADILLY.

1802.

The first work to contain literary criticism and reviews of books published for children, the editor being the formidable Mrs Sarah Trimmer. The work is discussed in the text.
23 × 12.5cm

stating in his preface that Gibbon would have 'desired nothing more ardently than the laying aside of the former editions of his history' in favour of that cleaned up by Dr Bowdler.

As Noel Perrin pointed out in *Dr. Bowdler's Legacy*, 1969 (Macmillan):

> With the turn of the nineteenth century, a new literary morality appeared in England. The old calm acceptance of most literature as suitable general reading rapidly faded, and an intense prudishness replaced it. One result was bowdlerism.

The next book to fall into the hands of Mrs Trimmer was *The History of Susan Gray, as related by a Clergyman, for the Benefit of Young Women going into Service*, 1802 (published anonymously), the third work of a lady who later achieved the astonishing total of over three hundred and fifty books, tracts and pamphlets to her credit. *The Traditions: a legendary Tale, written by a young lady*, 1795 (2 vols), had been followed by *Margarita*, 1799 (4 vols); neither of which had achieved much success for Mrs Martha Mary Sherwood (1775–1851). She was later to be in the thick of the fight which raged until the 1830s between the straitlaced moral and didactic juvenile tract and the fairy story. She proved herself very much on the side of Mrs Trimmer in opposing what she called the superstitious nonsense that children would persist in reading and presumably enjoying.

Although the two women had not at that time had the pleasure of meeting each other, and Mrs Trimmer had apparently been unable to identify the author of the book she was reviewing, she instantly perceived that here was a kindred spirit who could be relied upon to root out vice and lustful indulgence in whatever form it arrayed itself. *The History of Susan Gray* had her warmest approval:

> This exemplary tale furnishes a most seasonable and edifying lesson to girls of the lower order; and, with a little accommodation to circumstances, it might be applied with great propriety to the higher classes, for the *love of dress*, and the *desire of admiration*, to which it relates, are equally prevalent, in all the different ranks of which the female part of society is composed. This fatal propensity may, indeed, be justly considered as a pestilential disease of the mind, the baneful contagion of which is daily spreading till it is become almost universal. If any means can check its progress they must, we think, be such as this little book affords. . . It should also, we think, be put into the hands of mothers, with the view of checking in them that thoughtless vanity which frequently contributes to the ruin of their daughters.

At a village in Essex, not far from
nford, some children were playing
r a windmill: to see the sails go
nd was very amusing, but one lit-
boy going to examine them too
ely, was struck by one of the sails,
ch caught him up, and threw him
onsiderable distance, and when
d he was lifeless.

Printed by Darton, Harvey, and Co.
Gracechurch-Street, London.

MRS. SHERWOOD,

Now residing in the Neighbourhood of

WORCESTER,

Wishes to undertake the Education of a Few

YOUNG LADIES.

Her Terms are Eighty Guineas a Year when
the young Ladies go Home for the Holidays, and
One Hundred Guineas when they remain with
her the whole Year.

The young Ladies are taught—

ENGLISH,	HISTORY,
FRENCH,	GRAMMAR,
ASTRONOMY,	WRITING,
GEOGRAPHY,	CIPHERING,

And the Learned Languages if required.

⁎ A Quarter's Notice is expected before the Removal of any
Pupil.

Printed by Houlston and Son, Wellington, Salop.

(Left) *One of the anecdotes from* A Present for a Little Boy, *1816, issued in printed paper wrappers by Darton, Harvey & Darton. 15.7 × 9.5cm.* (Right) *Martha Sherwood combined her writing with the more certain financial returns that running a young ladies' boarding-school afforded. This advertisement of 1823 was tipped into several of her tales for the young. 14.2 × 8.8cm*

Despite the narrow-mindedness of its editor, *The Guardian of Education* is of inestimable value to the literary historian and bibliographer. Many of the books Mrs Trimmer reviewed have now been lost to sight. They are known only through the titles she gives and through advertisements contained in other works of the period. This rule applies especially to the many ephemeral little publications for children issued at prices ranging from one old-fashioned penny to threepence, for their only protection against dirt and damage was flimsy paper wrappers. No one bothered to keep such commonplace objects and their expectation of life must have proved very short indeed. Thanks to Mrs Trimmer we know of their plots and illustrations, and of their authors' and publishers' names.

In the meantime, Mrs Sherwood had sailed for India where her husband, Captain Henry Sherwood, was on military service. It was here that she fell under the evangelising spell of the missionary Henry Martyn, and from that time onwards her intensely righteous books demanded a standard of conduct from children that would have ultimately resulted in a juvenile population composed solely of cherubs. She had written nothing since 1802, but on her return to England she completed *The History of little Henry and his bearer*, 1814, published by F. Houlston & Son, Wellington, Shropshire, most of which she had written in 1809 in India. A second edition appeared in 1815, and from then onwards its success was phenomenal. Reflecting, as it did, Mrs Sherwood's missionary zeal, it passed through edition after edition, and was translated into a number of European and Eastern languages. Edward Carlyle, who supplied her biography for the DNB, compared its popularity to that of *Uncle Tom's Cabin* some thirty-eight years later.

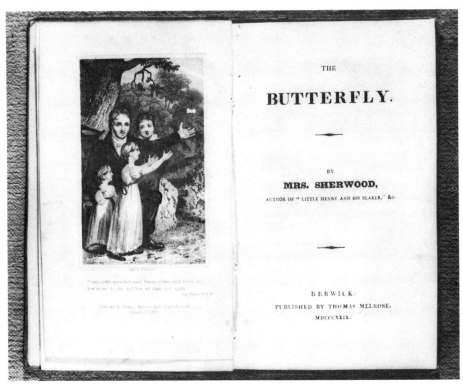

Martha Sherwood wrote over 350 books, tracts and pamphlets, mostly for children. Most were published outside London and are difficult to find in first-edition form. The Butterfly, 1829, was issued in a binding of printed paper-covered boards with a cloth spine, priced at an old-fashioned shilling a copy

The title was later changed to *The Story of Little Henry and his bearer Boosy*, with the result that the last two words are sometimes found transposed in ink or pencil, no doubt to the amusement of their later Victorian owners. In essence, the tale tells of dear little Henry's dogged perseverance in the face of all odds, ultimately leading to the embracing of Christianity by his capitulating and worn-down Indian servant. The title remained in print until after 1900, and the provincial firm of Houlston & Son, who published the vast majority of Mrs Sherwood's library of tales, owed much of their prosperity to her seemingly endless output. *The History of Lucy Clare*, 1815, *The Lady and her Ayah: an Indian story*, 1816 (under a Dublin imprint), *Memoirs of Sergeant Dale, his daughter and the orphan Mary*, 1816, and *The Indian Pilgrim: or the progress of the pilgrim Nazarene*, 1818, were followed by the (in many ways revolting!) book by which she is remembered today: *The History of the Fairchild Family; or, The Child's Manual; being a collection of stories calculated to show the importance and effects of a Religious Education*, a work published in three widely separated parts, dated 1818-42-47. She received the help of her daughter, Mrs Sophia Kelly, in writing the final part, and this lady was also responsible for a lively and readable biography of her mother, entitled *The Life of Mrs Sherwood, chiefly autobiographical*, 1854, most of which was extracted from the subject's voluminous diary which she kept throughout her life.

The History of the Fairchild Family enjoyed a vogue unsurpassed by any children's book for fifty years or more. The majority of middle-class children up to the mid-1850s may be said to have been subjected to its rigorous piety to an extent that finally led to a revulsion of feeling by the time they were married and had children of their own. Someone, somewhere, must have started to giggle, and giggles are infectious. Within a few years her book, intended for the interest and discipline of the young, was subjected to increasing ridicule, and was then so forthrightly condemned by critic after critic that all those with the true interests of children and young people at heart withdrew it from their shelves. Whatever Mrs Sherwood's aims and intentions may have been, the result of her Calvinistic moralising must surely have been to terrify and subdue, rather than edify and cheer, her young readers. The very sight of Mr Fairchild mincing towards them in their dreams would have chilled them with fear and roused them screaming from their beds. The smell and sight of death and damnation pervaded every scene he entered:

'Come with me to the gibbet,' said Mr Fairchild, taking the hands of his infants to where the corpse swung slowly in its casket of chains. It had not yet fallen to pieces although it had hung there for some years. However the face of the corpse was so shocking that the children could not bear to look at it.

'Oh! papa, papa! what is it? Let us go, papa!' cried the children, pulling Mr Fairchild's coat. 'Not yet,' said Mr Fairchild sternly. 'I must tell you the story of this wretched man before I allow you to leave this place.'

Another macabre scene relished with gloating piety by the authoress concerns a visit to a cottage in which Mr Fairchild's faithful old gardener, Roberts, has recently died. 'You never saw a corpse, I think?' says Mr Fairchild. 'No, papa,' answers Lucy, 'but we have a great curiosity to see one.' 'And so you shall, dear child.' Off they go through the garden, hand in hand, until they arrive at the cottage:

When they came to the door they perceived a kind of disagreeable smell, such as they had never smelt before; this was the smell of the corpse, which having been dead now nearly two days had begun to corrupt . . . the whole appearance of the body was more ghastly and horrible than the children expected . . . At last Mr Fairchild said, 'My dear children, you now see what death is; this poor body is fast going to corruption. The soul, I trust, is in God; but such is the taint and corruption of the flesh, by reason of sin, that it must pass through the grave and crumble to dust . . . Remember these things, my children, and pray to God to save you from sin.'
'Oh, Sir!' said Mrs Roberts, 'it comforts me to hear you talk!'

The works of Mrs Sherwood, and to a lesser degree those of her sister Mrs Lucy Cameron (1781–1858), became interwoven into the literary fabric of Victorian family life, and were the accepted Sunday afternoon reading of generations of nineteenth-century children. The extreme rigidity of Mrs Sherwood's theological stance made her works unacceptable to large sections of the reading public as the century drew to a close, but titles written early in the 1820s were still being presented as Church of England Sunday school prizes up to the start of World War I. Despite her manifest faults she possessed a great deal more literary talent than most of her female companions in the field of children's literature, and her often vivid descriptions of domestic life in the Fairchild family live on in the imagination long after her prayers and exhortations have mercifully faded and been forgotten.

One of the first books to show a markedly lenient attitude to the bubbling high spirits and the goodness of plain naughtiness in children was *Holiday House: a Series of Tales*, 1839, by Catherine Sinclair (1800–64), published in Edinburgh by William Whyte & Co., and containing a hand-coloured frontispiece after a design by the authoress. Miss Sinclair was the daughter of a Scottish politician, and came of so tall a family that the path leading to their home was nicknamed 'The Giant's Causeway'. Her first book for children was *Charlie Seymour; or The good aunt and the bad aunt*, 1832, published by Waugh & Innes, Edinburgh (second edition, enlarged, 1838, this time published by William Whyte & Co., Edinburgh), both editions having a hand-coloured frontispiece by the authoress. It is interesting to note that the second edition has the title changed to read *Charlie Seymour; or the Good Lady and the Bad Lady*. In her preface to the work Miss Sinclair stated that, when selecting books for her friend's children, she had been surprised to observe

> what a large proportion of the volumes recommended had frontis-pieces to represent a death-bed surrounded by the clergyman, the physician, and the afflicted relatives of a dying Christian; the memoirs of the children *especially*, which I examined, were almost invariably terminated by an early death.

She was determined, therefore, to write a cheerful story, containing concealed allegories. She was going to portray real-life children, wilful, mischievous, exasperating, stubborn, destructive, often dirty and untidy, often disobedient, and sometimes downright bad. She preferred her children to be like 'wild horses on the prairies, rather than well-broken hacks on the road'. In *Charlie Seymour* she based the boy's choice between right and wrong, and between living with his indulgent Aunt Jane or his upright and moral Aunt Mary, on actual conversations she had with 'a child of great intelligence'. We may assume this was her nephew, the Hon G. G. Boyle, son of the Earl of Glasgow, for whom she admitted writing her children's books. Naughtiness and disobedi-ence are shown by the do-as-you-would-be-done-by Aunt Mary to be foolhardy, and she expounds the inevitable moral when little Charlie is ill after having stuffed himself with raspberry cream, or nearly plunges over a cliff in a donkey-cart after missing church.

In *Holiday House*, written some seven years later, Catherine Sinclair is even more liberal-minded, and positively extols youthful high spirits and near-riotous behaviour in a way not countenanced in children's literature amongst *hoi polloi* for another fifty years. Harry and Laura Graham, the hero and heroine of the tale, start playfully setting their grandmother's house on fire before indulging in an orgy of destruction in which windows, clothes, toys and furniture all suffer in greater or lesser degree. Their guardian, Uncle David, discovers Laura cutting off all her hair, just for the fun of it, and calls the children together for a mild rebuke:

I am not so seriously angry at the sort of scrape Laura and you get into, because you would not willingly and deliberately do wrong. If any children commit a mean action, or get into a passion or quarrel with each other, or omit saying their prayers and reading their Bibles, or tell a lie, or take what does not belong to them, then it might be seen how extremely angry I could be; but while you continue merely thoughtless and forgetful, I mean to have patience a little longer.

Miss Sinclair was certain that the children of her age were far too severely disiplined, but she had no doubt that a strict religious up-bringing was their only ultimate hope of salvation. She did believe that each and every child was gifted with a personality that was individual, and the young people could not be drilled and dragooned into unquest-ioning obedience without extinguishing the joy for life and natural high spirits possessed by the youth of the world, and her attitude marked her as being far in advance of her time both as a writer and as an educationalist. *Modern Accomplishments: or the March of Intellect*, 1836, and *Modern Society*, 1837, forming a second part of the same work, were two of her earliest attempts to interest an adult readership in her views; but she also wrote novels, such as *Modern flirtations: or a Month at Harrowgate*, 1841 (3 vols) and *Jane Bouverie: or Prosperity and Adversity*, 1846, as well as books of local topography and history. She was also responsible for some 'picture letters' for children, supposedly hand-written letters where some of the words have be translated from pictures put there in their stead. These were published by James Wood, Edinburgh, from 1861 to 1864, that of 1861 being the first of a series of six which were printed in colours by W. H. McFarlane. According to F. J. Harvey Darton, five thousand copies were sold in a fortnight, and the figure of one hundred thousand was reached by 1863.

Other women writers still dominated the world of children's literature. Mary Hughes, née Robson, contributed *Aunt Mary's Tales; for the enlightenment and improvement of little Girls*, 1811 (second edition 1813, and third, 1817) *The Ornaments Discovered: a Story, in two parts*, 1815, *The Alchemist*, 1818, and, among many others, *The Orphan Girl: a moral tale*, 1819, in all of which the influence of her friend Maria Edgeworth is clearly visible. Mrs Lucy Littleton Cameron, née Butt (1781–1858), wrote her first book, *The History of Margaret Whyte: or, The Life and Death of a Good Child*, as early as 1798, when she was still only sixteen, but it was not published until several years later. *The two Lambs*, 1803, *The Raven and the Dove*, 1817, *The Holiday Queen*, 1818, and *The Willoughby Family*, 1824, are just a few of her scores of titles, many of which passed through twenty or thirty editions, rivalling her sister

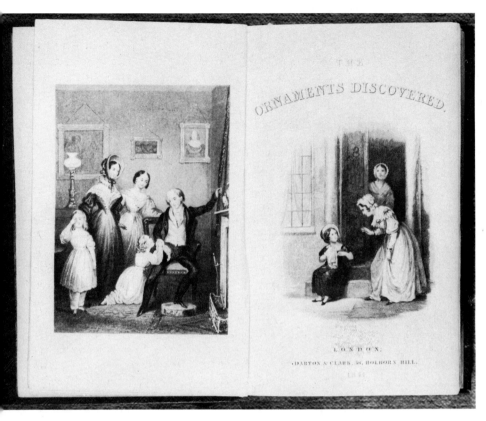

A story by Mary Hughes which first appeared in 1815. 14.3 × 8.4cm

Mrs Sherwood, in juvenile popularity.

Agnes Strickland (1796–1874) is remembered, if at all, for *The moss-house*, 1822, and perhaps for *The rival Crusoes, or The Shipwreck*, (1826), in which she collaborated with her sister Elizabeth. Her *Lives of the Queens of England*, 1840–8, which was finally completed in twelve volumes, achieved considerable success and was followed by a number of similar works, some of which, in abbreviated form, became established as school textbooks. Her other sister, Jane Margaret Strickland (1800–88), who later became the editor of *Fisher's Juvenile Scrap-Book* for the 1849 issue, wrote *National Prejudice: or, The French prisoner of war*, 1828, *Edward Evelyn: a Tale*, 1843, and a number of other juvenile historical tales.

The publications of the rival firms of John Harris, Taylor & Hessey, Longman, Hurst, Rees, Orme, Brown & Green, Harvey & Darton, A. K. Newman & Co. and Whittaker & Co. largely dominated the market as far as juvenile literature and children's books were concerned, at least up to the 1840s. Between them these firms produced a

The frontispiece, by Edward Burney, for The Affectionate Brothers (c.1833), *by Mrs B. W. H. Hofland, a work which first appeared in two volumes in 1816. 8.5 × 6.5cm*

complexity of titles issued in widely differing formats, with the quality of their binding styles, and of their illustrations, varying tremendously.

On the shelves immediately in front of me there is a wide-ranging selection of titles by the more prolific authors of the first half of the nineteenth century and a little before, and from these I can only make a random choice of representative works. The market for children's books had expanded many times during the last decade and had attracted an increasing number of writers to fill the demand. Amongst these was Elizabeth Sandham, whose birth and death dates remain a mystery. She used a variety of publishing houses after the appearance of her first title for children: *The Happy Family at Eason House. Exhibited in the amiable conduct of the little Nelsons and their parents*, 1799, which was itself issued under the imprint of Thomas Hurst; this being quickly followed by *Trifles; or, Friendly mites towards improving the rising generation*, 1800, *Juliana; or, The affectionate sisters*, 1800, *The Boys' School; or, Traits of character in early life* (1800), *The Godmother's Tales*, 1808, *The History of Britannicus and his sister Octavia*, 1819, and dozens of others until well into the 1820s, many being issued anonymously.

Next to the works of Elizabeth Sandham are those written by Mrs Barbara Hofland (1770–1844), née Wreaks, who had published a volume of *Poems* (1805) under a Sheffield, Yorkshire, imprint. But it was the appearance of *The History of an Officer's Widow and her young Family*, 1809, that first set her feet on the path of children's books, and it was succeeded almost immediately by *Little Dramas for Young People, on subjects taken from English history*, 1810, dating the preface from the boarding-school she ran at Harrogate, in which she said that they were merely meant for the play hours of her pupils, and certainly *not* for public performance by children, for which she entertained 'a decided disgust'. *The History of a Clergyman's Widow and her young Family*, 1812, proved extremely successful, selling well over twenty thousand copies in the space of ten years, no doubt having been written from the heart, Mrs Hofland being herself the widow of a wealthy Sheffield merchant, T. B. Hoole. She married T. C. Hofland, the artist, ten years later, having lost the fortune her first husband left her in the disastrous crash of the firm she placed it with. To support herself and her children (her boarding-school was also a failure) she wrote several books each year until her death in 1844, following *The Son of a Genius: a tale for the use of Youth*, 1812, by the first of several novels intended for an adult readership, in this case *Says she to her neighbour, What?*, 1812, issued in four volumes by A. K. Newman & Co., the authoress herself hiding behind the pseudonym of 'An Old-fashioned Englishman'. *The Merchant's Widow and her family*, 1814, published anonymously, was largely autobiographical, appearing in 1823 with its title changed to

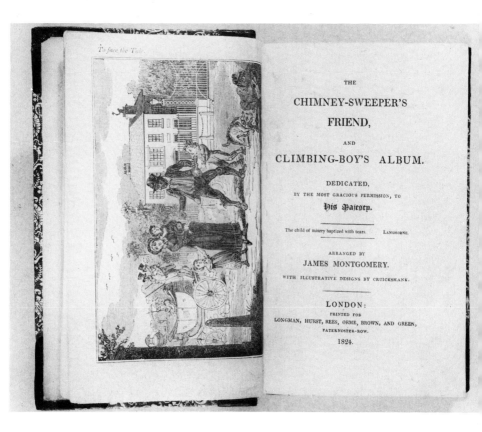

A volume of 428 pages devoted to bringing to public notice the sufferings of the hundreds of little boys pressed into service as climbing chimney-sweepers. The book contains the first separate printing of William Blake's The Chimney Sweeper *from his* Songs of Innocence. *16 × 9.5cm*

The History of a Merchant's Widow and her young family, in which form it passed through many subsequent editions. *The Affectionate Brothers. A Tale* first appeared in two volumes dated 1816, again going through many single-volume editions, and later she embarked on a moralistic series, mostly with single-word titles, such as *Integrity: a Tale*, 1824, *Patience: a tale*, 1823, *Moderation: a tale*, 1825, *Reflection: a tale*, 1826, *Self-denial: a tale*, 1827, and she was still at it late in the 1830s with *Fortitude: a tale*, 1835, *Humility: a tale*, 1838, finishing the series with *Farewell tales*, 1840.

Staying in Sheffield for the moment, we find *The Blind Man and his Son*, 1816, published anonymously by Samuel Roberts (1763–1848), the town's social reformer who became known as the 'Pauper's Advocate'. The profits from all his numerous books, pamphlets and broadsheets were always contributed to the various charities in which he had an interest, especially anti-slavery societies and those concerned with the abolition of child labour. *Tales of the Poor, or Infant Sufferings*, 1813, was his first book written for children. He had a close friend in James Montgomery (1771–1854), who had contributed the second part of 'The Four Friends—a poetical fable' to *The Blind Man and his Son*, and for that reason it stands next to *The Chimney-Sweeper's Friend and Climbing-Boy's Album*, 1824, mentioned earlier, a work compiled by Montgomery while in Sheffield. Although it has no real place in a chapter devoted to stories and tales for youth, so many children's authors contributed, including Charles Lamb, Sir John Bowring, Allan Cunningham and, of course, the Sheffield merchant's widow, Mrs Hofland, to say nothing of the illustrations by George Cruikshank, that I let it stay.

The adventures associated with travels in foreign parts were popular with children and young people from the earliest days. *The Wanderings of Tom Starboard; or the Life of a Sailor*, 1830, by Isabella Jane Towers

THE

BLIND MAN AND HIS SON:

A TALE FOR YOUNG PEOPLE.

THE FOUR FRIENDS:

A FABLE.

AND

A WORD FOR THE GIPSIES.

Any profits arising from the sale of this publication will be applied in aid of the Society for the relief of Aged Females in Sheffield.

LONDON:
PRINTED BY T MILLER;
FOR TAYLOR AND HESSEY, 93, FLEET-STREET.
1816.

THE BLIND MAN AND HIS SON.

Samuel Roberts, 'The Pauper's Advocate' as he came to be known, vowed never to publish for profit. This is his second book. 16.5 × 9.5cm

(1790–1867), née Clarke, relates, amongst other battles, the hero's fight with a rhinoceros, a creature described as standing some 'twelve feet high'. She was the sister of Charles Cowden Clarke (1787–1877), remembered for his *Readings in Natural Philosophy: or, a popular display of the Wonders of Nature*, 1828, *Tales from Chaucer in prose: Designed chiefly for the use of young persons*, 1833, *Adam the Gardener*, 1834, and several other children's books. One of the most sought-after of his books today is *The Young Cricketer's Tutor; comprising full directions for playing the elegant and manly game of Cricket*, 1833, the rules and regulations of which had been put together by John Nyren, with Clarke acting as editor-in-chief. It was originally issued in a binding of smooth green cloth, bearing on its front cover a printed paper label giving the title and price—2s 6d (12½p).

Fire-Side Stories; or, Recollections of my school-fellows, 1825, by an author who has never been identified, was issued by Harvey & Darton in a binding of printed paper-covered boards with leather spine. The only clue we have to who wrote the work is that it was admitted that he or she was the author of *The Picture Gallery*. *The Journies of Julius in North Africa*, 1823, was the first section of a two-part work by John Campbell (1766–1840), who continued it with *The Travels of Trophimus in North Africa*, 1824, both of which were fervently anti-slave trade and pro-Christian missionary service. These were issued some ten years before Sir John Bowring (1792–1872) published the first volume of *Minor Morals for Young People*, 1834, followed by two other volumes dated 1835 and 1839 respectively. As well as tales of travel and adventure this three-volume work contains a series of fairy-tales translated into English for the first time, but it is an extremely difficult title to acquire in first-edition form. The first two volumes were issued by Whittaker & Company, London, and the third volume some five years later (in a matching binding of glazed full-cloth, with paper-labelled spines) by William Tait, Edinburgh. All the full-page plates in the last two volumes were by George Cruikshank, but in the first volume he contributed only the frontispiece, with the rest of the illustrations by William Heath. *Minor Morals* was Bowring's only work for children.

In the USA, Jacob Abbott (1803–79), a Massachusetts educator and Congregational clergyman, was well into his final output of over two hundred titles, the first of which, *The Young Christian*, appeared in 1832. But he is remembered today for the twenty-eight books he wrote telling of the adventures of his hero Rollo, and Rollo's two friends Lucy and Jonas, of which *Rollo's Vacation*, 1839, published in Boston, is typical. The 'Rollo' books, as they came to be called, achieved an immense popularity, most being instructive stories in the genre of *Sandford and Merton*.

In Germany *Das Blumenkörbschen*, 1823, by Johann Christoph von Schmid (1768–1854), passed rapidly through edition after edition, although, surprisingly, it was not translated into English direct from the German edition until 1867. It was then that Frederick Warne & Company issued the story as *The Basket of Flowers; or, Piety and Truth Triumphant*. It was published in a full-cloth binding over bevelled boards, blocked in gold and black, undated, and with numerous coloured plates printed directly on to the text paper by Edmund Evans. This represented a new departure in colour printing, each chapter having a half-page coloured plate at its head. Earlier English editions of *The Basket of Flowers* had used a translation taken from the French by G. T. Bedell, or had used a modified translation taken from an American edition, with consequent inaccuracies. The story quickly became a favourite with children of many countries, and also lent itself admirably to the talents of illustrators and book designers. The tale itself is centred around a missing diamond ring that had apparently disappeared when Mary, a village girl and the daughter of a poor gardener, calls at the Count's castle with a basket of flowers to present to the Countess on the occasion of her birthday. Instead of being thanked, she is arrested on the evidence of a jealous maid, but, in spite of being cruelly whipped and tortured, she refuses to confess. Mary and her aged father are banished in disgrace from the Count's domain; but there is eventually a happy ending when a tree in the castle grounds is cut down and the missing ring discovered in a magpie's nest. Margaret, the covetous maid, is almost immediately struck down by a mysterious illness, apparently by Divine intervention, and dies 'at the age of twenty-three, a melancholy example of the misery that sin never fails to bring along with it. We cannot add that there was any hope in her death.' Meanwhile, Mary goes on to marry the son of the judge who had previously condemned her, and the diamond ring is given to her by the Countess for her wedding ring. All in all, a happy, well rounded ending, and one which many a young reader must have sighed over.

English editions of other of Johann Schmid's tales were *Eustace, the Christian Warrior, Genevieve, and other tales, Itha, Countess of Toggenbourg, The orphan child, or the story of little Sophia, The Pet Lamb, and other tales* and *The Two Brothers, and other tales*, all of which appeared originally in Germany in the 1840s before being issued in England in the 1850s. According to the publisher's advertisements, well over a million copies of *The Basket of Flowers* were sold in Britain before 1855, and it was undoubtedly the most popular tale to appear in English during that decade. The story remained in print well into the 1920s.

Viewed as a whole half-century of endeavour in the field of children's literature, one has to admit that the progress achieved during the period 1800–50 was in many ways unspectacular. Yet conventions were breached, inviolate rules were broken, and by the middle of the century the didactic age was all but finished. Entirely new kinds of books were being written for children, and adult fiction was also in an exciting state of transition. In books for young people, the day of the real-life romance and adventure story, unmoralised and unashamed, was close at hand. The energetic, questing, business-like spirit of the Victorians was gradually loosening the puritanical strait-jacket that had stifled almost all attempts at an honest portrayal of everyday life in juvenile books. The few exceptions that had thumbed their noses at the hell-fire and damnation school could be counted on the fingers of one hand. These few, however, had pointed the way to a new era, an era in which writers of the highest talent would give their best for young people, and in which a number of works specially written for children would eventually take their well earned places as classics of English literature.

By the mid-1850s, the changes that had been gradually taking place during the previous twenty years in the style and character of literature intended for young people had reached what, with hindsight, we can perceive to be a vital point in the time-scale. Children's books had altered, and to a degree that makes 1855 a dividing line between the old style and the new, between soul-saving didacticism and the modern children's book. The overlap either way was considerable; nevertheless, it can be stated that after that date the majority of children's books contained characters who resembled real children in their attitudes to the family and the world about them. They were no longer paragons of virtue with all the saint-like attributes; neither were they black-hearted little sinners plunging inexorably to hell.

There had been a considerable change of attitude on the part of responsive adults towards the obvious desire of intelligent young people for books which would amuse and entertain them, without at the same time seeking to impose a nagging load of moral responsibility on their unwilling young shoulders. This more liberal-minded view of the field of children's literature was soon reflected in the attitude of the progressive commercially minded publishing houses. It began to be realised that stories in which the action was less heavily clogged by the gum of piety sold better than those in which the youthful heroes and heroines were on their knees once or twice in every chapter as they prepared themselves for pious but early deaths. Sermonising no longer paid the dividends it did a few years back and a whole new generation of talented writers began to replace the black-browed divines and cam-phorated females who had haunted children's story books for so long. *Moralise less and sell more copies* became the unspoken watchword of the leading London publishers, and those in the provinces were not slow to follow their lead.

The literate population of Britain was growing at a pace that must have gladdened the hearts of the entire book-publishing trade, while the increasing use of the latest steam-driven printing presses was gradually bringing the price of books down to a level that made them readily accessible. Publishers began to understand more clearly the contrasting and varying needs of boys and girls in different age groups, while the calibre of writing improved to a degree that eventually gave the world a host of titles that became household names.

Children's books started to grow in size as well as contents. Bindings were restyled and spines and boards began to be pictorially blocked in gold on a rainbow of vividly coloured cloths, all to catch the eye of the youthful purchaser, albeit through the good offices of his or her parents, aunts, uncles or guardians. Boys and girls could now be expected to make their own choice of titles when they visited the

Both sides of the binding of one of Mrs Henry Wood's stories of c.1875, issued in pictorial cloth with vivid hues. The tale was first printed in The Golden Casket, *1861, edited by Mary Howitt. Size across both covers: 22 × 17cm*

bookshops or read the inserted advertisements in volumes they already owned. And for younger children books were designed in formats to appeal directly to the adults who made the selection and had to foot the bill. Led by Darton & Clark, London, and Thomas Nelson, Edinburgh, who were pioneers in the craft, extensive use began to be made of colour-printed illustrations in children's books. Many of the leading artists and engravers of the day were employed to supply the wood blocks and plates, and an industry expanded to supply the elaborately chiselled and incised brasses needed to hot-press the gold designs used to ornament the covers.

Books aimed at special categories of young people began to be written, and publishing houses gradually divided the market by concentrating on particular fields while leaving much of the rest to their rivals-in-trade. Works purely (the word is apt) for older girls in their teens were an innovation, and the lead was set by Charlotte Yonge (1823–1901), who, in the midst of her output of one hundred and fifty or so novels and tales wrote *The Daisy Chain*, 1856 (2 vols), a second edition (also in two volumes) being issued by Bernard Tauchnitz, Leipzig, the same year. Miss Yonge's first book, *Le Château de Melville: ou recréations du cabinet d'étude*, 1838, was published when she was only fifteen; then came *Abbey Church: or, Self-control and Self-conceit*, 1844; *Scenes and Characters: or, Eighteen months at Beechcroft*, 1847; followed by her first book written specially for children: *Kings of England: a history for young children*, 1848. She was now into her stride and from 1850 onwards turned out books at the rate of three or four a year to the day of her death, as well as acting as critic, reviewer and editor of the magazine *The Monthly Packet* from 1851 to 1894. Amongst her many works for children were *Henrietta's wish: or, Domineering—a tale*, 1850, *Langley School*, 1850, *The Little Duke: or, Richard the Fearless*, 1854, a work still in print in the 1890s and re-issued as late as 1910, *The Railroad Children*, 1855, *Little Lucy's Wonderful Glove*, 1871, and *P's and Q's; the Question of Putting upon*, 1872. She is remembered (and still read!) today for her novel *The Heir of Redclyffe*, 1853 (2 vols), three editions of which appeared the same year, the seventeenth edition being published in 1868; it has seldom been out of print since then. In 1965 it appeared again, this time under the editorship of C. Haldane.

Charlotte Yonge was one of the last of the old guard of children's writers, and to today's readers most of the characters she portrays would be merely ghosts of a bygone age, old-fashioned wax-faced dolls bowing and scraping at the pull of a string. Filial obedience was her constantly reiterated theme:

150

The things my parents bid me do.
Let me attentively pursue.

The Stokesley Secret, 1861, and *Countess Kate*, 1862, are arguably her two best books for girls, the latter giving what is probably a pen-portrait of herself as an excitable, wilful and headstrong child. The glimpses she gives us of mid-Victorian children released from the drudgery of the schoolroom and scampering home to tea are amongst the many vignettes of family life she recorded so vividly. The Merrifield children in *The Stokesley Secret*, while enduring the boredom of the classroom, are still recognisable as the ghosts of our own youth when school broke up for the holidays:

> What an entirely different set of beings were those
> Stokesley children in lesson-time and out of it!
> Talk of the change of an old thorn in winter to a
> May-bush in spring! that was nothing to it!
> Poor, listless, stolid, deplorable logs, with bowed
> backs and crossed ankles, pipy voices and heavy eyes!
> Who would believe that these were the merry
> capering creatures, full of fun and riot, clattering and
> screeching, and dancing about with ecstasy at Sam's
> information that there was a bonfire by the potatoe-house!

Ministering Children: A Tale dedicated to Childhood, 1854, by Maria Louisa Charlesworth (1819–80), seemed destined to become a best-seller from the day of issue. She was a vicar's daughter, and the children of the title of her book assiduously devote their every leisure moment to ministering to the needs of the indigenous poor. The book became enormously popular in the author's lifetime and, by the time the continuation of the work appeared some thirteen years later, nearly 100,000 copies had been sold. *Ministering Children, A Sequel,* 1867, is perhaps a little easier to acquire in first-edition form, but neither title is common in its original format. The last named was issued in a binding of full bead-grain cloth over bevelled boards, with the title oramentally blocked in gold on the front cover and spine. The frontis-piece and engraved pictorial title are particularly attractive, the work of C. H. Jeens after original illustrations by the well known artist J. D. Watson, whose work as a book illustrator of the ''Sixties' coffee-table volumes is now much sought after. Of Mrs Charlesworth's other works for children, her series of 'Reward Books', selected from *Sunday Afternoons in the Nursery*, comprised six little paper-wrapped Bible stories and sold in a packet at one shilling (5p) by Seeley, Jackson

& Halliday, London, remained as favourite Sunday school prizes for several decades. Her *The Old Looking Glass; or, Mrs Dorothy Cope's recollections of service*, 1878, was written near the end of her career.

The name of Charlotte Maria Tucker (1825–93) will be sought for in vain on the title-pages of any of her one hundred and sixty plus books and booklets. From the time of the publication of her first effort, *Claremont Tales; or, Illustrations of the Beatitudes* (1852), she insisted on using the pseudonym 'A.L.O.E.', the initials of the title 'A Lady of England'. *Sketches of the Life of Luther* (1853) was followed by *The White Shroud, and other Poems*, (1853); all published by Gall & Inglis, Edinburgh, a house which persisted in not dating the title-pages of the books it issued. Only the dated presentation inscription on the last named allows any bibliographical certainty of these issue dates.

One of her earliest children's books was *Wings and Stings*, 1855, followed by *Upwards and Downwards; or, The Sluggard and the Diligent; a Story for Boys*, 1856. But it was not until the publication of *The Rambles of a Rat*, 1857, issued by Thomas Nelson & Sons, Edinburgh, that she found her place in children's affections as a story-teller who could compel their interest. The adventures of 'Oddity' the piebald rat and his seven brothers, who lived in 'a large warehouse, somewhere in the neighbourhood of Poplar, and close to the River Thames', contained little moralising and was a story dear to the hearts of Victorian children. Like all her early books, this is a title very hard to find in acceptable condition in first-edition form. It was published in a full-cloth binding (usually red, but colour does not constitute a point of issue, the binders merely reaching down bolts of cloth as others were used up) blocked in blind on the covers and pictorially in gilt on the spine with a picture of a sheaf of corn around which three of the mischievous rats in the story are disporting themselves. *The Giant Killer*, 1856, and its sequel *The Roby Family*, 1857, were followed by *The Story of a Needle*, 1858, *The Mine: or, Darkness and Light*, 1858, *The Silver Casket: or, The World and its Wiles*, 1864, and *Fairy Know a-bit*, 1866, all published by Thomas Nelson & Sons.

This particular firm issued many titles which later became famous and continued in print for years, sometimes for generations, but collectors must be on their guard and exercise considerable care when acquiring what they believe to be first editions with Nelson & Sons imprint. The firm had a house rule that all editions should be dated on their title-pages, not just the first edition as was the practice with many other publishers at that particular period. The fact that they dated their title-pages, but gave no indication that the volume was a new edition or a numbered later edition has, in the past, made for considerable confusion in the ranks of bibliographers, not least for one of the greatest, the late Michael Sadleir (1888–1957). In his *Nineteenth Century Fiction*, 1951 (2 vols), he more than once fell into error with books published by Nelson & Sons, notably with *Martin Rattler*, 1858, by R. M. Ballantyne, which he dated 1859, as the publishers had given no indication of an earlier edition. Nelsons were one of the most prominent and successful publishers of children's books of the nineteenth century, and many of their cloth bindings are a delight to behold even today, when the patina of Time has dulled their lustre. But it is wise to be cautious when examining the many thousands of works for juveniles that appeared under their imprint before deciding on priority of editions.

It has been pointed out that Gall & Inglis, who were 'A.L.O.E.''s other main publisher, caused equal difficulty with their *undated* title-pages, and this observation applies with equal force to the many thousands of titles issued by the Religious Tract Society since its inception in 1799. The RTS, as it came to be known, published a number of best-sellers in the field of children's books, including the phenomenally successful *Jessica's First Prayer* (1867), by 'Hesba

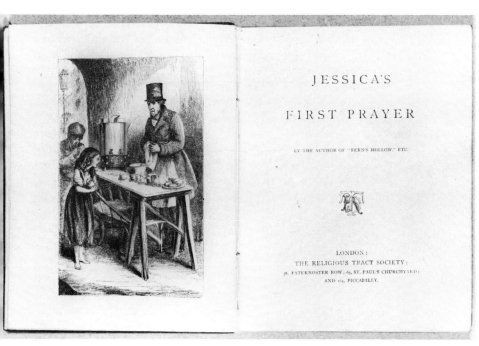

The first issue, with inscription dated December 1867, of a book which sold nearly two million copies. Later issues had more than one previous title quoted, and the title itself was wreathed by an ornamental frieze. Its author is discussed in the text. 15.5 × 12cm

Stretton', the pseudonym of Sarah Smith (1832–1911). She was the third daughter and fourth child (in a family of eight) of a Wellington, Shropshire, bookseller, and she lost her mother when only eight years old. Her education was chiefly gained by reading the books in her father's shop, and she began writing stories and poems at a very early age. In 1859, her sister Elizabeth, who became her lifelong companion, sent one of Sarah's stories 'The Lucky Leg', to Charles Dickens, who was then editor of the magazine *Household Words*. He accepted it, paid the authoress £5, and asked that she should submit anything else she wrote. A friendship sprang up between the two of them and many more of her stories, including the well known 'The Travelling Post Office', made their appearance in his periodical. She had earlier come to the conclusion that her own name sounded too commonplace and had adopted the pseudonym 'Hesba Stretton'. The word 'Hesba' represented the initial letters of the names of her brothers and sisters then living in order of age, and 'Stretton' was taken from the Shropshire village where, by the bequest of her uncle, her younger sister Ann had property. It was here that Sarah spent a holiday each year almost until her death.

It was not until *Jessica's First Prayer* was issued in book form in 1867, having first appeared in *Sunday at Home* in 1866, that she found herself famous, well over a million and a half copies in various editions being sold during the author's own lifetime. The girl heroine of the title, daughter of a brutal and vindictive mother, is found barefoot and dressed in rags as she shivers in the cold in the doorway of a fashionable chapel, having recently been beaten and turned out of doors by her mother. It is here that the minister's children discover her, but they are faced with a dilemma when they ask her inside the church to hear their father preach:

> The little outcast was plainly too dirty and neglected for them to invite her to sit side by side with them in their crimson-lined pew, and no poor people attended the chapel with whom she could have a seat.

Strange as they may seem today, these sentiments appeared quite rational to Hesba Stretton's young readers, who later rejoiced in Jessica's ultimate good fortune in being looked after by the chapel caretaker and his wife. She was even given a job by the minister: 'And many a happy day was spent in helping to sweep and dust the chapel, into which she had crept so secretly at first, her great delight being to attend to the pulpit and the vestry, and the pew where the minister's children sat.'

Hesba Stretton was undoubtedly one of the most gifted writers in what came to be called the 'street-arab school', a band of authors who excited pity on the part of their comfortable and prosperous readers with edifying stories of the horrors of the gin-sodden slums. In these, the charity of the wealthy enabled the most deserving and evangelical of the victims to be rescued for a life of hard-working thrift with ample opportunities to better themselves. These satisfying examples of the better-off caring for the lower orders remained firm favourites during the whole of the latter half of the nineteenth century, R. M. Ballantyne's *Dusty Diamonds Cut and Polished—A Tale of City-Arab Life and Adventures*, 1884, being continuously in print to 1914.

Hesba Stretton's first book, *Fern's Hollow* (1864), is rare (see illustration, below) and none of her other tales are easy to find as first editions. The most popular in her lifetime were probably *Little Meg's Children* (1868), *Alone in London* (1869), *Enoch Roden's Training* (1865) and *The Children of Cloverley* (1867). Other of her titles in my own

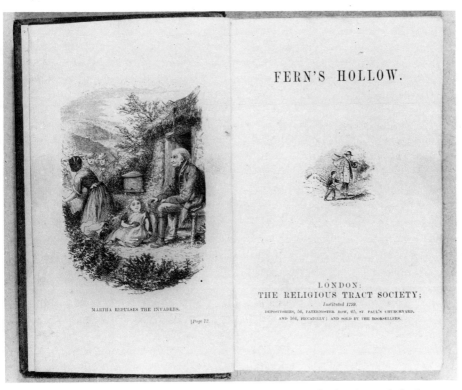

MARTHA REPULSES THE INVADERS.

[*Page 72*

FERN'S HOLLOW.

LONDON:
THE RELIGIOUS TRACT SOCIETY;
Instituted 1799.
DEPOSITORIES, 56, PATERNOSTER ROW, 65, ST. PAUL'S CHURCHYARD,
AND 164, PICCADILLY; AND SOLD BY THE BOOKSELLERS.

The first book written by 'Hesba Stretton', shown here as the first issue of the first edition, published undated in 1864. 16.4 × 9.8cm

collection are *Lost Gip*, 1872, this time published by Henry S. King & Company, *Max Krömer* (1871), *Pilgrim Street: a Story of Manchester Life* (1868), *Under the Old Roof* (1880) and *'No Place Like Home'* (1881).

School tales (rather, Public School tales!) made a tentative appearance as early as the 1840s, notably with the story of *The Crofton Boys*, 1841, by Harriet Martineau (1802–76), issued as the last of a four-volume series called *The Playfellow*, under the imprint of Charles Knight, London. It was published as a separate work in 1856. However, stories set in boys' schools did not gain prominence until the appearance of two works, separated by only a few months in time, each of which was destined to become internationally famous. *Tom Brown's School Days. By an Old Boy*, 1857, was published anonymously by Thomas Hughes, and issued by Macmillan & Co. over a Cambridge imprint. This was the first story which gave a genuine impression of what life was really like in an English public school, and was dedicated by the author to Mrs Arnold, the wife of the redoubtable Thomas Arnold. Thomas Hughes (1822–96) was himself educated at Rugby School, where Arnold was headmaster, and his first-hand knowledge of schoolboy cruelties and firm-chinned loyalties exercised there enabled him to depict school life in a way which swept the book into the best-selling bracket within a few months of its first appearance. The work revealed many aspects of boarding-schools' routine and punishments that parents and guardians had but dimly comprehended, and to have these secrets so vividly revealed, even in the form of a novel, came as a considerable shock. The work had a definite influence on the attitude of parents to such establishments and through them on the governing bodies from which reforms ultimately came. The sequel to *Tom Brown's School Days* was *Tom Brown at Oxford*, 1861 (3 vols), but, despite the fact that Hughes had himself been at Oriel, the work lacked the realism of its predecessor and can be accounted a failure. The only other work by Hughes which concerns us here is *The Scouring of the White Horse; or, The Long Vacation Rambles of a London Clerk*, 1859, illustrated in characteristic fashion by Richard Doyle, who also designed the gold-blocked pictorial covers. This was a book which must have been read by older children with considerable amusement, and is collected today by those interested in the evolution of publishers' binding styles and nineteenth-century book production, as well as those concerned with the text.

Within twelve months of the publication of *Tom Brown's School Days* the second notable title depicting life in a boarding-school made its appearance. *Eric or Little by Little—A Tale of Roslyn School*, 1858, by Frederick W. Farrar (1831–1903), was published by Adam & Charles Black, Edinburgh. It was the future Dean of Canterbury's first book and one that brought him immediate and lasting fame. Written when he was still a master at Harrow School, the work had little to do with the muscular Christianity of Hughes' earlier tale. The phrase 'little by little' sums up the gradual decline into sinful ways of the hero, Eric Williams, while a boarder at public school. The story has not progressed very far before Eric starts to use swear words, and then, another step down the ladder, secretly to smoke. Once on the slippery slope his pace quickens; before many more pages have been turned he is seen downing pints of porter at a low pothouse, punches a master on the nose, steals pigeons from a loft, and almost, but not quite, purloins some cash. Wrongly suspected of theft, he runs away to sea, to conditions of the utmost cruelty. It is in these scenes of physical cruelty that the author's powers of description seem perceptibly heightened, the schoolmaster with his bamboo cane tossing the whip to the Dean.

At last Eric falls and all but breaks his leg, but despite his injury the brutal captain of the ship orders him aloft with the rest of the crew to hoist the sail. The boy collapses under the effort and is immediately dragged across the deck, almost stripped naked, and tied to the mast. Then the captain and the crew stand in a semi-circle around the unresisting young boy while the author allows his imagination full play:

> Again the rope whistled in the air, again it grided across the boy's naked back, and once more the crimson furrow bore witness to the violent laceration. A sharp shriek of inexpressible agony rang from his lips, so shrill, so heart-rending, that it sounded long in the memory of all who heard it. But the brute who administered the torture was untouched. Once more, and again, the rope rose and fell, and under its marks the blood first dribbled, and then streamed from the white and tender skin.

This particular passage was suppressed in later editions; but it gives one something of the flavour of the rest of this remarkable work. It is a vivid example of the *maladie d'anglais* style of sexual sadism that lay close to the surface in so many tales of school life written by ex-schoolmasters and clerics and would-be schoolmasters and clerics of the period and of later days. An example by the Revd Henry William Pullen (1836–1903), vicar-choral of York Minster and later choirmaster at Salisbury Cathedral, will be enough to make the point, as repetition would be tedious. He first sprang to fame with a political squib published in Salisbury in 1870 called *The Fight at Dame Europa's School*, which presented the Franco-German War in easily understood parable form. Published anonymously in an initial printing of only five hundred copies, it had an almost unexampled success, selling no less than two hundred thousand copies during the next few years, with translations being made into almost every European language. It netted its author well over £3,000, enabling him to retire from his job of vicar-choral in favour of a life of travel, and to indulge his passion for writing stories for and about schoolboys. *Tom Pippin's Wedding*, 1871, *The Ground Ash*, 1874, and *Pueris Reverentia*, 1892, are typical, and an extract from the last named gives us an insight into his methods: Charlie Tremblett had been caned time and time again, at times so that he could barely sit in anything like comfort, but again he was up before his master for slow progress with his school work:

'I have tried caning, and impositions, and keeping you in. It is all of no use. Now we will see what a good sound flogging will do.'
'Please, sir!'
'Take this slip of paper; and, if the Doctor is busy, put it on his desk.'
'Please, sir!'
Dr Ajax was a big man, with a square brown beard and a fearful dignity . . . If there was a soft spot in his heart there was certainly none in his face . . . he seldom went home until the evening, and most of his leisure in the intervals between school hours was passed in his study on the ground floor of the Red House. To this snug retreat Charlie Tremblett now followed him, and knocked timidly at the door. On entering the room he found two prefects, specially told off for the purpose, in readiness to hold him down; and after a few unimportant observations from the Doctor . . . he was desired to assume a condition of disordered garments and group himself for the chastisement he so richly deserved. The prefects fell upon him gently and led him to a chair, assisting his unwilling fingers, with equal gentleness, to make things convenient for the Doctor. And very convenient indeed were all things made.

Charlie knelt gracefully forwards upon the soft leather seat of the high-backed chair, clutching at the chamfered edge of the old-fashioned furniture with the desperation of one who feels he is going to have a rough time of it, and would at least like to hold on to something. The prefects stood solemnly beside him, like supporters in a heraldic shield, each keeping Charlie at a proper angle with one hand, while the fingers of the other held up and twisted daintily the corners of the poor boy's shirt, lest the fluttering linen should get itself entangled with the twigs of the avenging rod, and temper the violence of the strokes to the shorn lamb.

Dr Ajax, who was propriety itself, waited half a minute or so until all things were decently arranged, coughing in a guttural whisper within himself, as if he wanted to make his throat believe

158

that he had never seen such a thing in his life before, and that it rather shocked him. He then unlocked a drawer, and took out from its inner depths two long thin wiry birches of rich autumnal brown, most picturesquely knotted, and fashioned with such consummate skill that I am inclined to think Mrs. Ajax must have had a hand in their fabrication . . . Dr. Ajax tucked the right side of his gown behind his back, measured his distance with approximate accuracy, and dealt his first blow. Poor Charlie winced, and shrank, and shuddered, but uttered not a sound. The prefects stood clear, bending the victim's body still further forward towards the back of the chair, that the Doctor's arm might have fair play, and that their own immaculate persons might be out of danger, in case he should deliver a wide. The birch went hissing through the air and fell once more, raising a long red freckled line. Charlie bit clean through the toffy till it stuck to his teeth like glue, and looked at the Head Master out of his great brown eyes . . . When nine cuts had been delivered the Doctor paused for a few seconds to examine the birch; and observing that the knots had worn off, and the extremities of the twigs peeled, giving the brush end of the instrument an altogether ragged and disreputable appearance, he changed his weapon, and fell to again. 'The boy is either very obstinate or very tough,' he said to himself; 'in either case, another half dozen strokes won't hurt him, and he shall have them well laid on.' The new birch stung most cruelly, cutting crisp into the blistered wounds. It was as much as ever Charlie could do to keep quiet; and, struggle as he would, he could not restrain his tears.

The Revd Pullen died a bachelor some seven years after completing a novel, *Venus and Cupid*, 1896, which he had published at his own expense. Young Cupid had to survive a flogging, as did all his young heroes, usually to sin and be flogged again. Eric in *Little by Little* also recovered from his vicious beating and returned home to be forgiven, finally dying repentant, an angelic smile on his lips. Farrar's other novels for youth include *Julian Home; A Tale of College Life*, 1859, *St Winifred's; or, the World of School*, 1862, and *The Three Homes; a tale for Fathers and Sons*, 1873, issued under the pseudonym 'F.T.L.'

Another exponent of the saga of school life was Talbot Baines Reed (1852–93), an author who reacted strongly against sentiments of both Hughes and Farrar by producing *The Fifth Form at St Dominic's* (1887), *The Cockhouse at Fellsgarth* (1893) and *The Master of the Shell* (1894), all of which appeared, undated, under the imprint of the Religious Tract Society, as did Reed's most famous book for boys, *The Adventures of a Three Guinea Watch* (1883).

159

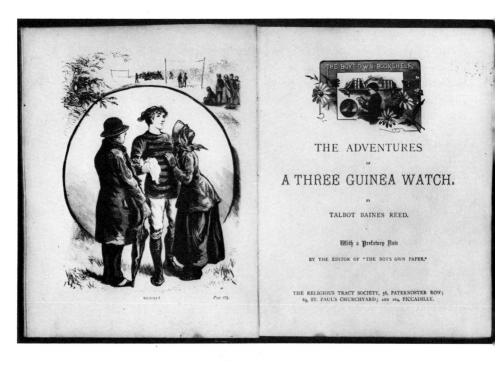

THE BOY'S OWN BOOKSHELF

THE ADVENTURES
OF

A THREE GUINEA WATCH.

BY

TALBOT BAINES REED.

With a Prefatory Note

BY THE EDITOR OF "THE BOY'S OWN PAPER."

THE RELIGIOUS TRACT SOCIETY, 56, PATERNOSTER ROW;
65, ST. PAUL'S CHURCHYARD; AND 164, PICCADILLY.

Published undated in 1883, in an elaborate binding of diagonal fine-ribbed cloth, heavily blocked in gold, silver and black, it was marked as No 1 in a series called 'The Boy's Own Bookshelf' issued by the RTS

It was finally left to Rudyard Kipling to upset all the accepted traditions of school stories with his memorable *Stalky & Co.*, 1899, a deliberately unsentimental and largely autobiographical tale of life in the United Services College in North Devon, a school which the author had attended himself. H. G. Wells was later to describe the heroes of the story as 'mucky little Sadists', and one feels the remark well justified after reading of the shooting of the school cat (later buried beneath the floorboards of a rival dormitory in order that the subsequent stench would make life unbearable to its inmates), and to the detailed, eight-page description of the slow torture of two tied-up bullies captured in a school ambush. The vigour and stark realism of *Stalky & Co.* had far-reaching effects, not least in seeming to expose the naïveté of all past and contemporary school stories for boys.

The wide diversity of stories and romances for children in particular and young people in general during the last few decades of the nineteenth century means that space can be found for only a thin cross-section of titles published during this extremely active literary period. The passing of the Elementary Education Act of 1870 and the consequent hunger for books by the increasing number of children who could now read and write led to expansion and prosperity for publishing houses, especially those specialising in children's books. The demand for school textbooks, school prizes in book form, library books for schools and a host of other literary needs created a thriving seller's market.

Women writers were still pre-eminent in the story-book world of children, but, with the solitary exception of Anne Bowman (q.v.), they left the field of boys' adventure stories clear for their masculine colleagues. In the USA, Louisa M. Alcott (1832–88) wrote *Little Women*, 1868, one of the most popular juvenile books ever published. Drawing on her memories of home, the authoress portrayed the daily lives and doings of four girls—Jo, Meg, Beth and Amy March—in a New England family. The influence of Charlotte Yonge's *The Daisy Chain*, 1856, is discernible in the character of Jo, who owes something to the Ethel May of the earlier book. In fact, in the third chapter of *Little Women* Jo is discovered in the attic, 'eating apples and crying over *The Heir of Redclyffe*'. *Little Women* and its sequels passed through countless editions and were translated into almost every foreign language. *An Old Fashioned Girl*, 1870, and *Little Men*, 1871, were the best of her later

(Left) *An illustration from* The Fifth Form at St. Dominic's *(1887), by Talbot Baines Reed, which epitomises the cruelties in the fagging system of an earlier public school era. 19 × 12.5cm. (Right) Published in 1902 by Macmillan & Co., this first edition was illustrated by the author, who also designed the pictorial cover. Size of cover: 24 × 18cm*

novels. She is also remembered as the editor of a successful children's magazine, *Merry's Museum*, started in 1867.

Juliana Horatia Ewing (1841–85) was the daughter of Mrs Margaret Gatty (1809–73), whose first book *The Fairy Godmother and Other Tales*, 1851, was followed by her frequently reprinted *Parables from Nature*, issued in five separate series during the period 1855–71, later being translated into almost every European language. Mrs Gatty was assisted by her daughter in preparing *Aunt Judy's Tales*, 1859, and the sequel *Aunt Judy's Letters*, 1862, illustrated by Clara Lane and published by Bell & Daldy, London. In May 1866 she founded *Aunt Judy's Magazine*, and her daughter Juliana became the Aunt Judy to whom the children addressed their letters. At the same time Juliana was writing books on her own account, starting with *Melchior's Dream, and Other Tales*, 1862, a work that had made its first appearance in the magazine *The Monthly Packet* the previous year. There was then a gap of nearly seven years before the publication of *Mrs Overtheway's Rememberances*, 1869, followed by *The Brownies; and Other Tales*, 1870, and *A Flat Iron for a Farthing*, 1872. These and most of her other tales for children, such as *Lob-lie-by-the-Fire*, 1874, *Six to Sixteen*, 1875, *Jan of the Windmill*, 1876, and *Jackanapes*, 1884, to name just a few, all made their first appearance as serials in *Aunt Judy's Magazine*.

Mrs Ewing took considerable pains over her many books, polishing their texts with infinite care and revealing a compassionate heart as far as juvenile misbehaviour was concerned, as well as an almost impish sense of humour. She married Major Alexander Ewing in 1867, and for many years was forced to live the unsettled existence of an army officer's wife. A number of her later works reflect this aspect of her career and had an army setting. These were the special favourites of Rudyard Kipling, who said of her *Six to Sixteen* (actually a story for girls), that he owed more 'in circuitous ways to that tale than I can tell you. I knew it, as I know it still, almost by heart.' All her stories found a wide readership, and all passed through several editions in the course of a very few years. *Daddy Darwin's Dovecot* (1884) and *Dandelion Clocks* (1887), published undated under an RTS imprint, were followed by the posthumous *Verses for Children*, 1888, which appeared in three volumes. Her works attracted the talents of the foremost book illustrators of her day, with George Cruikshank, Randolph Caldecott, Gordon Browne, Helen Paterson (afterwards Mrs William Allingham), J. A. Pasquier and R. André among the most prominent names.

Juliana Ewing's reputation as a writer for a juvenile audience seems to have worn less well than either of her two foremost rivals, although as picture story books of the mid-Victorian era they exert a charm that has had collectors pursuing them for many years. One tends to bracket

A set of ten volumes of the tales of Mrs Juliana Ewing, illustrated by R. André, published about 1880. Each 18 × 15.5cm

THE ADVENTURES

OF

H E R R   B A B Y

BY MRS. MOLESWORTH

" I have a boy of five years old ;
His face is fair and fresh to see."
WORDSWORTH.

ILLUSTRATED BY WALTER CRANE

London
MACMILLAN AND CO.
1881

"Oh look, look, Baby's made Peepy-Snoozle into 'the parson in the pulpit that couldn't say his prayers,'" cried Denny.—P. 5.

A Walter Crane frontispiece to one of Mrs Molesworth's most famous titles. 23.5 × 18cm

her as a writer in much the same category as Mrs Molesworth and Mrs Hodgson Burnett, the more so since the appearance of Marghanita Laski's *Mrs Ewing, Mrs Molesworth and Mrs Hodgson Burnett*, 1950, in which she reviewed their work and social backgrounds. The books of the same three ladies stand together on my own shelves, those of the last two names impressive in full-cloth bindings blocked pictorially in gold, while Mrs Ewing's slim little volumes stand rather primly in a corner in their paper-covered boards.

Mary Louisa Molesworth (1839–1921) was a formidable dreadnought of a woman, stately of carriage, precise and dignified in her demands on life and on those around her. As her cousin Mrs Dyson-Laurie later confessed, 'her manner was distant and one worshipped from afar'. Her earliest books were written under the pen name 'Ennis Graham' and her first children's book *Tell me a Story*, 1875, published by Macmillan & Co., London, and illustrated by Walter Crane, was the forerunner of over a hundred 'child novels'. *'Carrots': Just a Little Boy*, 1876, brought her work to the notice of a wider public, and from that time onwards hardly a year passed without at least one or two books

164

from her pen appearing on the booksellers' counters in time for the Christmas trade. She used a fairy-tale fantasy in many of her stories, including *The Cuckoo Clock*, 1877, *Four Winds Farm*, 1887, and *An Enchanted Garden*, 1892: this last title being published in T. Fisher Unwin's important series of little volumes, bound in blue 'pinafore' cloth, he called his 'Children's Library'. It was not long before her real-life tales of romance and adventure captured a wide readership, mostly of children in their early teens. The best of these were *The Tapestry Room, a child's romance*, 1879, *A Christmas Child*, 1880, *The Adventures of Herr Baby*, 1881, *Two Little Waifs*, 1883, *'Us', an Old-fashioned Story*, 1885, *Christmas Tree Land*, 1884, *The Old Pincushion* (1889), *Four Winds Farm*, 1887, *Nurse Heatherdale's Story*, 1891, *'Farthings'*, 1892, and *The Carved Lions*, 1895.

The last of our trio is Mrs Frances Hodgson Burnett (1849–1924), an Anglo-American novelist, born in Manchester, England, of poor parents, who emigrated to the USA with her family in 1865, settling near Knoxville, Tennessee. Her first work to be published in book form was *That Lass O'Lowrie's*, 1877, New York, which appeared as a serial in *Scribner's Magazine* the same year. *Haworth's*, her next novel, was published in 1879; but she is forever remembered by the title that has long since become a household name and a derogatory term of abuse: *Little Lord Fauntleroy*, 1886, again issued under a New York imprint, having first appeared as a serial in *St. Nicholas Magazine* there, running from November 1885 to October 1886. This saccharine picture of a beautifully bred child appeared in book form in 1886 in Britain, issued by Frederick Warne & Co., London, and promptly 'ran through England like a sickly fever', to quote F. J. H. Darton in his *Children's Books in England*, 1932 (third edition 1982, by Cambridge University Press, and still in print). The story was dramatised in 1888, and a film version appeared in the late 1930s. In less than four years twenty editions of the story were issued in England alone, and it was subsequently translated into nearly every European language. The author's other successful children's books included *Sara Crewe; or, What happened at Miss Minchin's*, 1888, *The Captain's Youngest*, 1894, *Piccino; and other stories*, 1894, *Two Little Pilgrims' Progress*, 1895, *In the closed room*, 1904, *Racketty Packetty House*, 1907, and *The Secret Garden*, 1911, all of which made their first appearance in the USA, followed by London editions dated the same year. *The Secret Garden* displayed her insight into child psychology and is probably the book deserving pride of place amongst her many works. *The One I knew best of All*, 1893, deserves an honoured place in any collection devoted to the evolution of publisher's binding styles, the first English edition, published the same year as the true first, being issued by Frederick Warne & Co.

*A title published in 1895 in a heavily gilt pictorial binding. Size of front cover:
20.6 × 14.5cm*

in a diagonally striped full-cloth binding over bevelled boards. The front cover and spine were blocked in gold and colours with pictures and emblematic designs by the American artist Reginal Birch, and is a delightful volume to own and admire. It was Birch who created the familiar figure of the obnoxious Fauntleroy from a photograph of the author's second son Vivian. Frances' marriage to Dr Swan Burnett ended in divorce, and she married again, this time a Mr Stephen Townsend. She called her novels 'fairy tales of real life'.

Susan Bogart Warner (1819–85) was an American novelist who wrote under the name 'Elizabeth Wetherell'. She sprang to immediate and lasting fame with her *The Wide, Wide World*, 1850 (2 vols), published in New York. This pious and sentimental story, in which the principal characters are in tears on almost every page, had only a paper-thin plot and very little action of any kind. Despite this, her description of the emotions of her characters apparently more than compensated for the lack of incident in this and her other stories. They were works to sigh over, and tens of thousands did just that.

The Wide, Wide World became a national best-seller within a few months of issue and it proved almost as popular in Britain as it was in the USA. *Queechy*, 1952 (2 vols—New York), her next book, was also a success, the first English edition being published the same year by James Nisbet, London, to be re-issued, dated 1853, the following year. In order to be first in the field, Nisbet rushed copies into the booksellers without having time to commission any illustrations, the two volumes appearing in a binding of wavy-grained cloth, with the title blocked in gilt on the front covers and spines. The first English illustrated edition was published by George Routledge & Co., London, as a single volume dated 1853, and contained a pictorial title-page and frontispiece. The same firm also issued a single-volume edition of *The Wide, Wide World*, dated the same year and containing illustrations by William Harvey.

Susan Warner's other works for teenagers include *The Old Helmet*, 1863, *Melbourne House*, 1864, and *Mr Rutherford's Children*, 1853–5 (2 vols). With this last title her sister Anna Warner (1827–1915), who used the pseudonym 'Amy Lothrop', acted as co-authoress. Anna also wrote books on her own account, including *Dollars and Cents*, 1852, and *My Brother's Keeper*, 1855.

During the years 1851–2, the American magazine *National Era* serialised the story of a noble, high-minded, devoutly Christian slave who is eventually flogged to death by his brutal master, amid the tears of many of the hundreds of thousands of readers who followed the tale in periodical and book form. *Uncle Tom's Cabin, or, Life Among the Lowly*, 1852 (2 vols), was published by John P. Jewett & Company,

UNCLE TOM'S CABIN;

OR,

LIFE AMONG THE LOWLY.

BY

HARRIET BEECHER STOWE.

VOL. I.

BOSTON:
JOHN P. JEWETT & COMPANY.
CLEVELAND, OHIO:
JEWETT, PROCTOR & WORTHINGTON.
1852.

Chicago
A. C. McClurg & Co.
1914

Edgar Rice Burroug

(Left) *The first issue of the first edition of a book which hastened the outbreak of the American Civil War. Mrs Stowe's famous anti-slavery novel appeared as a serial before publication as a two-volume work. 19 × 12cm.* (Right) *Pictorial title of the first edition of a world-famous book. 19 × 12.5cm*

Boston, in a binding of black cloth, blocked in gold (in later issues black cloth was abandoned in favour of brighter colours). The author was Harriet Beecher Stowe (1811–96), who must have been gratified to learn that, during its first year of publication, well over three hundred thousand copies were sold in the USA alone. And it was a book which children the world over annexed as one of their own favourite tales. Within a few years, children's illustrated editions were legion on both sides of the Atlantic, the text often abbreviated and amended.

The first English edition of Mrs Stowe's internationally famous anti-slavery novel was issued by Clarke & Co., London, dated 1852, who rushed out the text unillustrated in order to beat their rivals-in-trade. Most other British publishing houses pirated the text of Clarke & Co., and over twenty different editions, all dated 1852, were on sale in Britain that same year. Within months, elaborately illustrated editions had made their appearance, the foremost book illustrators of the day being pressed into service, while some of the cloth bindings were blocked so ornately they seemed ablaze with gold. Within five years of its original publication the story had been translated into twenty-three languages. Mrs Stowe was not immune from attacks by her critics, and to counter these she published *A Key to Uncle Tom's Cabin*, 1853, in which she quoted facts and figues to support her arguments. At the height of her fame in 1853 she made a trip to Britain, where she was enthusiastically received and which led to her writing *Sunny Memories of Foreign Lands*, 1854. *Dred; a tale of the Great Dismal Swamp*, 1856, was her attempt to show the demoralising influence of slavery upon whites of the South.

The tradition of 'man the friend of animals' was a favourite theme in children's books, and nowhere better illustrated than in *Black Beauty: the Autobiography of a Horse* (1877), by Anna Sewell (1820–77). The work was published, undated, by Jerrold & Son, London, and has never been out of print since its original appearance. It was a story told in the equine first person singular and its tremendous success brought an immediate crop of similar works employing every type of animal, reptile, insect, and even plants. The authoress, a Quaker, had been crippled by a leg injury since the age of fourteen, and, by the time she came to write *Black Beauty*, her one and only book, she was bedridden. She died a few months after its publication, too early to realise the extent of its phenomenal success.

Another famous title in the same field was *Tarzan of the Apes*, 1914, by Edgar Rice Burroughs (1875–1950), a first edition of which must bear the imprint of A. C. McClurg & Co., Chicago. The book remained in the best-selling lists for years and it has been estimated that over 25 million copies of it and its sequels have been sold to date. The first issue of the first edition is now a very valuable book, and can be distinguished by the fact that 'W. F. Hall Printing Co., Chicago' is printed in Old English type at the foot of the copyright page, and that there is *not* a picture of an acorn blocked on the spine, new evidence having contradicted Burroughs' bibliographer's original assumptions. All copies of the first edition of this seminal work, for Tarzans now abound, no matter what the issue, are avidly sought after.

Amongst Burroughs' many later titles were *The Return of Tarzan*, 1915, *The Beasts of Tarzan*, 1917, *Tarzan and the Jewels of Opar*, 1918, *Tarzan the Terrible*, 1921, *Tarzan the Invincible*, 1931, and *Tarzan the Magnificent*, 1939, all of which were first issued under American imprints. He was also early in the field of science fiction and contributed *A Princess of Mars*, 1917, *The Warlord of Mars*, 1919, and *Lost on Venus*, 1935, amongst many more.

In complete contrast, my collection of the works of Kate Greenaway (1846–1901) may lack the robustness of the titles of the previous author, but have a charm widely appreciated and internationally acclaimed. They occupy half a shelf, mostly slim little volumes in assorted sizes, starting with the first book she illustrated, *Infant Amusements*, 1867, by W. H. G. Kingston, whose works are discussed later. Probably the first of her illustrations to be colour printed appeared in *Aunt Louisa's Nursery Favourite*, 1870, in which six unsigned pictures of Kate Greenaway's were used for the story 'Diamonds and Toads'. The work was printed in colours by Kronheim and published by Frederick Warne & Co., London. 'Aunt Louisa' was the pen name used on many occasions for similar works by Laura Valentine, and her *London Toy Books* had a wide sale. In *Aunt Louisa's Ships, Birds and Wonder Tales* (1872), Kate Greenaway contributed six full-page quarto-sized illustrations for the story, and it is in this set of pictures, for the first time, that one can discern the stylised mode of dressing her children which makes her work instantly recognisable. *School Days in Paris* (1874), by Margaret S. Jeune, contains four full-page illustrations by her in the undated edition of 1881, as does the 1882 edition of *The Children of the Parsonage* (dated this time!) by Henry C. Selous, both titles being published by Griffith & Farran, London.

When *Under the Window* (1878) made its appearance in its glazed pictorially printed paper-covered boards, engraved in colour by Edmund Evans, her quaintly dressed little girls and boys instantly captured the public's interest, displaying a fluency of style that has made her books collector's pieces ever since. A first edition of twenty thousand copies was printed and sold, but, despite this much larger than normal run, the quarto volume is extremely difficult to find in clean original condition. *A Day in a Child's Life* (1881), *Mother Goose* (1881), *Language of Flowers* (1884) and *The Pied Piper of Hamelin* (1888) were all illustrated in the inimitable style that soon made her an equal favourite with children and adults. *The Queen of the Pirate Isle* (1886), by Bret Harte, was one of the most successful examples of her talents as a book illustrator and was described by her friend John Ruskin as 'the best thing you have ever done—it is so real and natural', repeating his praise when the *Pied Piper* appeared two years later.

Also collected by the children of her day, but now in a price bracket which puts them well beyond the reach of collectors of moderate means, is her series of little almanacs. A complete set, from its beginning in 1883 to the conclusion of the series in 1897 (missing the year 1896 for which there was no issue), comprises a total of fourteen miniature volumes. Most of them were originally issued in envelope dust-jackets, marked ready for the post. The issue of 1897, bound in leather, is much the rarest, and that for 1889 is also difficult to find. A full set is much prized, and is now priced in bookseller's catalogues at close to four figures sterling. Her *Queen Victoria's Jubilee Garland*, issued in illustrated wrappers in 1887, was published and engraved by Edmund Evans, whose press was responsible for all her important work. *Kate Greenaway's Carols*, printed in colours on stiff board for hanging on a nursery wall, is a rare item. George Routledge & Sons, London, published the majority of her first editions; those bearing the imprint of Frederick Warne & Co. are usually late editions of little value. Finally, I must mention the definitive work that has long been a collector's item in its own right: *Kate Greenaway*, 1905, by M. H. Spielmann and G. S. Layard, published by Adam & Charles Black, London. The edition-de-luxe of this magnificent work was limited to only five hundred copies, each of which contains an original pencil drawing by Kate Greenaway inserted at the front of the book, thus enhancing the volume's value many times. Probably the finest collection of her original drawings and first editions and inscribed editions is to be found in the Rare Book Room, Detroit Public Library, USA. *Kate Greenaway—A Catalogue of the Collection*, 1977, compiled by Susan Ruth Thomson, is finely illustrated and is an indispensable bibliography for the collector. *Kate Greenaway—A Biography*, 1981, by Rodney Engen (Macdonald, London), telling of her unrequited love affair with Ruskin, deserves a place on every collector's shelves.

An American author who found his most popular works pirated by British publishers was John Habberton (1842–1921), who is today remembered almost exclusively for his best-selling novel *Helen's Babies*, 1876, which he published anonymously as being 'by their latest victim, Uncle Harry'. He was one of the first writers to amuse his readers with his own special vocabulary of baby language and the lisps and inversions of early youth. *Helen's Babies* can be read today with almost the same amusement one finds in reading *The Diary of a Nobody* (1892), by George and Weedon Grossmith, a work quickly discovered by teenage children as a hilarious piece of domestic strife, although never meant for their eyes. The first English edition of *Helen's Babies*, 1877, was published in December 1876, by David Bryce & Son, Glasgow, complete with a pictorial title-page, and issued as a square octavo in a smooth-cloth binding with gilt leaf-edges. Another edition, also dated 1877, appeared later in that year and was published in a pictorial binding (but without illustrations) by William Mullan & Son, London. But to find any early edition in good condition is difficult, the book being so popular that it was literally read to death.

Much the same fate was accorded to the first edition of *The Story of the Treasure Seekers*, 1899, by Edith Nesbit (1858–1924), afterwards Mrs

The Aerial Burglars, *1906, by James Blyth, had deep-buttoned leather seats for both cars and aircraft! The illustrator was Harry Piffard. 19 × 13cm*

Hubert Bland. She had previously tried her hand at several styles of writing with little success, but the enthusiastic reviews of Andrew Lang brought her to the notice of a wide public. Although she aspired to be recognised as a poet, her children's books were what ultimately brought her fame. From the time *The Story of the Treasure Seekers* appeared, she was established as a leading writer of what came to be known as 'modern' children's stories of family life. The book was episodic, and various chapters previously appeared in the *Pall Mall Magazine, Windsor Magazine, The Illustrated London News* and *Nister's Holiday Annual* during 1898. The adventures of the Bastable children in search of a fortune (to quote the subtitle of the work) continued in *The Would-be-Goods*, 1901, dedicated to the authoress's son, Fabian, who died suddenly in his sixteenth year, and ended with the last of the trilogy, *New Treasure Seekers*, 1904. It should be mentioned that Edith Nesbit and her husband were founder members of Fabian Society, after which her son was named. All three volumes were published by T. Fisher Unwin, London, and illustrated by Gordon Browne and Lewis Baumer. Her stories, which seemed to have a direct appeal to the imagination of children, have been popular ever since, and are still in print today. Of the thirty or so which followed, the most popular were probably *The Story of the Amulet,* 1906, *The Railway Children*, 1906, *The Enchanted Garden*, 1907, *The Magic City*, 1910, *Wet Magic* (1913) and *Five of Us—and Madeline*, 1925.

Vice Versa: or A Lesson to Fathers, 1882, is another difficult first edition to acquire in anything like good condition, and for the usual reasons—its popularity meant each copy was read scores of times by succeeding generations. The author, Thomas Anstey Guthrie (1856–1934), better known by the pseudonym he always used of 'F. Anstey', frequently changed his publisher, but insisted that all his title-pages should bear the legend 'By the author of *Vice Versa*'. It was a runaway best-seller in its day, and can still be read with amusement now. *Paleface and Redskin*, 1898, and *Only Toys*, 1903, are the best known of his later books for children. He also achieved a considerable reputation as a novelist with such titles as *Voces Populi*, 1890–2 (2 vols), *The Man from Blankley's*, 1893, and *The Brass Bottle*, 1900, all of which appealed to older children.

John Meade Falkner (1858–1932) wrote only four books, the last of which, just completed and still in manuscript form, he inadvertently left in a railway carriage. He never saw it again and had not the heart to set about the task of rewriting it, with the result that the reading public was almost surely deprived of a book which would have passed through many editions. His other three did, and each has been reprinted during the last few years. *The Lost Stradivarius*, 1895, *Moonfleet*, 1898,

and *The Nebuly Coat*, 1903, have each been read by generations of older children and adults, the second having established itself as a near-classic adventure story in the tradition of Stevenson's *Treasure Island*. *Poems*, 1933, appeared posthumously.

Entirely different in concept were the stories and tales of G. E. Farrow (1866–1920), who achieved considerable success with *The Wallypug of Why* (1895), and its six sequels, of which *The Wallypug in London*, 1898, and *In Search of the Wallypug*, 1903, are typical examples. *The Missing Prince*, 1896, *The Little Panjandrum's Dodo*, 1899, *Baker Minor and the Dragon*, 1902, and *Professor Philanderpan*, 1904, are amongst his many other stories, most of which were published by C. Arthur Pearson, London.

Two other minor authors whose books were widely read by children in the older age groups were E. H. Knatchbull-Hugessen (Baron Brabourne) (1829–1923), a great-nephew of Jane Austen, and Sir Edward Abbott Parry (1863–1943), most of whose works were inscribed as by 'His Honour Judge Parry'. Knatchbull-Hugessen contributed stories derived from folk-tales and legends, including *Stories for my Children*, 1869, *Tales at Tea-Time*, 1872, *Queer Folk*, 1874, *Whispers from Fairyland*, 1875, and *River Legends*, 1875, this last title with illustrations by Gustave Doré. Judge Parry's tales covered a wider spectrum: *Katawampus: its treatment and cure,* 1895, was followed by a sequel entitled *Butterscotia; or, a cheap trip to Fairy Land*, 1896. *The First Book of Krab*, 1897, was illustrated by Archie MacGregor and published by David Nutt, London, as were the author's first two titles. *The Scarlet Herring*, 1899, and *Gamble Gold*, 1907, are both fine examples of avant-garde cloth binding styles of the period. *Don Quixote of the Mancha, retold by Judge Parry*, 1900, is perhaps one of the titles illustrated by Walter Crane most difficult to find in acceptable condition.

Standing at the end of this particular shelf is a solitary title, *Toyland*, 1875, by Arthur and Eleanor O'Shaughnessy. This was the Irish poet's only book written for children, and one in which his wife was co-author.

Opposite:
(Above left) *The first edition of a popular children's book by 'F. Anstey' (T. A. Guthrie), published in 1903.* (Above right) *Angela Brazil was herself once head girl at a boarding-school, and is distinguished as the founder of a genre of girls' school stories, of which she wrote over sixty. 18.5 × 12cm.* (Below) *Moonfleet, 1898, by John Meade Falkner, established itself as a near-classic adventure story in the tradition of Stevenson's* Treasure Island. *The latter's* Black Arrow, 1888, *was originally conceived as a serial for* Young Folks. *Both 19 × 12.5cm*

The name of Kenneth Grahame (1859–1932) must now be almost as well known as the book which brought him lasting fame, *The Wind in the Willows*, 1908, published by Methuen & Co., London, with a frontispiece by Graham Robertson. The first edition is, as one can imagine, now an expensive book to acquire, and is almost indistinguishable from the second (published in October 1908). In the past, copies have been sold to collectors as 'firsts' when in fact they were later editions, so a word of warning is necessary. There is one sure method to tell the difference between a true 'first' and a sophisticated fake or made-up copy. The first edition of 1908 is blocked on the front cover pictorially in gold, while all later editions are blocked in blind only. Otherwise the spine and the rest of the volume are much the same, although in unsophisticated copies the words 'second edition' (or later) are printed on the title-page, and the number of impressions on the verso of the same leaf.

Toad of Toad Hall, 1929, by A. A. Milne, was the first printing of the dramatised version of Grahame's book, and is now also sought after. *Pagan Papers*, 1894, which has a title-page designed by Aubrey Beardsley, is a collection of essays and stories and his first publication, while *The Golden Age*, 1895, reprints part of it. Grahame's last book for children was *Fun O' the Fair*, 1929, and was adapted from his essay *Sanger and his Times*. It is a very difficult title to find, having been published by J. M. Dent & Sons in a binding of orange-coloured paper-wrappers as one of their *Elian Greeting-Booklets*, and its fragile nature ensured that few copies survived.

Women authors I must not ignore include Mrs Gene Stratton-Porter (1863–1924), a very popular novelist during the early part of the twentieth century, many of her books becoming firm favourites on both sides of the Atlantic. *Freckles*, 1904, *A Girl of the Limberlost*, 1909, *Laddie*, 1913, and *The Keeper of the Bees*, 1925, are typical of her titles in which idealism, sentimentality and the joys of the outdoor life receive equal prominence. *A Girl of the Limberlost* has never been out of print since its first appearance, telling the tale of Eleanora, the companion of an Indiana waif called Freckles, who together hunt the Florida swamps for rare moths, which they sell to provide money for an education.

Bertha Upton (1849–1912) supplied the text for a distinctive series of oblong story books in verse, while her daughter, Florence K. Upton (1873–1922) brought them to life with her pictures of wooden dolls and the little shock-headed nursery favourite she christened 'Golliwogg'. Florence invented the name, and the black-faced doll in his striped pinafore trousers made his first appearance in her mother's tales, all of which were published by Longmans, Green & Co., London. *The Adventures of Two Dutch Dolls* (1895) was the first of the many titles

176

on which Mrs Upton and her talented daughter co-operated, all issued in oblong-quarto format, in bindings of glazed pictorially printed paper-covered boards with cloth spines, and each having sixty-four pages of text and illustrations. *The Golliwogg's Bicycle Club* (1896), the first issue of which has the copyright declaration printed on the front cover but has no mention of other titles in the series, *The Golliwogg at the Seaside* (1898), *The Golliwogg in War* (1899), *The Golliwogg's Polar Adventures* (1900) followed in similar style, and *Golliwogg in the African Jungle* (1909) was the last Golliwogg adventure. Two books issued in identical format, but not featuring the Dutch dolls Sarah Jane, Peg, Meg, Wed and the Midget, the last named being a tiny version of her bigger sisters, lacked the magic which endeared the rest of the titles to several generations of children: *The Vege-Men's Revenge* (1897) and *The Adventures of Barbee and the Wisp* (1905) were experiments not repeated. Due to their unusual size and shape, and the fact that the glazed covers easily soil, Golliwogg books are difficult to find in good condition and dealers ask high prices for those which have managed to survive intact. During World War I, Florence Upton gave her entire collection of manuscripts, drawings and the original model Golliwogg and Dutch dolls to the Red Cross. They were auctioned in London and fetched nearly £500, the money being used to buy an ambulance. The purchaser, Miss Faith Moore, donated the collection to Chequers, the British Prime Minister's official country residence in the Chilterns, and there Golliwogg and his friends have found a permanent home in an illuminated glass case in the Long Gallery.

Another woman writer of an internationally famous title was Helen Bannerman (1863–1946), who married an army doctor and spent much of her life in India. It was while on a tedious journey by ox-cart between Kodai and Madras that she wrote *The Story of Little Black Sambo*, 1899, finishing the brightly coloured illustrations and making a fair copy of the text when she finally arrived at her destination. Her daughters, Janet and Day, then five and two, were with her and loved the story from the start, and its popularity with the children of her friends persuaded her to send the manuscript to London in the hope of finding a publisher. Grant Richards bought it outright for the price of a single £5 note, and it appeared in diminutive format in 1899, bound in striped light green cloth as No 4 in his series of *Dumpy Books for Children*. Five hundred copies were printed, complete with twenty-seven colour-printed wood engravings, and these sold at such a speed that a second, then a third, edition were called for within a few months. By October 1900 over twenty thousand copies had been sold, but despite the book's continuing success during the next thirty years Grant Richards refused to pay the author a penny in royalties.

177

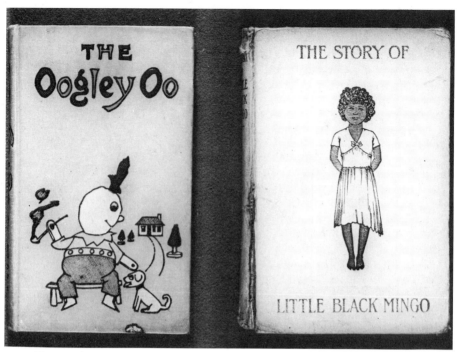

Two small first editions exceedingly difficult to find in their original cloth bindings as shown. The Oogley Oo *(1903) was illustrated by Gerald Sichel, with text by S. C. Woodhouse.* The Story of Little Black Mingo, *1901, by Helen Bannerman, followed her best-selling* The Story of Little Black Sambo, *1899. Height of covers: 13.5cm*

The Story of Little Black Mingo, 1901, followed, this time under a James Nisbet & Co., London, imprint (as were all her other titles), Frederick A. Stokes Co., New York, issuing her works in the USA, usually dated a year later than the British editions. *The Story of Little Black Quibba*, 1902, *The Story of Little Degchiehead*, 1903, *The Story of the Teasing Monkey*, 1906, and *The Story of Little Black Quasha*, 1908, were amongst her later titles, but none of these achieved anything like the success of her first book for children. It was about 1950 that her choice of the word 'Sambo' and incidents in the story itself came under increasing criticism as being racist in character, so much so that many librarians withdrew the title from their open shelves. Due to Grant Richards' claim that for the original payment of £5 he owned the copyright, Mrs Bannerman had lost control of the book's appearances in the United States. Her original sympathetic figures of the coloured family were vulgarised by American illustrators and Sambo was depicted as a capering coon or the idiot of some Nigger Minstrel postcards. By the time all this happened Mrs Bannerman had been laid to rest untroubled by the storm which subsequently broke over the little book she had copied out and coloured for her two small daughters.

Beatrix Potter (1866–1943) also wrote and illustrated little books, insisting that they should remain tiny to suit the little hands into which they were meant to find their way. *The Tale of Peter Rabbit* (1901) was her first book, and, as she was unable to find a publisher, she had it privately printed by Strangeways & Sons in an edition of 250 copies. It was bound in green boards, the spine flat, and illustrated with a frontispiece in colour and forty-one illustrations in monochrome, eleven of which were not used in subsequent editions. The book must have been well received for she had a second privately printed edition produced, this time of 200 copies, which appeared in February 1902. The binding was similar to the first edition, but the spine was rounded, while the text had been revised and corrected. It was only when the first trade edition appeared, undated, in 1902, under the imprint of Frederick Warne & Co. that it became apparent that the general public appreciated the tale and the pictures. The grey end-papers had only a leaf pattern, and it was not until four printings had been exhausted that the famous pictorial end-papers came into use.

In the meantime Beatrix Potter had written and privately published *The Tailor of Gloucester*, 1902, a story she described as her 'favourite among the little books'. It, too, was later published by Warne, dated 1903, continuing the run of her works that later became famous as the 'Peter Rabbit' books. First editions can be identified through carrying the Warne imprint and are also dated on the *front* of their title-pages, as well as having a dated copyright inscription on the verso. The early titles in first (regularly published) form are expensive and hard to find, while the earlier privately printed editions fetch far more than the average collector would be able to afford.

The Tale of Squirrel Nutkin, 1903, *The Tale of Benjamin Bunny*, 1904, *The Tale of Two Bad Mice*, 1904, *The Pie and the Patty-Pan*, 1905, were all written when Norman Warne, her publisher, to whom she became engaged to be married in 1905, was her confidant and adviser. Within months he had died of leukaemia, and soon afterwards Miss Potter took her sorrow with her and bought the remote 'Hill Top Farm' as she called it, a smallholding in the Lake District, near Ambleside, in Westmorland. *The Tale of Jeremy Fisher*, 1906, had been written in London, but *The Tale of Jemima Puddle-Duck*, 1908, *The Tale of the Flopsy Bunnies*, 1909, *The Tale of Timmy Tiptoes*, 1911, and *The Tale of Mr. Tod*, 1912, were all products of Hill Top Farm, the pictures often mirroring the village life of Sawrey, the interior of the farm itself and its gardens and animals. Two of her titles were issued in a larger format: *The Roly-Poly Pudding*, 1908, and *Ginger and Pickles*, 1909; while

A selection of the first published editions of tales by Beatrix Potter, which became known as the 'Peter Rabbit' books. Size of Squirrel Nutkin: *14.5 × 10.5cm*

The Tale of Little Pig Robinson, 1930, was a late addition to her tales for children. Her last book to appear was published posthumously in 1956 by Frederick Warne & Co., under their New York imprint, and was titled *The Tale of the Faithful Dove*.

Few children's stories of the 1920s seem genuinely alive in the sense of being continually reprinted for modern reading, or even achieved sufficient success in their own decade to be sought after by literary historians and bibliographers. The long series of 'William' books from the pen of Miss Richmal Crompton Lamburn (1890–1969), who wrote under the pen name Richmal Crompton, is an exception. Born in Lancashire, the daughter of a Church of England parson, she turned to teaching as a career, spending years as Classics mistress at Bromley High School for Girls in Kent. It was there that she began to write short stories, including one featuring a rumbustious, mischievous, untidy schoolboy, William Brown. These first appeared in *Home Magazine* in February 1919, continuing at monthly intervals before being transferred to the *Happy Magazine*. It was in 1922 that the publishers, George Newnes, decided to issue a collection of her stories in book form. *Just William*, 1922, was the first title in a series that brought its author both fame and fortune, a series which continued for over forty-five years and ultimately totalled thirty-eight books. *More William*, 1922, *William Again*, 1923, and *William the Fourth*, 1924, are typical of her hilarious tales about the hateful little schoolboy her readers quickly came to love. Miss Lamburn also produced no less than thirty-nine adult novels none of which even began to approach the success of her William books.

Long before this, the 'Oz' books had appeared in Britain, though never achieving anything like the sales figures reached in the USA. L. Frank Baum (1856–1919), journalist and dramatist, had told the story of his heroine Dorothy and her dog Toto, both of whom had been whisked away by a cyclone from their cheerless Kansas home to a land of fantastic adventure, peopled by such creatures as the Cowardly Lion, the Tin Woodman, an animated Scarecrow, and the Wizard himself. *The Wonderful Wizard of Oz*, 1900, with illustrations by W. W. Denslow, was published in Chicago by George M. Hill, in a binding of light green cloth pictorially blocked in green and red, with twenty-four coloured illustrations, and has never been out of print from that time onwards. The success of this book, and Baum's musical extravaganza adapted for the stage in 1902, led to thirteen sequels, including *Dot and Tot of Merryland* (1901), *The New Wizard of Oz* (1902), *The Marvellous Land of Oz*, 1904, *Ozma of Oz* (1907), *Dorothy and the Wizard of Oz* (1908), *The Road to Oz* (1909), *Patchwork Girl of Oz* (1913), *Scarecrow of Oz* (1915) and *The Magic of Oz* (1919).

181

Baum also wrote dozens of other children's stories, including *Father Goose: His Book* (1899), *Mother Goose in Prose*, (1897), *The Life and Adventures of Santa Claus* (1902), *The Enchanted Island of Yew* (1903), *Sea Fairies* (1911) and *Once Upon a Time and other Stories* (1917).

The early 1930s witnessed the beginning of a new and exciting trend in children's literature in Britain with the appearance of *Swallows and Amazons*, 1930, by Arthur Ransome (1884–1967). The book was written when he was forty-six, by which time he already had over a quarter of a century of authorship behind him, all books for adults. The first edition of *Swallows and Amazons* was not illustrated and caused little stir; but the publication of the second edition, with illustrations by Clifford Webb and with end-paper maps by Steven Spurrier, was immediately noticed by reviewers and highly praised. *Swallowdale*, 1931, was followed by *Peter Duck*, 1932, a title enthusiastically received by the critics. The trio of works now began to sell really well, reprints being constantly called for. By the time that *Winter Holiday*, 1933, had

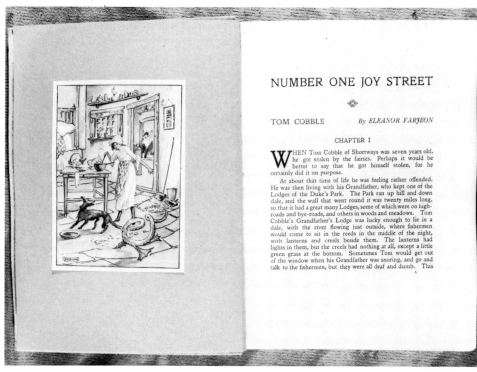

The first of the series of 'Joy Street' books, published by Basil Blackwell, Oxford, in 1923. They contained a medley of prose and verse by leading writers of the day, with coloured plates tipped in on tinted paper. 24.3 × 18cm

made its appearance, Arthur Ransome found himself established as one of the foremost writers for young people of the period. *Coot Club*, 1934, *Pigeon Post*, 1936, *We Didn't mean to go to Sea*, 1937, *Secret Water*, 1939, *The Big Six*, 1940, *Missee Lee*, 1941, *The Picts and the Martyrs*, 1943, and *Great Northern*, 1947, include all his children's holiday stories, now universally known as the 'Swallows and Amazons' books. They well deserve a place in any comprehensive collection of juvenile literature.

Space permits only a brief mention of some of the most important of the later writers in the genre, but Alison Uttley (1884–1976) will be remembered for her *The Squirrel, the Hare, and the little Grey Rabbit*, 1929, the first of a long series of 'Little Grey Rabbit' tales. Elsie Oxenham (1885–1960), whose books of girls' stories are now looked for and collected, wrote *Goblin Island* (1907), *A Princess in Tatters* (1908), *Mistress Nanciebell*, 1910 and *Girls of the Hamlet Club*, 1914, amongst a host of other titles. Hugh Lofting attained fame with his *The Story of Dr Dolittle*, 1920 (New York), followed by a series of sequels, such as *Dr Dolittle's Post Office*, 1923, *Dr Dolittle's Circus*, 1924, *Dr Dolittle's Garden*, 1927, and *Dr Dolittle's Return*, 1933, all first published in New York, with British issues following soon afterwards.

That prolific writer 'Marjorie Bowen' (ie Gabrielle Margaret Vere Campbell—1886–1952) found time to produce, amongst her scores of adult novels, *The Winged Trees: a Tale for Boys*, 1928, and *The Trumpet and the Swan*, 1938; while some of the works of Richard Thomas Church (1893–1972), such as *A Squirrel called Rufus*, 1941, *The Cave*, 1950, *Dog Toby* (1953), and *The Bells of Rye*, 1960, passed through several editions. William Earl Johns (1893–1968) sprang to fame with his series of 'Biggles' books, starting with *Wings: a book of Flying Adventures* (1931) and continuing a very long line of titles, such as *The Camels are Coming* (1932), *The Cruise of the Condor* (1933), *'Biggles' of the Camel Squadron* (1934), *Biggles Hits the Trail*, 1935, and *Comrades in Arms*, 1947.

Enid Blyton (1897–1968) published her first book, a series of short poems, *Child Whispers*, in 1922, and later went on to edit and largely write *Sunny Stories*, a magazine she was associated with for nearly twenty-five years. By the 1940s she had become well known as the author of the *Famous Five* and *Secret Seven* series of books, but it was not until 1949 that she became a really famous public figure by the creation of what was, to many critics, her obnoxious little hero 'Noddy'. With Big Ears, Mr Plod the policeman, and the other characters of Toyland Village, her 'Noddy Books' sold hundreds of thousands of copies, *Little Noddy goes to Toyland*, 1949, being the first. By the time of her death, Enid Blyton had written and had published over four hundred titles. Many librarians banned her work from their shelves on the grounds that her moralising in such black-and-white terms deterred young children from enjoying more subtle literary values, but there is no gainsaying the fact that children themselves wanted to read her books, and did so in their tens of thousands. Noddy, by the way, never allowed anyone a ride in his car unless they first paid him a fee.

Mary Atkinson (b. 1899) had success with her *August Adventure*, 1936, and followed it with *Mystery Manor*, 1937, *The Compass Points North*, 1938, and, amongst her many adventure stories, *Crusoe Island*, 1941; while William Suddaby (1900–64) produced *Lost Men in the Grass*, 1940 (under the pseudonym 'Alan Griff'), *The Star Raiders*, 1950, *The Moon of Snowshoes*, 1956, and *A Bell in the Forest*, 1964.

Josephine Elder (b. 1900) specialised in school stories, starting with *Erika Wins Through* (1924) and continuing with *The Scholarship Girl* (1925), *The Scholarship Girl at Cambridge* (1926), *Barbara at School* (1930) and *Strangers at the Farm School*, 1940, amongst many other titles. Mary Norton (b. 1903) achieved success with her series of 'Borrowers' books, such as *The Borrowers*, 1952, *The Borrowers afield*, 1952, *The Borrowers afloat*, 1959, etc. Her first real seller was *The Magic Bed-Knob*, 1945, but nearly all her titles passed through several editions, both here and in the USA.

Graham Greene (b. 1904), so well known for his novels and other works, also found time to write several entrancing books for children. *The Little Train*, 1946, was actually published under the name of the illustrator Dorothy Craigie; but *The Little Fire Engine*, 1950 (published in New York, dated 1953, as *The Little Red Fire Engine*), *The Little Horse Bus*, 1952, and *The Little Steam Roller*, 1953, are now sought by collectors on both sides of the Atlantic.

Terence Hanbury White (1906–64) wrote *The Sword in the Stone*, 1938, and followed this success with *The Witch in the Wood*, 1939 (New York), plus several other titles; while Joan Kiddell-Monroe (b. 1908) is remembered for her quaintly named 'Black Waistcoat' books, with titles such as *In his little Black Waistcoat*, 1939, *In his little Black Waistcoat to China*, 1940, *In his little Black Waistcoat to India*, 1948, and *In his little Black Waistcoat to Tibet*, 1949, etc.

Geoffrey Trease (b. 1909) started his career as a children's writer with *Bows against the Barons*, 1934, a work almost instantly translated into Russian and published in Moscow that same year; following on with *Comrades for the Charter*, 1934 (Moscow, 1935), *The Unsleeping Sword*, 1934, *The Call to Arms*, 1935, and many other historical and adventure stories.

The revival of interest in literature for the amusement and instruction of children, both in Britain and the USA, is shown by the number of medals and awards for writers and others concerned in the production of books for juveniles. The Newbery Medal, awarded annually in the

USA to the author judged to have made the most notable contribution to children's literature in that country, was first won by Hendrik Willem van Loon for his *The Story of Mankind*, 1921. The following year Hugh Lofting received the award for his *The Voyages of Dr Dolittle*, 1922. The Caldecott Medal has been awarded annually since 1938 to the best American picture book for children. Britain has two principal awards in the field of children's books, both presented annually by The Library Association. The Carnegie Medal has been awarded annually since 1936 (when it was won by Arthur Ransome with *Pigeon Post*) for an outstanding book for children published during the preceding year and written by a British subject living in the United Kingdom. The Kate Greenaway Medal, inaugurated in 1955, is awarded to the British artist who was judged to have produced the most distinguished illustrations of children's books during the preceding year. The first winner was Edward Ardizzone for his book *Tim All Alone*. Finally, it should be mentioned that the magazine *The Junior Bookshelf* has been a most useful and successful publication since its first number in 1936.

7

BOYS' ADVENTURE
STORIES

A debt is owed by many British writers in the field of boys' adventure stories to their American counterparts who had earlier helped blaze the trail. James Fenimore Cooper (1789–1851) had listened to the tales of the Indian Wars told by his father Judge William Cooper, with much the same fervour that had kept young Walter Scott silent and attentive while grey-bearded old warriors recounted their personal adventures in the troubles of '45. As Scott later used his first-hand knowledge of the Highlands and Borders of Scotland when writing his long series of historical novels, so Cooper added life and colour to his father's tales by his own exploring expeditions in the backwoods and prairies of North America.

The result was a series of adventure stories that came to be known as *Leather-Stocking Tales,* starting with *The Pioneers,* 1823 (2 vols, New York), and continuing with *The Last of the Mohicans,* 1826 (2 vols, Philadelphia); *The Prairie,* 1827; *The Pathfinder,* 1840 (2 vols, Philadelphia); and *The Deerslayer; or, the first War-Path,* 1841 (2 vols, Philadelphia). All of these ostensibly adult novels were adopted within a few years of their first appearance by children as adventure reading. Most of Cooper's titles were published in England within a year of their first being issued in the United States, although certain of his works, notably *The Water Witch; or, the Skimmer of the Seas,* 1830 (3 vols, Dresden, Germany) were actually first published in Europe. His first book, *Precaution,* 1820 (2 vols, New York) is, as one would expect, now a very rare and valuable work.

By the mid-1830s Cooper's name was internationally famous, and he is now credited, more than any other writer of his day, with having created the legend of the Redskin and Paleface that gave birth to the the 'Cowboys and Indians' saga that continues in children's games, Western novels and films, and the never-ending television presentations of today.

It was Frederick Marryat (1792–1848), sea captain and novelist, who first intentionally created plots and characters aimed as adventure stories at a specifically juvenile audience. Cooper's works had been discovered and read by at least one generation of children before the

186

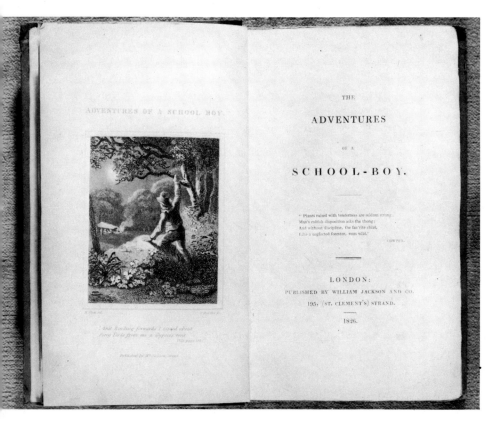

A rare title, dated 1826, whose author has so far escaped identification. 18.5 × 11cm

publishing houses woke up to the fact that they had a ready-made series of tales for which the teenage youth of the day was eagerly waiting. Before long *The Last of the Mohicans* and several other of his novels were being issued in single-volume form, dressed in a variety of brightly gilt cloth bindings specially designed to attract the young. Marryat, however, made it quite clear on his title-pages that it was children and young people he had in mind when he wrote these particular books. *Masterman Ready; or, The Wreck of the Pacific*, 1841 (3 vols), had the words 'Written for Young People' across its title-page; as did *The Settlers in Canada*, 1844 (2 vols), and *The Mission: or, Scenes in Africa*, 1845 (2 vols), all first published in London by Longman, Orme, Brown, Green, & Longmans. His earlier works, such as *The Naval Officer*, 1829 (3 vols), *The King's Own*, 1830 (3 vols), *Peter Simple*, 1833–4 (3 vols—Philadelphia), *Japhet in Search of a Father*, first issued in four separate parts, 1835–6 (New York), and *Mr. Midshipman Easy*, 1836 (3 vols), plus several other titles, were all taken from personal experience during his naval career both ashore and afloat. They made an instant appeal to young readers, although the original format of several of these novels had been designed to attract an adult readership. With *The Children of the New Forest* (1847), published in two volumes by H. Hurst, Charing Cross, London, Marryat apparently insisted that modifications be made to their usual bindings so as to attract young people to buy the work or have it bought for them. The result was that eye-catching title-pages were designed, printed in glowing reds and greens, and the same was done for his *The Little Savage*, 1848-9 (2 vols), and this time he also had the words 'The Juvenile Library' blocked in gold on the front covers.

The tentative beginnings of a specialised publishing industry channelled into providing books for teenagers only, rather than trying to cover the needs of all ages of children, can be discerned in this particular decade. However, it was to be another thirty years or more before firms almost solely devoted to satisfying the demands of this age group flooded the Christmas counters of the bookshops with vividly bound pictorial cloth covers of adventure stories for the twelve- to eighteen-

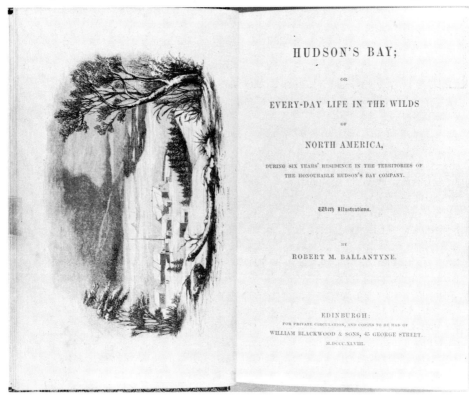

The first (privately printed) edition of Ballantyne's first book, dated 1848. 19 × 12.5cm

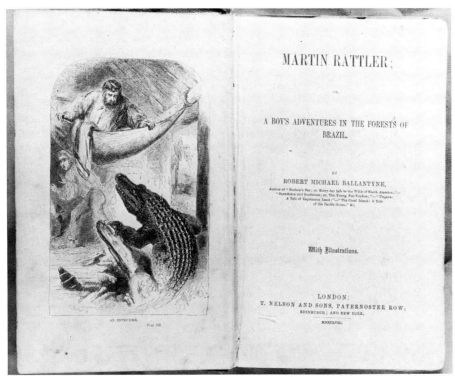

MARTIN RATTLER:

OR,

A BOY'S ADVENTURES IN THE FORESTS OF
BRAZIL.

BY

ROBERT MICHAEL BALLANTYNE,

Author of "Hudson's Bay; or, Every-day Life in the Wilds of North America;"—
"Snowflakes and Sunbeams; or, The Young Fur-Traders;"—"Ungava;
A Tale of Esquimaux Land;"—"The Coral Island; A Tale
of the Pacific Ocean," &c.

With Illustrations.

LONDON:
T. NELSON AND SONS, PATERNOSTER ROW;
EDINBURGH; AND NEW YORK.
MDCCCLVIII.

AN INTRUDER.   *Page 130.*

The first edition of one of Ballantyne's most famous books for boys. Dated 1858, it was later reprinted several times. 16.5 × 10cm

year olds. This rapidly growing group of literate young readers, all of them at an age when reading was a primary and most absorbing pleasure, discovered to their delight that whole walls of freshly printed titles were available for their personal pleasure and enjoyment.

In 1825, Edinburgh was the birthplace of a Scot who was destined to be the first writer for boys who allowed his youthful heroes to wander at will, usually far from home, in any upright and God-fearing manner they liked, unrestrained by the curbing hands and stifling platitudes of accompanying adults. Robert Michael Ballantyne (1825–94), was apprenticed by his father as a clerk in the Hudson's Bay Company of Canada at the age of sixteen. He returned to his native Scotland some six years later in 1847. It was then he discovered that his mother had carefully preserved all the long and intimate letters he had written home during his years in the backwoods of Rupert's Land. These letters formed the basis of his first book, the first of more than a hundred titles, *Hudson's Bay; or Every-Day Life in the Wilds of North America*, 1848. Unable at first to find a publisher, he and his family and friends clubbed together to find the money to have his work privately printed and published at their own expense, although the title-page bore the imprint of William Blackwood, Edinburgh. A full account of what happened can be read in his published biography, *Ballantyne the Brave*, 1967 (Rupert Hart-Davis), and of his subsequent doings, but it is sufficient to state here that a second (or, first published) edition appeared the same year, bearing a similar date. The work was an exciting account of the young author's experiences in the snow and ice of the Far North, but was far from being a financial success. Blackwoods were at fault in not designing a more interesting-looking binding for the volume that might catch the eye of young readers as well as adults. In fact, both editions appeared in bindings of austere plain-grey cloth, unrelieved by any gold-blocking on either cover. This was far too dignified a format to attract prospective young purchasers and the remainder of the copies languished on Blackwood's shelves until 1853.

Any hopes Ballantyne may have had of establishing himself as an author received a severe set-back and it was not until some eight years later that his next book for young people appeared. *Snowflakes and Sunbeams; or, The Young Fur Traders*, 1856 (the first part of the title was dropped after three editions), was an immediate success and went far to establish the man who was later to be described as the hero of Victorian youth, and, as a consequence, the first of the best-selling authors in the teenage market. However, it was not until the publication of the work with which the reading public will always associate his name that he finally decided to make writing his future career. *The Coral Island: A Tale of the Pacific Ocean*, 1858, issued with a series of eight full-page coloured plates by T. Nelson & Sons, Edinburgh, at 6s (30p) a copy, has been almost continually in print to this present day. Yet despite the fact that the title must have earned the company many thousands of pounds in profit, Ballantyne himself received a total of only £90, having sold them the copyright for what turned out to be a mere fraction of its true value. Such was the fate of many an impecunious author in the mid-nineteenth century, despite the protection which the Copyright Act of 1842 should, in theory, have provided.

Ballantyne was careful to set all his fictional tales against a factual and well researched background, visiting whenever possible the regions and localities in which the action of his stories was supposed to take place. *Ungava: A Tale of Esquimaux-Land*, 1858, *The World of Ice*, 1860, *Silver Lake; or, Lost in the Snow*, 1867, *The Giant of the North*, 1882, *The Big Otter*, 1887, *The Buffalo Runners; a Tale of the Red River Plains*, 1891, and *The Walrus Hunters*, 1893, plus several other titles, were written with the knowledge derived from his experiences in the service of the Hudson's Bay Company, as, of course, were *Hudson's Bay* and *The Young Fur Traders*.

Four Ballantyne first editions in their original pictorial cloth bindings. Each 19 × 12.5cm

Much travel and research went into his other titles, especially *The Lifeboat*, 1864, *Freaks on the Fells*, 1865, *The Lighthouse*, 1865, *Fighting the Flames*, 1867, *Deep Down; A Tale of the Cornish Mines*, 1868, *The Floating Light of the Goodwin Sands*, 1870, and *The Iron Horse; or, Life on the Line*, 1871. To enable him to write accurately about such diverse subjects Ballantyne spent weeks inside Bell Rock Lighthouse; worked as a crew member of a fire brigade; made a series of underground visits to the Botallack Tin Mine, St Just, Cornwall; took trips on the footplate of an express train; and spent days of sea-sickness on the heaving lightship off the Goodwin Sands. He had learned his lesson after writing *The Coral Island*, having been forced to rely on evidence which was second-hand, with the result that he made several factual mistakes, notably in describing coconuts growing on palm trees in exactly the form in which he had seen them in the greengrocers' shops in Edinburgh. Before settling down to write what proved to be his most famous

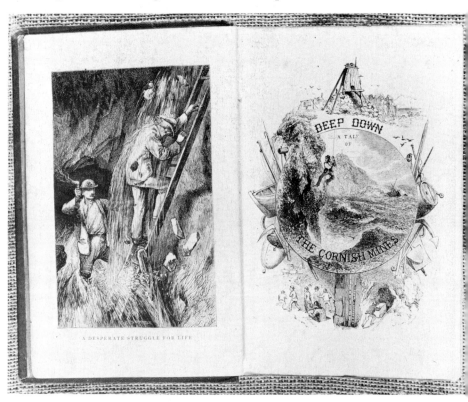

Ballantyne supplied illustrations for the vast majority of his many titles, Deep Down; A Tale of the Cornish Mines, *1868, being typical of the style of pictorial title-page he favoured. 17 × 11.5cm*

book, Ballantyne had read up the subject of the South Seas and desert islands from file copies on the shelves of his publisher Nelson & Son. He obtained much evidence from *Recent Exploring Expeditions to the Pacific, and the South Seas*, 1853, by J. S. Jenkins; but his most fruitful source book was *The Island Home; or, The Young Cast-Aways*, by an American writer, James F. Bowman, first published in Boston, USA, in 1851, although Ballantyne used the text of the first British edition, dated 1852, published by Nelson & Son. Bowman was a Californian author who wrote under the pseudonym of 'Christopher Romaunt'. He was for many years the editor of the *San Francisco Chronicle*, a journalist rather than an author by profession, for the only separate publication of his which has survived in book form appears to be *The Island Home*. Despite that, he has more than earned his place in the annals of English literature, for a reading of both works makes it immediately clear that Ballantyne had lifted a great deal of the plot of

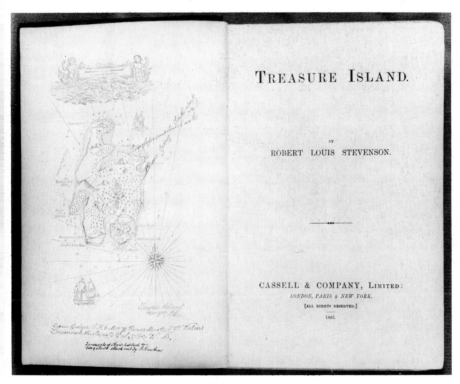

The first edition of a classic among adventure stories for boys of all ages. The wording on the map frontispiece was printed in four contrasting colours. 19.2 × 12.2cm

193

The Coral Island from Bowman's earlier title. It was *The Coral Island* that young Robert Louis Stevenson knew almost by heart, once confiding to Ballantyne, when a boy of sixteen, that he had read the work at least six times. It was this book that instilled in him his longing to visit the South Seas, a trip which led to him settling in Samoa in 1888. Without the stimulus of *The Coral Island* it is possible that the immortal classic full of romance and adventure for boys of all ages, *Treasure Island*, 1883, might have taken another form or never have been written. It made its first appearance as a serial in *Young Folks* from late in 1881, under the title 'The Sea Cook; or, Treasure Island'. From the time when the narrator, the lad Jim Hawkins, takes up the tale at the start of the book, until that plausible but likeable one-legged old schemer and double-dyed villain, Long John Silver, slips over the side of the *Hispaniola* to safety, leaving the squire's party the vast bulk of the treasure, the tale grips and thrills each succeeding generation of young readers to a degree unequalled by almost any other adventure story of this or any age. All this was kindled by Stevenson's many readings of the adventures of Ballantyne's three heroes, Ralph, Jack and Peterkin, as they fought the cannibals and braved the dangers of their remote coral strand. *Treasure Island* is unsurpassed as a straightforward adventure story for boys, unmoralised and not ashamed to be so. One must remark that Ballantyne's own debt to James Bowman can be equated to some extent to Bowman's obligation to Daniel Defoe and to Johann Wyss, the latter's *Swiss Family Robinson* having been first published in two parts in Zurich, 1812–13, with an English translation appearing a year later.

W. H. G. Kingston (1814–80) was a Londoner by birth, but spent many years in Oporto in his father's business, his frequent voyages between England and Portugal instilling a love of the sea that was later reflected in the many seafaring stories he wrote. Unlike Ballantyne, who never attempted any fictional work for the adult market, Kingston started his literary career with the publication of several three-decker novels. *The Circassian Chief*, 1843, *The Prime Minister*, 1845, and *The Albatross*, 1849, all made their appearance in this multi-volume style, while his books of travel, such as *Lusitanian Sketches*, 1845, and *Western Wanderings; or, a Pleasure Tour in the Canadas*, 1856, were each issued in two volumes.

The first of well over a hundred books for young people was issued in 1851, and is his most famous title. *Peter the Whaler*, 1851, is still a most readable book in its class, a second edition, this time with plates, making its appearance two years later. From that time onwards he devoted almost all his time to writing and editing books for boys in particular and young people in general. Among the better known of his

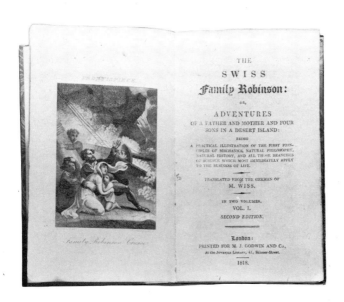

Any early edition of this series of desert island adventures commands high prices at auction and elsewhere

stories are *Adrift in a Boat*, 1869, *Ben Burton; or, Born and Bred at Sea*, 1872, *Cruise of the 'Frolic'*, 1860 (2 vols), *Digby Heathcote*, 1860, *Ernest Bracebridge*, 1860, *In the Rocky Mountains*, 1878, *In the Wilds of Florida*, 1880, *Manco; the Peruvian Chief*, 1853, and *Old Jack: A Tale for Boys*, 1859; but there are scores of other titles that could be as easily mentioned, and I could have continued this alphabetical procession to 'Z' and back again.

Kingston was the editor of several magazines, including *Kingston's Magazine for Boys*, 1860–3 (5 vols), the final volume being published in several monthly parts, but never issued as a book; and *The Union Jack*, 1880–3 (4 vols), a magazine he founded as well as edited, handing over the chair to G. A. Henty after the appearance of the eighteenth number in April 1880, just a few months before he died. Kingston translated into English for the first time several of Jules Verne's futuristic stories, including *The Mysterious Island*, 1875, and *Michael Strogoff*, 1877. He was a most prolific writer, churning out as many as five or six full-length books a year. His works occupy a full eight pages in the British Library Catalogue, but despite his output he never managed to achieve anything approaching the popular esteem and youthful reputation of his contemporary, Ballantyne. He is remembered today, if at all, solely for his first boys' book *Peter the Whaler*, yet the interest now being shown in the writers of minor Victorian fiction probably means that several collectors are attempting the all but impossible task of putting together a complete library of all his titles in the form of first editions. Unlike Ballantyne, Kingston and many other writers in the same field lack anything approaching an accurate bibliography, so that the sifting of evidence regarding points of issue, first-edition dates and binding styles needs careful personal research.

Meanwhile, in the USA, the novelist and humourist 'Mark Twain', pseudonym of Samuel Langhorne Clemens (1835–1910), was writing some of his most famous books, notably that enduring favourite *The Adventures of Tom Sawyer*, 1876, followed later by *The Adventures of Huckleberry Finn*, the first edition of which appeared under a London imprint in 1884, with a New York imprint, dated 1885, shortly afterwards. *Tom Sawyer* in its original state is a rare and expensive title to acquire, and much the same could be said for *Huckleberry Finn*, yet both are cornerstones of any wide-ranging collection of early children's books.

Clemens' later work was of very uneven quality, *Pudd'nhead Wilson*, 1894, and *Personal Recollections of Joan of Arc*, 1896, ranking with the best; but his two later books for young people, *Tom Sawyer Abroad*, 1894, and *Tom Sawyer, Detective*, 1895, are only feeble shadows of the earlier classic.

Thomas Mayne Reid (1818–83), an Irish emigrant to the USA, later obtained a commission in the New York Volunteers and was badly wounded during the Mexican War while attempting to storm Chapultepec. As Captain Mayne Reid, as he afterwards called himself, he put his experiences to good account when writing his first novel, *The Rifle Rangers: or, Adventures of an Officer in Southern Mexico*, 1850 (2 vols). The book sold well, and from that time onwards he devoted himself solely

Frontispiece to the first edition of The Adventures of Huckleberry Finn, *1884, by 'Mark Twain'*

to writing. *The Scalp-Hunters*, 1851 (3 vols), *English Family Robinson*, 1851, *The Desert Home*, 1852, *The Boy Hunters: or, Adventures in search of a White Buffalo*, 1852, *The Young Voyageurs: or, The Boy Hunters of the North*, 1854, *The White Chief: a legend of Northern Mexico*, 1855 (3 vols), and *The Forest Exiles*, 1855, were some of his earlier works. Novels and adventure stories continued to appear at least once or twice a year until his death in 1883, and even after that his widow brought out post-humous works she had found in manuscript form. Many, indeed *most*, of his two- and three-volume novels now command high prices, such as *The Wood-Rangers*, 1860 (3 vols), *The Child Wife*, 1868 (3 vols), and *The Flag of Distress,* 1876 (3 vols), some of which were remaindered as three volumes bound as one in publishers' cloth. *The Headless Horseman; a Strange Tale of Texas*, 1866 (2 vols), is perhaps Mayne Reid's most famous work, and one of the most difficult to find complete with all its twenty-four full-page plates. But his rarest work is a title quite out of the general run of his writing, and almost unobtainable in an acceptable state in its original limp orange-cloth binding blocked in gold on the front cover with the title and the author's name. *Croquet*, 1863, with a frontispiece of the layout of the game, contains a preface dated from

The Ranche, Gerrard's Cross, Buckinghamshire, his home at the time, and where he eventually ruined himself financially by foolhardy building speculations. Things got so hot for him that, in 1867, he left hurriedly for New York, and it was there that he founded and conducted *The Onward Magazine*. For those keen to attempt a collection of Mayne Reid's works, I will mention that *Croquet* was published as a slim, forty-six-page octavo, by Skeet, of Charing Cross, London, and not the author's usual publisher at that period, Routledge, Warne & Routledge; his earlier works were issued by David Bogue, Fleet Street.

To explain why certain titles in an author's canon of work should be so rare one has to consider several factors. One of these is undoubtedly the publication of a single work by a publishing house which did not normally handle the output of a well read and relatively successful writer. One can cite many instances of the application of this factor: R. M. Ballantyne's *Life in the Red Brigade* (1873), published by George Routledge & Sons at a time when Ballantyne's regular publisher was James Nisbet; G. A. Henty's *The Young Colonists*, 1885, again published by Routledge and not Henty's usual publisher Blackie & Son, thus making this particular title one of the rarest of his single-volume adventure stories for boys. The reason why titles issued by houses other than the author's usual publisher are often so rare is that an established outlet had been built up over the years, often with a regular readership buying each and every title as it appeared in the bookshops. These same bookshops had standing orders of so many copies of authors whose works sold well, placed, of course, with his or her usual publisher. Librarians, too, often used much the same system, so that any work issued outside normal channels suffered a handicap. Less copies were sold in the days when the book was new, and correspondingly less copies have survived to the present day.

But many other factors weigh in the balance: the popularity of any given title—some works are quite literally read to death; the type of binding the book was originally issued in; the physical make-up of the book (a thick and dumpy octavo in a comparatively fragile binding quickly falling to pieces after it had been dropped or mishandled a few times—the first edition of Mrs Isabella Beeton's *Book of Household Management*, 1861, being a notorious example); even the type of paper on which the work was printed; all these and several other attributes play their part in deciding how many copies will survive the years. And with books produced for children and young people these factors weigh even more heavily: the expectation of life of any book for juveniles is always much less than that of its adult counterparts.

Croquet, by Mayne Reid, and such titles as *Environs and Vicinity of Edinburgh*, 1859, or *Handbook to the New Goldfields . . . of the Fraser and*

198

Thompson River Gold Mines, 1858, both by Ballantyne, or *Rujub, the Juggler*, 1893, (3 vols), and *The March to Magdala*, 1868, both by Henty, have no proper place in this chapter, or in a work purporting to deal exclusively with children's books. One is, however, faced with the difficulty that almost every collector of juvenilia, once he or she has become really interested in a particular author, nearly always ends up attempting to make a complete collection of his or her works, usually, if they can afford it, in the form of first editions. Very few writers were content to stick rigidly to a straight and undeviating literary path— poets wrote prose; novelists wrote verse; essays in political philosophy came from the pens of detective-story writers; historical novelists have been known to write science fiction; and almost every writer of fairy stories, nursery rhymes, folk-tales and juvenile romances and adventure stories has made at least one attempt to break into the grown-up world of the circulating and subscription libraries and the shelves reserved for *belles-lettres*, travel and topography, or the novel. Especially the novel! However, space can be found here for no more than a passing mention of the more important works in the adult field by the better known of the writers of children's books: those collectors seeking a complete set of any particular author's works in the original state must consult the relevant bibliography if there is one, or have the satisfaction of under-taking personal research. I mention this as writers of boys' adventure stories were particularly prone to stray from the narrow path by which they derived the bulk of their literary income.

Friedrich Gerstäcker (1816–72) was a German writer and traveller in both America and Africa, whose subsequent narrative descriptions of his trials and tribulations in the wilds enjoyed considerable popularity, besides acting as source books for many English writers, notably W. H. G. Kingston. One of the most successful translations of his works was *The Little Whaler,* which appeared under a London imprint in 1857, with eight full-page illustrations by Harrison Weir.

As far as I am aware, the only woman novelist of the Victorian era who specialised in writing adventure stories for boys was Anne Bow-man (1801–90). She was the daughter of Thomas Bowman (1772–1862), whose wife, Anne Pulleine Bowman, had originally lived in New York, before the two of them settled in Richmond, Yorkshire, where Thomas carried on his job as clerk and book-keeper. Here, in the Marketplace, Anne and her brother Thomas (neither of them ever married) set up business as printers and booksellers, with the stationery side of the shop also selling 'genuine patent medicines and perfumery'. They printed and published *Bowman's Guide to Richmond*, 1836, and other works of local interest, living over the shop itself until 1850, when the two of them moved with their parents to a private house in the French-

199

The only known portrait of the only woman novelist of mid-Victorian days who specialised in writing adventure stories for boys. Miss Anne Bowman was born and spent her entire life in Richmond, Yorkshire

gate district of Richmond. It was here that Anne settled down to writing full-length novels and romances, soon turning her attention to compiling adventure stories for boys.

Her books were invariably published by George Routledge & Sons, London, under such titles as *Charade Dramas for the Drawing Room*, 1855, *The Castaways*, 1857, *The Kangaroo Hunters; or, Adventures in the Bush*, 1859, *The Boy Voyagers; or, Pirates of the East*, 1859, *Among the Tartar Tents*, 1861, *The Young Yachtsmen; or, The Wreck of the Gipsy*, 1865, *Tom and the Crocodiles,* 1867, *The Young Nile-Voyagers*, 1868, and *The Boy Forester*, 1868. *Travels of Rolando*, which first appeared in English as a four-volume work in 1804, having been translated by Lucy Aikin from the French of Louis François Jauffret (1770–1850), was issued as a two-volume set in 1853, having been corrected and revised by Cecil Hartley. Miss Bowman wrote the second volume, this being one of her first ventures into print.

She was an excellent cook, and her *The New Cookery Book . . . comprehending carefully tried Receipts for every branch of the Art* (c. 1860) passed through numerous editions to become one of the most popular recipe books of its day. Here, for the first time, the secrets of Yorkshire black puddings, Yorkshire goose pie, Yorkshire whigs, Yorkshire girdle cake and Yorkshire fritters were revealed, as well as what was to become almost the definitive method of turning out real, honest Yorkshire puddings. Her first book, after moving from the shop in Marketplace, was *Laura Temple*, 1851, a novel for girls. *Clarissa* and *The Rector's Daughter*, both 1864, were in similar vein, but it is as a writer of boys' adventure stories whose work can be favourably compared with her masculine rivals in the same field that she is remembered today.

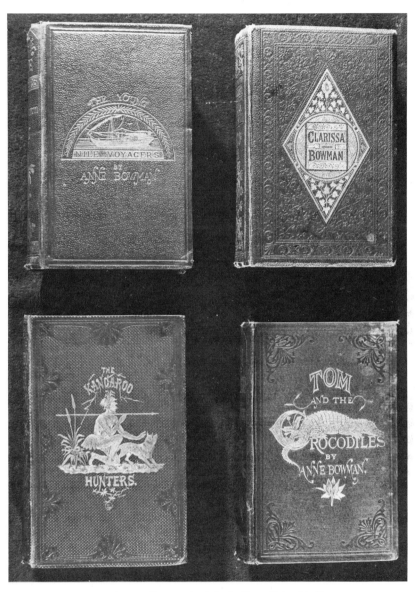

Four of Anne Bowman's titles in first-edition bindings

Across the Atlantic, Horatio Alger, Jr. (1834-99), a Unitarian minister, had been forced to quit his pulpit due to his alleged relationship with several of the better-looking choirboys of his church, and 1866 found him in New York City. There, rather like a fox amongst the chickens, he moved into the Newsboys' Lodging House to act as chaplain. He had already published *Frank's campaign; or, What boys can do on the farm*, 1864, and the novel on which he pinned high hopes, *Helen Ford*, 1866. But it was his interest in, and close observation of, the half-starved young inmates of the juvenile doss-house for the penniless street urchins of the city that ultimately brought him great rewards. His first best-seller was *Ragged Dick: or, Street Life in New York with the Boot-Blacks*, published, undated, in 1868, by Loring Inc., Boston, in a binding of green cloth. From that time onwards Alger produced several books about boys every year, the vast majority having as their theme from-rags-to-riches, or how a little capitalist street arab can rise to millionaire. *Rough and ready; or, Life among the New York newsboys* (1869), *Luck and Pluck; or, John Oakley's inheritance* (1869), *Mark the match boy*, 1869, *Ben, the luggage boy; or, among the wharves* (1870) and *Sink or Swim; or, Harry Walton's resolve* (1870) were the first of a rapid succession of titles, all of which carried the same message. He sentimentalised the life of the underprivileged young waifs of New York, telling his readers that to struggle against poverty and temptation inevitably leads a boy to wealth and fame. His most noted hero was the central figure in the 'Ragged Dick' series, while his 'Luck and Pluck' series and 'Tattered Tom' books were a close second in popularity. He widened his net to include such titles as *The young Julius; or, the street boy of the West* (1874), *The young miner; or, Tom Nelson in California* (1879) and *Bob Burton; or, the young ranchman of Missouri* (1888).

Alger sometimes varied his theme by producing idealised versions of the biographies of famous men, far more like hagiographies than factual accounts. *Abraham Lincoln; the backwoods boy* (1883) was typical of several similar titles, all of which concentrated on the boyhood years, the author seeming to lose interest in his subject as soon as his hero approached maturity. His favourite theme remained to the end of his life the penniless newpaper seller who typifies the American dream by achieving great riches. Thus we have *Do and Dare; or, a brave boy's fight for fortune* (1884), *Adrift in the City; or, Oliver Conrad's plucky fight* (1895), *Adrift in New York; or, Tom and Florence braving the world* (1900), the latter part of the title being changed to 'Dodger and Florence braving the world', *Adventures of a New York telegraph boy; or, 'Number 91'* (1900) being one of the few books he published under the pseudonym 'Arthur Lee Putnam'; and finally back to the Lodging House with the posthumous *Ben Bruce. Scenes in the life of a Bowery newsboy* (1901).

Alger is known to have written a total of 142 titles, and seventy different American publishing houses gave their imprint to his works. About fifty of these issued his books in pictorially printed paper wrappers in the style of the *Dime Novels* that E. S. Ellis, the writer of 'Westerns', so often appeared in. Joseph de Mello, writing in the American magazine *Western Collector*, has estimated that there are well over four thousand known collectors of the first and early editions of Horatio Alger's works, so it is hardly surprising that they now command high prices at auction and elsewhere.

There are at least the same number of collectors of the works of George Alfred Henty (1832–1902), a man who was ridiculed by his classmates at Westminster School for writing poetry. He said he was born at Trumpington, near Cambridge, the son of a wealthy mine-owner, and that, soon after the outbreak of the Crimean War, he enlisted in the Hospital Commissariat. Before long he was established as one of the earliest war-correspondents, covering events for *The Morning Advertiser* and, during the decade which followed, found himself in the thick of several minor European wars as correspondent for *The Standard*. Henty covered almost a dozen colonial compaigns of varying degrees of bloodiness. The crushing of native revolts, and the flag-planting and empire building that went with it, stood him in good stead when he at last established himself as a historical novelist.

The Fight with the Puma.—*Page 59.*

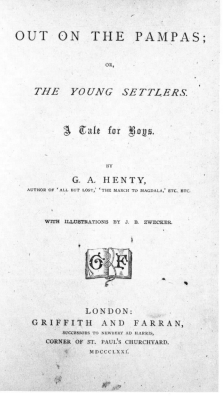

OUT ON THE PAMPAS;

OR,

THE YOUNG SETTLERS.

A Tale for Boys.

BY

G. A. HENTY,

AUTHOR OF 'ALL BUT LOST,' 'THE MARCH TO MAGDALA,' ETC. ETC.

WITH ILLUSTRATIONS BY J. B. ZWECKER.

LONDON:
GRIFFITH AND FARRAN,
SUCCESSORS TO NEWBERY AD HARRIS,
CORNER OF ST. PAUL'S CHURCHYARD.
MDCCCLXXI.

The first edition of Henty's first book for boys, dated 1871. 19 × 12.5cm

203

His first attempts as a writer of romantic three-volume novels were failures, and made not the slightest impact on the readership of the circulating and subscription libraries. *A Search for a Secret*, 1867, and *All but Lost*, 1869, fared as badly as his later attempts to interest adults with *Rujub the Juggler*, 1893, *Dorothy's Double*, 1894, and *The Queen's Cup*, 1897, all of which appeared as three-deckers in publisher's cloth bindings, blocked in gold. Autobiographical accounts of his experiences as a war correspondent were given in *The March to Magdala*, 1868, and *The March to Coomassie*, 1874, which still make quite interesting reading. But it is with his adventure stories for boys that Henty's reputation as a writer stands or falls. The first two he produced, *Out on the Pampas*, 1871, and *The Young Franc-Tireurs*, 1872, were only moderately successful, and it was not until he took over the editorship of *The Union Jack* from W. H. G. Kingston in May 1880 that his name became a household word with young teenagers throughout Britain. *The Union Jack*, a weekly magazine 'for British boys', cost an old-fashioned penny a week, or sixpence monthly (the monthly issue having tinted or colour printed illustrations). It ran during the period 1880–3, and four annual volumes, bound in pictorial cloth, were issued for those wishing to have the work in hardback form.

As soon as he took over as editor, Henty started running as a serial his story *The Young Franc-Tireurs*, a tale which had appeared in volume form some nine years earlier. The magazine was soon to contain stories by all the best-known writers in the field, including Kingston, Ballantyne, Harry Collingwood and Henty himself, six of whose full-length tales were serialised before their issue in volume form. From the time that *The Young Buglers*, 1880, made its appearance in the bookshops, until *With Kitchener in the Soudan*, 1903, issued after his death, hardly a year passed without at least two (sometimes as many as five!) of his adventure stories being published for an eager young readership. *The Cornet of Horse,* 1881, *Facing Death*, 1882, *With Clive in India*, 1884, *The Young Carthaginian*, 1887, *With Lee in Virginia*, 1890, *A Woman of the Commune*, 1895, *With Roberts to Pretoria*, 1902, are a few of titles from a list of a hundred or so stories for boys. A complete checklist would contain nearly two hundred and fifty references for those collectors (and I know several of them) intent on tracking down each and every reference and contribution to magazines and periodicals. A Henty Society has been formed, many of whose members collect only this one particular author, not only in first-edition form, but in subsequent editions almost to the present day. A narrow field, but, to them, a satisfying one, their shelves having space for no other writer.

Ballantyne and Henty wrote quite different sorts of books, yet they had much in common. Both portrayed a world in which there were no shades other than black and white; the good invariably being terribly good and the bad acting in a totally un-British manner. Neither for a moment doubted the innate benevolence of British imperialism, coupled, as sooner or later it always was, with the blessings which Anglo-Saxon-style Christianity would visit on the subject races of the Queen's vast dominions. The work of both of them suffered from their inability to tell a straightforward adventure story that was free from the moralising of their puritanical predecessors, and youth had to wait for Stevenson's *Treasure Island* for a tale of adventure without sermons and unashamedly cheerful in tone. As already stated, Ballantyne carefully researched his factual backgrounds before weaving his fictional plots against a realistic setting. A boy could smell the tar and taste the salt, duck at the twang of a bow-string, shovel coal on the footplate of a swaying express, maroon himself on a lighthouse, play the part of a detective in the underground cellers of the General Post Office, or choose any of a dozen different roles from a diversity of titles covering every aspect of adventurous, youthful endeavour.

Henty, unlike Ballantyne, chose a historical background for his themes of dash and daring and owed much to Scott. But both authors projected into lives that were often drab and humdrum a realistically

The Young Colonists, 1885, published by George Routledge, is one of the most difficult Henty first editions to find in acceptable condition; By Sheer Pluck, 1884, is also hard to find

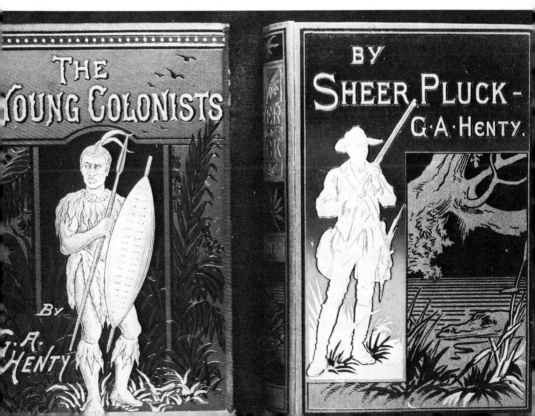

coloured adventure image, mirroring their readers in the figures of their young heroes. They opened for the sons of middle- and working-class families an exciting new vista of a world spiced with danger and romance, a world which lay waiting for the young men of Britain to grow up and explore. Both could be said to have supplied more self-education to willing and intelligent youth than years at school were able to instil; and, through the scrambling feet and inquisitive eyes of boyhood heroes whose exploits with Clive in India, with Buller in Natal, with Gascoyne, the sandal-wood trader, or Martin Rattler in the forests of Brazil, taught geography and history unobtrusively and persuasively. They revealed a world which generations of young men would never have known otherwise. Several of the best of Ballantyne's stories are still in print today. Henty has not worn so well; but his fellow member of the Savage Club, George Manville Fenn, a contemporary author of juvenile fiction, was correct in his assertion that a debt was owed to Henty for teaching 'more lasting history to boys than all the schoolmasters of his generation'.

The Manville Fenn just mentioned (1831–1909), was another of the prolific writers, publishing three or four titles a year, that the final decades of the nineteenth century produced so readily in the genre of juvenile fiction. He wrote well over a hundred full-length novels and adventure tales, including a number of three-volume fictional works aimed at the adult market. Many of his boys' books bear intriguing titles, such as *The Golden Magnet*, 1884, *Quicksilver; or, The Boy with no Skid to his Wheel*, 1889, *The Rajah of Dah*, 1891, *Walsh, the Wonder Worker*, 1903, and *Marcus: The Young Centurion* (1908), among a long list of works from the same pen. His first editions are not always easy to identify, for many appeared undated under the imprint of Ernest Nister, or that of the SPCK. He is closer to Ballantyne than to Henty, and several of his titles, such as *Menhardoc: A Story of the Cornish Nets and Mines*, 1885, owe a considerable debt to his rival. *Hollowdell Grange; or, Holiday Hours in a Country House*, 1866, is one of the most difficult of his works to find.

William Gordon Stables (1840–1910) had voyaged to the Arctic while still a medical student, later achieving the rank of naval surgeon. Soon after his retirement from the sea in 1871 he began to fabricate story after story for boys, averaging close on four books a year for the next thirty years. *Wild Life in the Land of the Giants*, 1888, *Our Home in the Silver West* (1896, pulished by the RTS, undated as usual), *Remember the Maine*, 1899, *Kidnapped by Cannibals*, 1900, and *'From Greenland's Icy Mountains.' a tale of the Polar Seas* (1892) are a few titles from a list of works that would nearly fill this page if stated in full. Less prolific was David Ker (1842–1914), a writer who specialised in adventure stories set in the wilder and unexplored regions of the earth: *On the Road to Kiva*, 1874, *The Boy Slave of Bokhara*, 1875, *Lost amongst the white Africans*, 1886, and *O'er Tartar Deserts*, 1898, are representative of his output. Closer to home were the works of James F. Cobb (1829–*c*.95), who was born in Margate, Kent, but spent much of his life in Torquay, Devon. It was his visits to Cornwall which prompted *A Tale of Two Brothers—A Cornish Story* (1866) followed by *Silent Jim. A Cornish Story*, published, undated, in 1871 (both these titles under the SPCK imprint), and his most famous title, *The Watchers on the Longships* (1878), a work which passed through at least twenty editions before the turn of the century. Others by him were *Martin the Skipper* (1883) and *Off to California* (1884), this last title being a free translation from the Dutch of Hendrik Conscience's *Het Goudland*, 1862.

To enumerate every boy's author of note during a period in which writers jostled to crowd a rapidly expanding market is beyond the scope of this work. Young people in their teens were not only literate, but were eager to devour with impartial vigour almost everything set before them—just for the sheer joy of being translated from the formalised surroundings and pomposity that characterised so much of late Victorian everyday life. Until the outbreak of World War I in 1914, when children who could read were leaving school in their hundreds of thousands, those publishers who had made a speciality of issuing books for older children were sometimes hard put to it to cope with the incessant demand.

A whole fresh crop of writers sprang up to occupy territory that was once the preserve of Ballantyne, Mayne Reid, Kingston, Manville Fenn and G. A. Henty. W. J. C. Lancaster (1851–1922), who wrote under the pseudonym of 'Harry Collingwood', produced his first book for boys, *The Secret of the Sands*, in 1879. Although the majority of his tales were about the sea (he was an ex-naval officer), he produced some of the earliest adventure stories featuring aerial warfare and bombing attacks. Typical titles are *The Log of the 'Flying Fish'*, 1887, *The Congo Rovers*, 1886, *With Airship and Submarine*, 1908, and *A Middy of the Slave Squadron*, 1911.

Army and navy officers on retired pay crowded the publishers' lists: two in the Harry Collingwood vein were Captain F. S. Brereton (1872–1957), with his *Under the Spangled Banner; a tale of the Spanish-American War*, 1903, *The Great Aeroplane*, 1911, and its sister volume, *The Great Airship*, 1914, as well as at least forty other titles; and also Captain Charles Gilson (1878–1943), who wrote *The Lost Column*, 1909, *The Lost Island*, 1911, *The Race round the World*, 1914, *Submarine U-93*, 1916, *In Arms for Russia*, 1918, and *In the Power of the Pygmies*, 1919.

One other notable author of the genre, picked from a host of deser-

LIEUTENANT MILDMAY RUNS FOR HIS LIFE.

"'HELLOA! WHAT'S THIS?'"

(Above left) *From* The Log of the Flying Fish, *1887, by Harry Collingwood, a science-fiction story which passed through several editions. The artist was Gordon Browne. 19 × 13cm.* (Above right) *Captain Brereton was one of the first to introduce scouting into his novels, with* Tom Stapleton —The Boy Scout, *1911*

From Under French's Command, *1915, by Captain F. S. Brereton. All illustrated World War I novels, adult or juvenile, are now rapidly appreciating in price. 19 × 12.5cm*

ving names, is 'Herbert Strang', the pseudonym of a partnership between George Herbert Ely (died 1958), and James L'Estrange (died 1947). Their first book, *Tom Burnaby*, 1904, was the forerunner of well over fifty full-length stories, covering the field of historical novels, science fiction, military and naval epics, adventures in the Wild West and the Frozen North, school stories, and every other aspect of teenage interest. *Boys of the Light Brigade*, 1905, *Kobo—A Story of the Russo-Japanese War*, 1905, and *The Adventures of Harry Rochester*, 1906, between them brought forth admiring criticism from reviewers, several of whom drew attention to the gap in the realm of juvenile fiction left by G. A. Henty's death in 1902, now filled by Herbert Strang. *The Cruise of the Gyro-Car*, 1911, *The Flying Boat*, 1912, *The Air Patrol*, 1913, a book containing the first coloured pictorial representation of a bombing attack by a conventional (as opposed to a science-fiction) aeroplane, and *With Haig on the Somme*, 1918, were amongst their wartime titles. They also achieved what is probably a unique distinction in the annals of adventure stories for boys, that of having several of their titles issued in special limited editions as large-paper copies. These were published simultaneously with the ordinary trade editions.

First English editions of two of Jack London's most popular titles, soon adopted by boys as their own. They are dated 1905 (left) and 1907. Cover size: 20 × 13cm

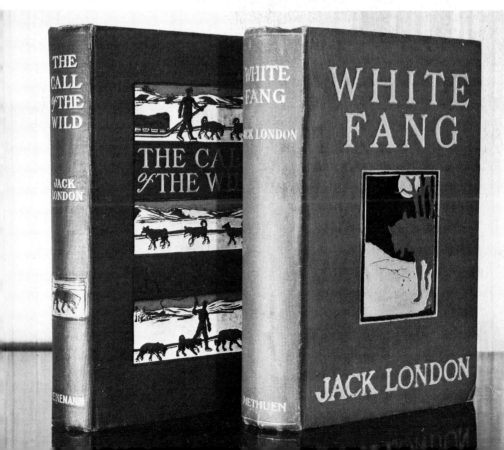

Few specialist book collections look more impressive on the shelves than fine copies of first or early editions of adventure story books issued during the period 1860–1910. One can allow a few years extra at either end of this time scale; but, with the outbreak of World War I, the glitter began to fade as the real gold blocking rapidly gave way to tinted aluminium substitutes which tarnished within a few months of purchase. Even today, the fiercely coloured pictorial spines ablaze with gold blocking of books issued during this earlier fifty-year period and their covers of gilded magnificence and startling eye-catching designs in their bright war-paint make a fine sight, and this after use and exposure for some three-quarters of a century. Publishing houses of the period vied with each other in their efforts to produce the most arresting styles, some of which can be seen illustrated in this present work. Many of the more progressive firms, such as Blackie & Son, who were the first to use the varnished lure of shiny olivine edges to attract prospective young purchasers, and T. Nelson & Sons, who embellished their children's books with high-quality chromo-lithographed plates as early as the 1850s, were pioneers in the evolution of publishers' binding styles. The volumes they issued found a shoal of imitators eager to take part of the market of the 5s (25p) adventure story book, most of which were issued in dust-jackets that usually bore quite different designs from those found on the books themselves.

First editions of two Edwardian science-fiction stories. Height: 19.5cm

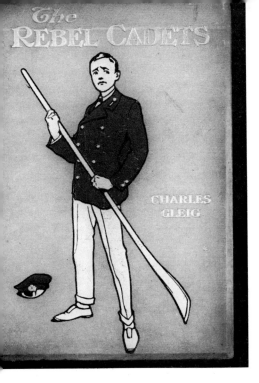

THE
REBEL CADETS

CHARLES
GLEIG

Smooth cloth over bevelled boards, blocked pictorially in gilt and colours: this being a typical Edwardian binding, dated 1908. 19.5 × 13cm

It is only in the last few decades that the attention of book collectors and literary historians has been switched to what was once almost unexplored territory. First editions of Ballantyne, Henty, Mayne Reid and W. H. G. Kingston could be obtained in almost pristine condition for a few old-fashioned shillings each, with the less well known writers such as Edward S. Ellis, Herbert Hayens, Andrew Hilliard, Bertram Mitford, Kirk Munroe, J. Macdonald Oxley, S. Walkey and Percy F. Westerman hardly warranting shelf room. Those short-sighted days are gone forever, and better-known titles such as *The Coral Island* or *Out of the Pampas* in their original cloth bindings are now making hundreds of pounds each.

But there is still ample scope for collectors of only moderate means to acquire a representative collection of first editions of the works of writers whose vocation it was to produce the kind of book for boys that has been the subject of this chapter. Sisters often read them as well, and many a young lady learned a deal of her history from Henty, and as much geography and exotic natural history from Ballantyne as she obtained from years at school. The importance these authors had in moulding young minds at their most impressionable age has been emphasised more than once. The young men who devoured the annual Christmas tales, with their too-good-to-be-true heroes and often threadbare plots, were the boys who, in their turn, became the soldiers and sailors, the explorers and trail-blazers, the merchant adventurers of the great British Empire on which the sun never set.

8

TOY-BOOKS, MUSICAL BOOKS, PEEP-SHOWS AND MOBILES

Lodged safely in nearly every large collection of early children's books are a few examples of toy-books, specially manufactured little volumes which booksellers displayed in their shop windows with the view of attracting the attention of young customers. John Newbery, far back in the eighteenth century, offered various little gifts to his young subscribers; toys such as fans, pincushions, spinning-tops, whips and dolls. These were sold on the persuading principle of 'book alone—sixpence—book and pincushion together eightpence'. The gifts could be purchased separately if the client so desired.

When Robert Sayer became owner of a bookshop opposite Fetter Lane in Fleet Street, London about 1765, he set about finding novel and attractive items to sell side by side with his stock of books and prints. Some of the leading theatres of the time featured pantomimes, then often termed 'harlequinades' after the part of the show in which the harlequin and clown play the principal roles. Sayer had been experimenting with little 'turn-up' books, composed of single pictorially printed sheets folding perpendicularly into four. Hinged to the head and foot of each fold was the picture, cut through horizontally across the centre to make two flaps that could be opened up or downwards. When raised, they disclosed another hidden picture below, each having a few lines of verse to tell the story—finishing with the words 'Turn Up' or 'Turn Down', so that another picture came into view. These 'harlequinades', as they soon came to be called (for Sayer had featured the adventures of Harlequin in many of his titles) were one of the first toys in book form. Children referred to them as 'turn-up books'. By the end of 1770 Sayer had published four and, no doubt to his delight, they soon became a craze with young people. By the turn of the century there were scores of titles to choose from. They sold at an old-fashioned sixpence plain ($2\frac{1}{2}$p) or one shilling coloured (5p). It was not long before his rivals in the trade, including Thomas Hughes, Ludgate Street, and George Martin, of 6 Great St Thomas Apostle, Bow Lane, Cheapside, were putting out their own versions. Martin seems to have published only coloured versions of his 'turn-up' books, and had brought the price down to sixpence. Typical of his titles were *The Woodman's Hut, Blue Beard, The Miller and his Men, Bertram* and *Philip and his Dog*, all of which were issued undated about 1810.

These fragile relics of a bygone age were the forerunners of what was termed 'The Juvenile Drama', a form of printed toy in sheet form that was almost certainly invented by John Green, a publisher of children's books at 121 Newgate Street, London. The earliest sheets of the juvenile drama can be dated to about 1810, and they have many affinities with the theatrical tinsel pictures of the same period. These tinsel pictures were a favourite form of recreation for both young and old on wet afternoons and winter evenings. They comprised a printed sheet depicting the backdrop of a well known play, plus an envelope or small box containing a variety of shaped and coloured tinsel and other materials, as well as the head and shoulders of the favourite actor or actress of the day. The figure of the actor was gradually built up on the pictorial background by lightly glueing into place the bits of dress material, tinsel, feathers, beads, silver paper, silk scraps and velvet that were shaped to make the body. The finished picture, with such wording as 'Mr Almar—as Steel Cap the Outlaw' or 'Mrs Egerton as Helen MacGregor' printed underneath, made an extremely colourful exhibit for the drawing-room wall when framed and glazed.

With young people, the juvenile drama became one of their most popular indoor pastimes. Sheets of scenery, flats, wings and drop scenes, both interior and exterior, became available for children to construct their own miniature theatres. The proscenium arch itself and the cardboard stage were on sale in bookshops ready for young purchasers to construct and paint. By 1830 there were over fifty publishers who advertised *Juvenile Drama Sheets*, printed and ready for the scissors, and for sale in book-form portfolios to protect them from wear.

From these theatrical sheets stemmed a new development that was promoted by the firm of S. & J. Fuller, at Rathbone Place, London, who intrigued children by calling their premises 'The Temple of Fancy'. Here they displayed an assortment of peep-shows, panoramas, children's books and toys, and their novel and newly invented paper doll figures which were accompanied by stories in verse. A series of loosely inserted cut-out figures took the place of the conventional pictures in these little stories. They were sold in the form of printed boards tied with silk ribbons and issued in a board case to match. When the lucky child opened her present she discovered several hand-coloured paper dolls representing the hero or heroine of the tale—but all minus their heads! However, this could soon be put to rights, for a set of heads, and an assortment of hats to put on them, accompanied the dolls, and they fitted into place on the bodies with paper tags. They were delightful toys to own, for a child could change the dress of the doll, and its face, by substituting new sets of clothes, heads and hats.

S. & J. Fuller catered only for the 'carriage trade'; their carefully hand-constructed wares were expensive purchases, selling in this instance at from five to eight shillings each (25p to 40p), putting them far beyond what the average parent would be prepared to pay. They were playthings for children of the comparatively wealthy, or bought for very special occasions.

The History of Little Fanny, 1810, was Fuller's most successful venture in this field, and no less than four separate editions were called for in the first year of issue. As might be expected, very few of these fragile paper dolls have survived complete with all their bits and pieces to the present day and it is usual to find that at least some of the separate heads and hats are missing. Complete examples fetch very high prices at auction and elsewhere.

Other much sought-after examples to enhance and lend wider interest to collections of early children's books are the *Toilet Books* of the 1820s and later. Stacey Grimaldi (1790–1863), son of the miniature-painter William Grimaldi (1751–1830), discovered a set of his father's drawings which the artist had made of a dressing-table and its contents. These depicted nine toilet articles, each hinged to a flap. As each flap was raised an apt moral observation was found beneath it. A bottle marked 'A Wash to smooth wrinkles' disclosed the word 'Contentment', and when the looking-glass above the table was lifted with the finger, the word 'Humility' came into view. William had painted the little pictures and designed the flaps for the amusement of the younger members of his own family, and it was his second son, Stacey, then aged thirty, solicitor and Fellow of the Society of Antiquaries, who conceived the idea of turning them into a book. He provided verses to go beneath each of the nine pictures and wrote a preface to the work which made use of paraphrased quotations from *Visions in Verse*, by Nathaniel Cotton. *The Toilet; a book for Young Ladies* was published at his own expense (dated 1821), and was put on sale at the shop of William Sams, a bookseller who had gained the distinction of supplying volumes ordered for the Duke of York's library. The entire stock of *The Toilet* sold out, and Grimaldi had the satisfaction of seeing a second and then a third edition of the same work, both also dated 1821, go the way of the first. He was so pleased with the success of his enterprise that he persuaded his father to design a similar book for boys. He called this *A Suit of Armour for Youth*, 1824, this time published by Ackermann, with the plates engraved by Armstrong after William

Grimaldi's designs. In this version the pieces of body armour could be raised to reveal the maxims and morals. The one marked 'The strongest Breastplate', when raised, disclosed George III addressing the House of Lords, with the word 'Virtue' printed beneath; while that labelled 'Admirable Plume', the name attached to the Prince of Wales' feathers on the top of the helmet, was 'Loyalty', a reference to the future King George IV. Both titles continued to be published well into the 1840s.

For many years, publishers specialising in children's books had tended to hive off their activities from the general bookselling trade. Now came further divisions of enterprise, some catering almost exclusively for younger children while others looked after the interests of teenagers or concentrated their attention on the provision of textbooks and primers for use in schools.

The firm of Thomas Dean, later Dean & Munday, of Threadneedle Street, London (after 1846, Dean & Son), were early suppliers of toy books and were also one of the first publishing houses to make extensive use of lithography, and later chromo-lithography, when supplying illustrations for the children's books they issued. From about 1858 onwards they all but established a monopoly in the trade for movable and flap books. They set up a special department of skilled craftsmen to prepare the complicated and exacting systems of stiff paper levers which made the pictures in their books dissolve into fresh and unexpected scenes at the pull of a tab. Many were extremely complex and could only have been marketed at prices the public could afford because the skilled hand labour each little volume needed was available so cheaply. As Iona and Peter Opie have pointed out, the first book to contain pictures in which the characters could be made to move was almost certainly *The Moveable Mother Hubbard*, published in 1857, as No 1 in a list of thirteen titles later advertised by Dean & Son. Typical of their ingenuity were *Dean's Moveable A.B.C.* (*c.*1860), with the subtitle 'Prince Arthur's Alphabet', each letter of the alphabet being accompanied by a hand-coloured illustration, the figures of which moved their heads or limbs when a tab at the bottom of the page was pulled; *Dean's New Moveable Book of the Boy's Own Royal Acting Punch and Judy* (*c.*1858); *Dean's New Book of Dissolving Pictures* (1862), in which one picture slides over another at the pull of a tab to give a transformation scene; and *Dean's New Dress Book* (1860), telling of Rose Merton's adventures with the gipsies. The six hand-coloured pictures of Rose showed her clothed in actual dress materials of brightly coloured fabric. In *Moveable Pictures of our Four Footed Friends* (*c.*1878) the animals in the six coloured pictures moved their heads and legs when the book's youthful owner operated the cardboard levers.

Books illustrated with silhouette and shadow pictures, or those con-

A GREEDY PIG.

One of the lithographic illustrations from Shadows (1856), by Charles H. Bennett, the first of many similar works from his pen that were issued both plain and coloured. 18.6 × 13.3cm

taining illusion scenes, were once very popular with young people. One of the best exponents of the shadow technique was Charles Henry Bennett (1829–67), whose numerous picture books, produced during a short life terminated by consumption of the lungs, were extremely popular, most passing through several editions. The first of these proved to be one of the most successful, and copies of the first edition are increasingly difficult to find. *Shadows* (1856) was published by D. Bogue, London, in a binding of pictorially printed paper-covered boards, a fragile protection for a much-read work. The twenty-four leaves were printed by lithography on one side only, with circular pictures depicting comical figures of the day, each casting shadows on the walls behind them (see illustration, page 216). The shadows show no human likeness to their owners, except in so far as they depict their characters and desires. *The Fables of Aesop and others translated into Human Nature* (1857) was a slim volume issued by Kent & Co., London, at six shillings plain (30p) or half a guinea coloured (52½p). It contained some of Bennett's finest and most vigorous work. The same year saw the publication of *Shadows—Second Series*, while *Proverbs and Pictures*, 1859, published by Chapman & Hall, was a picture book he designed throughout, the entire work, both text and pictures, being printed by lithography. In *Shadow and Substance*, 1860 he collaborated with Robert B. Brough, who supplied the text. The 'shadows' in this work are generally acknowledged to be the best illustrations Bennett achieved in any of his books.

The Stories that Little Breeches told, 1863, had the pictures etched on copperplates and then hand-coloured; being followed by *The Book of Blockheads*, 1863, *The Nine Lives of a Cat; a tale of wonder* (1863), *The Fairy Tales of Science* (1864), with text by J. C. Brough, *Fun and Earnest*, 1865, with text by Darcy W. Thompson, *Lightsome, and the Little Golden Lady*, 1867, and his satirical *London People: Sketched from Life*, 1868. Bennett's books are collected as much by those interested in the history of book illustrations as by those adding to their collection of early children's books. He also edited and illustrated *Old Nurse's Book of Rhymes, Jingles and Ditties*, 1858, with the coloured plates engraved by Edmund Evans, and supplied a remarkable set of portraits for an edition of Bunyan's *Pilgrim's Progress*, 1860, to which Charles Kingsley contributed the preface. Finally, one last title that must have been a special favourite with older children: *The Surprising, Unheard of and Never-to-be-surpassed Adventures of Young Munchausen*, 1865, which Bennett related and illustrated in twelve very tall stories. The book was published by Routledge, Warne & Routledge, and the hand-coloured plates were engraved by the Dalziel Brothers.

Probably the best of the silhouette books was *Karl Frölich's Frolicks*

217

A GREETING TO HIS READERS.

PAPER AND SCISSORS

(Above) *Silhouette illustrations from* Karl Frölich's Frolicks with Scissors and Pen, *1879. 11.5 × 8.2cm*

A self-portrait by Karl Frölich taken from his Frolicks with Scissors and Pen, *1879*

with Scissors and Pen, 1879, translated from the German by Clara de Chatelain (1807–76), and published by R. Worthington, New York. Frölich had made a living for many years in his native Germany as an expert silhouettist, quickly cutting the sitter's portrait in profile with scissors from coloured paper. Before the advent of photography this was a cheap and speedy way of having one's likeness taken. Military men and travellers, embarking for overseas, often had a head and shoulders silhouette taken, then enclosed it in a letter home, complete with a lock of their own hair, as a token of remembrance for their families. Frölich, whose first silhouette book appeared in Germany in 1852, was able to compete with the more popular camera by virtue of the excellence of his art, the title quoted above (see illustrations, page 218) allowing a glimpse of his consummate skill.

Illusion books were popular in the 1860s, and some of the best of the children's versions were produced by J. H. Brown of Brighton, Sussex. *Spectropia; or, Surprising Spectral Illusions*, 1864, contained sixteen full-page plates of ghostly phenomena hand-painted in vivid colours. If the printed directions were followed, images were seen on ceilings and walls in complementary colours. This was due, of course, to persistency of vision and the retention of the image on the retina of the eyes. It did not take children long to learn how to make their own 'ghosts', but *Spectropia* proved popular for many years and passed through several editions.

No firm ever equalled, much less surpassed, the technical brilliance of the animated picture books devised by Lothar Meggendorfer (1847–1925). Starting his working life as a magazine illustrator in Munich, he turned in the late 1880s to designing books with movable figures. Most of these were originally published by Braun & Schneider, Munich, and later by J. F. Schreiber, of Esslingen, near Stuttgart. They were marvels of ingenuity, a single tab at the side or bottom of the page making apes swing from trees, crocodiles swallow little boys, umbrellas open, boats roll and houses collapse. Usually several movements took place at the same time: a horse rearing would throw its rider while its companion would successfully jump a fence.

The 'works' which operated the various figures consisted of a series of interconnecting cardboard levers sandwiched between the coloured illustration on the front of the oblong leaf and the dummy pasted behind it. The animated limbs and heads were cut-out models on the front of the picture, and moving the tab set the whole scene in motion. Titles included *Reiseabenteuer des Malers Daumenland und seines Dieners Damian* (1889), with the little artist Daumenland displaying a startling likeness to the classical figure of Little Lord Fauntleroy created by the artist Reginald Birch. The English version was published in London by

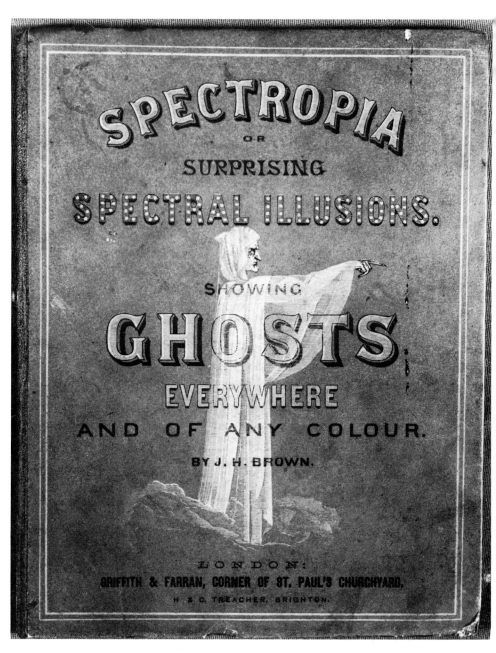

Spectropia, *1864, was an illusion book, discussed in the text. 25 × 19.5cm*

(Opposite) *The eight dramatically coloured scenes from* Daumenland und seines Dieners Damian, (1889) *by Lothar Meggendorfer, change position when the protruding tabs are moved. 33 × 25.5cm*

H. Grevel & Co., under the title *Travels of Little Lord Tom Thumb and his man Damian* (1892), and versions appeared in French and several other languages, as did most of his titles. *Schau mich an!* (1891) was a series of comic indoor scenes; there were also *Lach mit Mir!* (1889), *Lustige Ziehbilder* (1899) and *Lustige Automatentheater* (1890). Meggendorfer's *pièce de résistance* was his magnificent *Internationaler Zirkus* (1889), containing more than four hundred and fifty separate pieces in the form of performers and animals, and issued complete with a circus-ring tableau beneath which were the tabs to bring the circus to life. It sold at 7 Marks 50 pfennig, as against the usual 5 Marks for the more conventional animated books. H. Grevel & Co. acted as Meggendorfer's London agents, and a large number of his titles were translated and made their appearance in Britain.

As Maurice Sendak said in his appreciation of the master animator, given as a foreword to *The Publishing Archive of Lothar Meggendorfer*, 1975, (Justin G. Schiller, New York):

Meggendorfer enlarged the child's visual pleasure in a way that probably will never be duplicated. His work stands alone. What came after, the pretty pop-ups of my own childhood, were skimpy in comparison and, more to the point, they were directed to a profitable, publishing-concocted child audience. Meggendorfer never condescended to children. He granted them, as he granted himself, a lively intellect and cultivated visual taste. He knew, as did all the great writers and illustrators, that children observed life more shrewdly than adults; that they enjoyed with a kind of sensual gusto the delights of color, shape and movement. What he had to offer was the very best on the highest level. It is no miracle that children delighted in his work, as did the adults who had the grace to remain children.

Today, very high prices are paid whenever a Meggendorfer book comes on the market, for few have survived intact. Children invariably tugged a little too hard, or tried to adjust a figure which obstinately stuck and refused to perform its antics, with catastrophic results for the master's hidden machinery. Provided all the bits and pieces are still in place repairs can be carried out, but finding these intriguing relics of the showman is another matter. The expectation of life for an animated book must be considerably lower than its literary counterpart and, once utterly broken down, its probable fate was consignment to the dustbin at the next spring-clean.

Another German responsible for a host of children's books imported into Britain and the USA was Ernest Nister. His firm in

Nuremberg also specialised in movable and toy books, and he went to great lengths, through his London-based subsidiary, to see that the English texts were accurate. All the books he issued started life in Germany, the English text not being added to the printed pictures until the British writers he employed had completed their work. His 'dissolving picture-books' and 'stand-up' books were very popular, as were his more conventional but beautifully produced picture books for children, many of them being cut into the shape of dolls or houses, etc, as shown in the illustration on page 224.

Most of Nister's transformation scenes were contrived by means of sliding slats, so that one picture was replaced by another as the colour-printed slats moved into place at the pull of a tab. *Pleasant Pastime Pictures* (*c*.1895) and *More Pleasant Surprises*, of about the same date, were typical of the slim, folio-sized books that told a story in verse, while the extremely well executed oil-colour-printed illustrations dissolved from the heat of a summer's day to a snow-covered Christmas scene in the twinkling of an eye. Sometimes the slats were arranged to operate by a circular movement, as in *Magic Moments* (*c*.1892) or in *Twinkling Pictures* of the same year, with verses by L. L. Weedon.

One of Nister's finest three-dimensional 'stand-up' books was *Peeps into Fairyland* (*c*.1895), a panorama picture book of fairy stories, including an English text devised by F. E. Weatherly (1849–1929), a

A page from More Pleasant Surprises (c.*1896*) *by F. E. Weatherly, a movable book produced by Ernest Nister, Nuremberg, Germany. When a tab at the bottom is pulled the first picture disappears and the other takes its place. Pictorial area: 17.3 ×* *12.3cm*

I don't think black suits him, do you?
And soon a great change you will view.

Books with shaped covers are still with us today; but the earlier models, such as these two examples from the 1890s, are difficult to find. Size of the little girl: 25.5cm high

writer and versifier extensively employed by Nister. This oblong folio operated its three-dimensional grottos and fairy-tale scenes as the leaves were opened and the book laid flat. Linen slips pulled the integrated pictures upright, with as many as four different levels of scenery to give the scene real depth. *The Land of Long Ago* was a similar production of about the same date. All these early examples were carefully made, artistically designed, and printed in harmonious selections of colours that blended with the colour-printed backgrounds. Those which have survived intact are no doubt treasured by their lucky owners, for they call to mind the more leisurely age in which they were painstakingly designed and produced by the craftsmen of Nuremberg.

Later versions with the same basic ideas, produced in Britain and the USA, were called 'pop-up' books. The pictures automatically erected themselves into fairy castles or woodland scenes when the volume was opened at any particular section. Those of the 1920s and 1930s were mass produced to sell cheaply in the bookshops, the pop-up models being printed in the most garish of contrasting colours. Nevertheless, they supplied a need and were no doubt treasured in equal degree by the children who received them as birthday or Christmas presents. Now, in the 1980s, artists and craftsmen of the talent of Jan Pienkowski, Jane Walmlsey, Tor Lokvig and James Roger Diaz, amongst others, are once again producing collector's pieces of the future with their complex and intricately designed pop-up books, such as *Haunted House*, 1979, and *Robot*, 1981, the first of which won the Kate Greenaway Medal awarded by the Library Association.

Pride of place in my own collection of toy-books has been given to *The Speaking Picture Book* (*c*.1875), a musical toy in the form of a book that has never failed to fascinate young visitors (to say nothing of my own six children!) whenever they have been allowed near enough to it to see and hear the action. It consists of a folio-sized box (32 × 24cm) that outwardly looks very much like a large thick children's book. Where the edges of the leaves would normally be is a carved fascia of gold-coloured wood made to resemble the gilt edges of the leaves of a book. On the fore-edge there is a series of nine little ivory tassels attached to strings that disappear into the interior of the volume. The front cover is blocked pictorially in colours, showing a little girl reading a book, surrounded by various birds of the field and hedgerow and watched attentively by her dog and cat. The spine has the title blocked in gold, and in the bookcase would be indistinguishable from a real folio-sized volume. When the 'book' is opened the first eight leaves are much like those of any other children's picture book, except that they are printed on very stiff paper, with the text in verse form on one side and each picture on the other. In the outer margin is a printed arrow which points to each tassel as the leaves are turned. The title-page announces that this is *The Speaking Picture Book*, and that it will reproduce 'the voices of the cock, the donkey, the lamb, the birds, the cow, the cuckoo, the goat, and the baby', if the reader will gently pull out and release the appropriate tassel opposite each picture in the book. The sounds reproduced are extremely life-like, almost startlingly so, each picture having a different 'voice' that issues from between the carved wooden top and bottom edges of the 'leaves' of the book. The cords operate a system of miniature bellows concealed in the interior of the book. The final two tassels cause the two children in the accompanying picture to call out 'Mama!' 'Papa!' as they wait at the lakeside for their parents to reach the shore. *The Speaking Picture Book* was yet another product of that famous German toy centre, Nuremberg. The original edition, issued about 1870, had a German text, but it proved so popular at home that it was soon being exported to most European countries and the USA in the appropriate languages. H. Grevel & Co. were the London agents, and in New York F.A.O. Schwarz. A London example, very similar in format, was titled *The Speaking Toybook*, 1893, while its rival was going through edition after edition, the fifteenth appearing in 1898, with the subtitle changed to read: 'With Pictures, Rhyme, & Sound for Little People'.

Finally, mention must be made of those delightful book-like toys which can be classed under the embracing title of peep-shows. Folded flat and usually boxed, they resembled books in shape, but when the front cover is lifted the rest of the body concertinas out into a serrated tube that instantly gives the impression of great depth when one's eye

Front cover of a peepshow of 1851, the back of which extends like a concertina to form a tube. The child then looks at the view by placing his or her eye at the hole in the centre

is applied to the round hole cut in the cardboard pictorial title. The earliest *dioramas d'optiques* seem to date from the second quarter of the eighteenth century, with Augsburg, in Bavaria, producing some of the best of the period. *An Army Marching in Battle Array*, with six hand-coloured sections extending into a long tube about 100cm long, showing the troops and cavalry with standards erect and guns at the ready, was turned out by the same craftsmen who produced *The Boar Hunt, A Hare-Chase Scene, Park Scene, Room in Grand Café Paris, Three Views of Sieges and Pillage* and many others, all luridly illustrated in three-dimensional perspective.

Peep-shows seemed to have fallen into neglect for some considerable time after that, few being produced elsewhere, but with the cutting of the first tunnel under the River Thames in London enterprising publishers were quick to offer views that purported to show what it would look like when finally completed. *A View of the Tunnel under the Thames*, 1827, was perhaps the most popular title ever produced, rendering itself admirably to a peep-show effect, and it took the opening of the Great Exhibition in 1851 to produce rivals which sold in anything like the same numbers (see illustration, page 226). *Lane's Telescopic View of the Ceremony of Her Majesty Opening the Great Exhibition*, 1851, was a favourite, extending when fully opened to nearly 60cm, although many young ladies must have sighed for the chance to enjoy the elegant delights so vividly depicted in the dancing figures seen when their eyes were gazing at the extended panorama entitled *Interior of a Ball-Room*. It is perhaps unnecessary to add that the casualty rate amongst these ephemeral little peep-shows was probably even higher than movable books, and the few that have survived now command high prices at auction and elsewhere.

9

PERIODICALS, ANNUALS AND PENNY DREADFULS

The earliest magazines for young people took the form of weekly or monthly paper-wrapped pamphlets and tracts of an extremely pious and usually evangelical nature. At the end of each year of issue there was usually a special Christmas number with which was given a pictorial title-page showing the year of issue's date and the volume number. This, and the collected parts, would then be bound up by the owner into a volume, but with the wrappers which protected the individual parts removed.

One of the earliest of these periodicals for youth was *The Juvenile Magazine*, edited by Lucy Peacock. It ran for only twelve months, the last monthly number being dated December 1788. In the fashion of the times it was illustrated with folding maps, engraved sheets of music and numerous copperplate illustrations, and the contributors included several well known writers of children's stories, including Dorothy and Mary Kilner. *The Youth's Magazine; or, Evangelical Miscellany*, 1816, which started what it described as its 'New Series' at the beginning of that year, was issued monthly as a thirty-six page periodical for children. In addition to a large woodcut illustration on the front page, each issue had a full-page engraving that took the form of a sheet of music, a map (usually folding) or a picture to illustrate an incident in the accompanying text. Mingled with the usual religious exhortations and moral platitudes were stories, tales of travel and adventure in foreign lands, potted biographies, poetry, songs and hymns, and numerous instructional articles with intriguing titles, such as 'The Surprising Vigour of the Whale', 'Death at a Card Table', 'The Snares of Youth' and 'The Depravity of the Morlachians'. The quality of many of the articles was higher than one would expect to find in a children's magazine of that period, and a number of well known writers of the day can be identified by their initials or pseudonyms. Jane Taylor of Ongar contributed some of her most successful juvenile tales during the period from February 1816 to the end of 1822, signing them with her pseudonym 'Q.Q.' These were later collected by her brother Isaac and published in two volumes as *The Contributions of Q.Q. to a periodical work*, 1826. *The Forget Me Not*, 1823, was the first Christmas annual for adults, quickly followed by dozens of rival publications stimulated by its amazing success. However, the first annual that made any pretensions of having young people's welfare and entertainment at least partly in mind followed within months. Issued in time to catch the Christmas trade in October 1824 (although dated forward to the following year, as was commonly the custom) *Blossoms at Christmas and First Flowers of the New Year*, 1825, was published by J. Poole, Newgate Street, as a joint venture with Simkin & Marshall, Stationers Court, London. The proprietors stated in their preface to the work that they hoped it would rank with the 'tokens of affections to young persons, [which] have for some years been greeted with the strongest manifestations of public favour on the Continent'. The engraved title-page and the presentation leaf were both hand-coloured, and there were full-page copperplate engravings showing portraits of the famous, and views of cities and towns. The articles and tales made few concessions to the taste of young people, however, but there were 'humorous anecdotes', fables and instructional tit-bits on such subjects as 'The origin of duelling' which teenage children may have read with some measure of interest. The enterprise could not have been a commercial success, for the second annual volume, dated 1826, was the last to appear.

In the meantime, *The Children's Friend* had been growing from strength to strength. It had started as a penny monthly magazine in January 1824, and was published as an annual at the end of each year, complete with a specially printed title-page and woodcut frontispiece, as well as the usual engravings which accompanied the text. This periodical continued without interruption until 1860, a new and enlarged series commencing in 1861. Until 1850, it was edited by Revd William Carus Wilson, Rector of Whittington, who had the magazine printed at Kirkby Lonsdale, Westmorland. It was here, at Cowan Bridge, that he founded the ill-omened Clergy Daughters' School which the unfortunate Brontë sisters were forced to attend in 1824. Charlotte Brontë had some measure of revenge by modelling Mr Brocklehurst in *Jane Eyre* on her late schoolmaster.

The same year that Wilson's magazine appeared saw the birth of *The Child's Companion; or, Sunday Scholar's reward*. It was published monthly by the RTS from 1824 onwards, an annual volume being issued at the end of each year. In January 1832 they published a 'New Series' in a similar format; and a third series, this time enlarged, came out from 1838 to 1844. It turned out to be one of the longest-running children's periodicals, continuing as *The Child's Companion and Juvenile Instructor*, from 1846 to 1928, and then under a number of modern-sounding

No. 186.
June 1876.

THE CHILDREN'S FRIEND.

Price One Penny.

SALLY SUNBEAM.

An illustration by Robert Barnes for the front of the monthly penny magazine The Children's Friend, 1876, published by S. W. Partridge & Co, London. It commenced publication in 1860 and was issued as an annual every year

230

titles until it finally ceased publication in 1932. It had the distinction of being the first magazine for children to contain examples of the colour printing of George Baxter (1804–67), even though it was issued at the price of one old-fashioned penny a month. The first of these coloured plates was given with the December issue of 1846, and was used as a frontispiece in the annual volume of that year. Altogether a total of six of Baxter's pictures were used, and with the second, a view of 'Her Majesty's Marine Residence, Isle of Wight', which was a frontis-piece to the 1847 volume, the inventor of the process was at pains to explain to his young readers how the plate was produced:

At first sight it will be seen that it is a picture not like those commonly found in books. It is a new invention, and it is printed, not with ink, but with oil colours, the same as used in painting. It is done with ten different engravings, on steel plates, each of which prints a separate colour, and altogether they form the picture as it now appears.

From 1852 onwards the Religious Tract Society awarded the contract to J. M. Kronheim, a licensee of the process, probably on the grounds that a more competitive price was quoted. The first children's *book*, as opposed to a magazine, to contain colour-printed illustrations is discussed later in this chapter.

Another monthly publication for young people was *The Infant Scholar's Magazine*, which commenced in January 1827, published by John Stephens, London. With the third annual volume, dated 1829, the title was changed to read *The Child's Repository, and Infant Scholar's Magazine*. It lasted only as long as the earlier *National School Magazine*, which was issued fortnightly by C. & J. Rivington, London, from April 1824 until December 1825. Yet another, in much the same style, was *The Nursery Infants' School Magazine*, a monthly edited by Mrs L. L. B. Cameron under the supervision of the publishers, Houlston & Son, Wellington, Shropshire. It ran from 1829 to 1832, after which it was known as *The Nursery Magazine*.

The Boy's Own Book, 1827–8 (2 vols), published by Vizetelly, Branston & Co., sported a single colour frontispiece printed in a bright shade of blue. The subtitle announced to its readers that it was 'A Complete Encyclopaedia of all the diversions, Athletic, Scientific, and Recreative, of Boyhood and Youth'.

The Christmas Box; an Annual Present for Children was closely modelled on adult annuals and was a much more tasteful and sumptuous prod-uction than other juvenile works in the same category. Nevertheless, it survived for only two issues, those of 1828 and 1829, despite the

This copperplate engraving was one of eight plates to illustrate The Juvenile Album, *first published by Ackermann & Co, 1841. The text was by Sarah Bowdich Lee, but the main interest lies in Thomas Woolnoth's fine engravings. 24 × 20cm*

talents of its editor, Thomas Crofton Croker, whose collections of fairy- and folk-tales were well known. *The Juvenile Keepsake*, edited by Thomas Roscoe, fared no better, for the volumes dated 1829 and 1830, issued in a binding of pictorially printed paper-covered boards, were all that appeared. *The New Year's Gift, and Juvenile Souvenir*, 1829, was one of the first children's annuals to have a woman with full editorial powers, Mrs Alaric Watts, who was married to the editor of the long-running *The Literary Souvenir*, 1825–36, first of the annuals to be available in a large-paper edition, with the plates printed on India paper selling side by side with the ordinary trade edition. *The New Year's Gift* completed a total of eight annual volumes during the years 1829–36, the earlier numbers being issued in a binding of glazed paper-covered boards with green morocco spines on which the title and the year of publication were blocked in gold. Its distinguished list of contributors in both prose and verse included Mrs Hofland, Mary and William Howitt, Mrs Amelia Opie, Agnes Strickland and Mrs Felicia Hemans, while the tissue-guarded engravings used to illustrate the work were of a quality that compared very favourably with those found in the expensive adult annuals. It deserved its success, as did *The*

Juvenile Forget Me Not, edited by the redoubtable Mrs S. C. Hall, which was issued in an almost exactly similar format (although an inch or so taller). It ran from 1829 to 1837.

One other early annual which deserves a mention was *Marshall's Christmas Box*, published by William Marshall, London, whose pocketbooks and almanacs always found a ready sale. The first of the two volumes he issued gained the distinction of being the earliest fully cloth-bound book for children. Marshall issued it in a binding of red watered silk, with the title and the year of publication, 1831, blocked in gold on the spine. However, the fabric proved much too tender for youthful hands and the second, final volume, dated 1832, was published in a binding of full morocco, blocked in gold and blind.

The publishers of annuals were nothing if not innovators, both as regards the binding styles they employed and the contents of their yearly volumes. In 1835, William Darton & Son published *The New Year's Token; or, Christmas Present*, a pretty little annual much in the general run of others in the field. It was in the next issue, published in

A selection of children's annuals in their original publishers' bindings, 1829–50. Size of left-hand volume on shelf: 18cm

October 1835, but dated forward to 1836, that we find the first colour-printed illustration ever to appear in a children's book. The frontispiece shows a delicately tinted view of Virginia Water, Surrey, with George IV's fishing temple in the background, while the ornamental title-page has a colour-printed vignette of a little boy examining a bird's nest. Both these illustrations were printed in oil colours from wood blocks by George Baxter after designs by the artist John Brown. The view of Virginia Water was later used in other books, but the picture of the little boy is now one of the rarest of Baxter's famous prints. *The New Year's Token* ran for only two years, so that the second volume is the target for several classes of collectors.

One other rarity that a few lucky children must have received for Christmas was the *Geographical Annual or Family Cabinet Atlas*, 1832, a choice and highly finished work which was designed and engraved throughout by Thomas Starling. All the maps on the ninety-six engraved plates were coloured by hand. In their preface to the work the

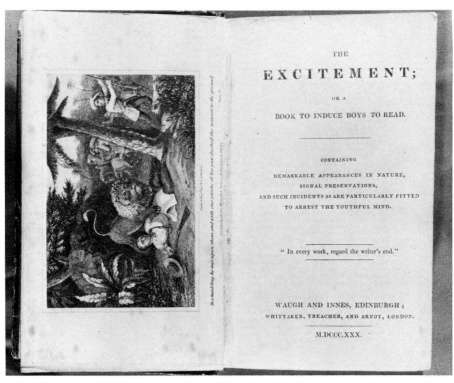

The first issue of the first annual specially produced for the amusement of young people, a title which appeared each winter for over ten years. 14.5 × 9cm

publishers expressed the hope that 'on account of its enduring interest, the present publication may justly lay claim to the title of a Perennial rather than an Annual & be valued as a lasting Gift of Friendship rather than a Pastime offering.' The following year they published the *Biblical Annual or Scripture Cabinet Atlas*, 1833, again engraved throughout by Thomas Starling, and with all the maps hand-coloured. Both volumes were issued in bindings of full morocco, blocked in blind with the titles and year of publication in gold.

The first children's annual in the modern sense was *The Excitement*, 1830, published by Waugh & Innes, Edinburgh, in pictorial paper-covered boards with a morocco spine blocked in gold. It was first published in December 1829, dated forward to 1830, and was edited by Adam Keys, an Edinburgh schoolmaster. Whereas the children's annuals which had so far been published were really scaled-down models of the volumes intended for adults, often using the same engravings and interspersed with prose and verse that was almost indistinguishable both in style and content from that used in their more expensive counterparts, *The Excitement* set out with the avowed intention of printing adventure stories and romances solely for the interest and amusement of young people. According to the editor, there was the allied hope that, by so doing, children would be induced to read more than they did and thus take more interest in literature as a whole. Keys was a forward-thinking man, and he stated plainly in his preface to the first volume of the series that by printing adventure stories founded on fact the books would be read

> by boys particularly, with the greatest attention; and also narratives of such striking incidents as are fitted to rouse the most slothful mind —incidents in which the reader cannot fail to imagine himself identified, as it were, with the parties concerned, and to enter with the deepest interest into all their various feelings.

This reference to reader identification with the characters and scenes depicted in the work is an interesting comment at so early a period. As Richard Gilbertson pointed out, the books were 'an early reaction against the Holy-Joe school, the stories being of adventure with no moral aptitude tests called for except courage and endurance'.

But Keys was later to run into serious opposition from some of the more evangelical elders of the Scottish Kirk. He had allowed almost no sermonising, and the titles of the stories were as zestful as their contents, with no concessions being made to the religious dogmas and bigotries of the day: 'A Lion Hunt in Africa'; 'Boiling Springs of Iceland'; 'Whale Ship destroyed by a Whale'; 'Sufferings endured in the Black-Hole of Calcutta'; 'An account of a Boa-Constrictor swallowing a Goat'; 'The Reign of Terror, and Fall of Robespierre'; 'The Lion Fight'; and 'The Inquisition at Goa', etc, being enough to stimulate the imagination of any boy lucky enough to possess a copy.

Complaints from the more puritanically minded of his critics caused Keys to insert a paragraph in the preface of the volume for 1837, and several of those which followed, to the effect that it had 'been hinted that it might be well to mingle more of pious sentiment with' the details presented in the *Excitement*. 'But', he went on, 'it does not appear to us essential that *every* work put into the hands of the young should necessarily contain something of a religious nature.' The opposition eventually proved too strong, however. Waugh & Innes were taken over as a business, for unspecified reasons, by John Johnstone, of Hunters Square, Edinburgh, and Adam Keys was dismissed from the editorship of *The Excitement* in 1838. The new editor was Revd Robert Jamieson, a dour Scot and minister of Westruther. He considered it his duty to state in the preface of the first volume he issued that, in future, the annual's leading design would be 'to combine pleasure with instruction; and to give the mind a relish for truth, rather than to excite and vitiate its taste by embellishments of fiction'.

Adam Keys was determined to carry on, and, with William Innes as publisher, started *The New Excitement*, 1838, on much the same lines as before. Both annuals ran side by side for a few years, the former turning more and more to the tribulations of missionaries amongst the unconverted heathens. Not so Adam Keys! He kept doggedly along his secular path, serving his young readers such tit-bits as 'Rat Eating', 'The Dead restored to Life', 'Attempt to steal the Regalia from the Tower', 'A Combat between two Beetles', 'Funeral of a Dog' and so on, all of which, he told his readers, were strictly founded on truth.

The Comic Annual, 1830, edited by Thomas Hood (1799–1845), although aimed at the adult market, was very popular with the young. It was full of excruciating puns, comical stories in which one or other of the characters came to summary grief, and contained the sort of easy-to-understand humorous illustrations beloved by children of all ages. Hood wrote most of it himself, and the series continued until the ninth volume appeared dated 1839, all bound in pictorially printed paper-covered boards with red morocco spines. There was no issue for 1840 or 1841, but the work briefly re-appeared with the issue for 1842, this time put out in a full-cloth binding blocked pictorially in gold. His son, Thomas Hood the younger (1835–74), known as Tom Hood, was later the editor of the comic periodical *Fun*, 1865, and in 1867 began *Tom Hood's Comic Annual*, which was popular with older children and continued for some years after his death.

To complete the period leading up to the appearance of the first *Peter Parley Annual* discussed earlier, mention must be made of *Fisher's Juvenile Scrap-Book*, 1836, a successful enterprise which survived until 1850 with a total of fifteen yearly volumes under a succession of editors. *My Own Annual* deserved a longer run than its two years of 1847–8. It was edited by 'Mark Merriwell', whoever he might have been, and was larger in size than most of its predecessors, had hand-coloured title-pages and frontispieces, and was issued in a full-cloth binding blocked pictorially in gold.

By the 1860s there was a wide choice of juvenile annuals. They were now issued as an integral part of children's magazines. Usually a full set of the weekly or monthly parts was issued by the publishers in December as an annual volume, in cloth binding, bright with gold blocking, but there were so many that only the most important can be mentioned.

The Halfpenny Picture Magazine for Little Children commenced publication in January 1854, and almost immediately changed its name to *The Pictorial Magazine for Little Children*, 1855–8, then to *The Little Child's Picture Magazine in Easy Words*, 1859–62, and finally to *The Picture Magazine*, 1863–5, all under the editorship of J. F. Winks. More important than the foregoing in the quality of its contributors, and for setting a standard that dozens of competitors later imitated, was one of the first of the boys' magazines issued in the size we are familiar with today. *The Boy's Own Magazine* was published monthly from 1855 to 1874, edited and published by S. O. Beeton, who boasted that, in 1863, its circulation had reached 40,000 copies a month. It was then enlarged and its price raised to sixpence ($2\frac{1}{2}$p). *The Boy's Penny Magazine* was started so that poorer children might not be deprived of periodical reading matter. Contributors to the *Boy's Own* included Austin Dobson, Thomas Hood, Mayne Reid, Mrs Harriet Beecher Stowe and W. H. G. Kingston, while Gustave Doré, Harrison Weir, J. A. Pasquier and J. B. Zwecker were amongst the illustrators. At midsummer and at Christmas, cloth-bound volumes were issued under titles whose names varied during the ensuing years. *The Boy's Own Volume* and *Beeton's Annual* had the longest run.

A rival publication was *The Boy's Journal*, published by Henry Vickers and edited by C. P. Brown, which was published monthly from 1863 to 1871 before being absorbed into *The Youth's Play-Hour*. *Every Boy's Magazine*, 1862–4, was incorporated into *Routledge's Magazine for Boys* in January 1865, and issued as *Routledge's Every Boy's Annual* complete with a series of colour-printed plates by Leighton Brothers. The name changed to *The Young Gentleman's Magazine*, 1869–73, and to *Every Boy's Magazine*, 1874–89, when it was finally absorbed into *The Boy's Own Paper*. R. M. Ballantyne was a regular contributor at one stage.

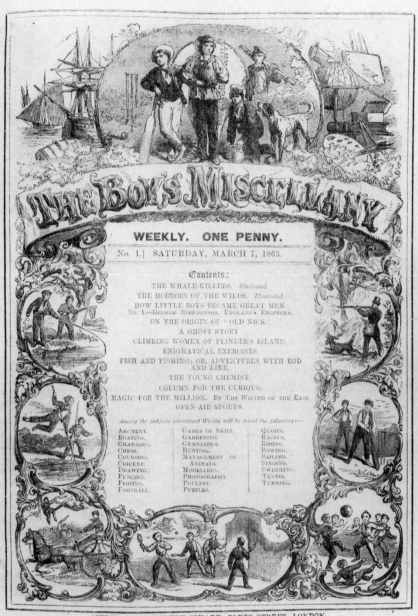

One of the most difficult of the penny magazines to find in original condition, the first number being illustrated here. 'Sixteen-String Jack' made his first appearance in September 1863

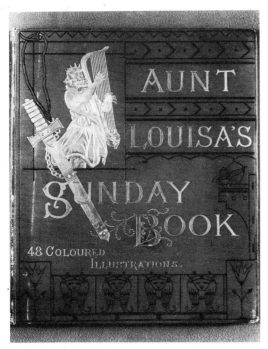

The most difficult of the early boy's magazines for a collector to find is *The Boy's Miscellany*, the first weekly issue appearing on Saturday, 7 March, 1863, priced at a penny a copy. Although it was never published as an annual it was possible to buy four of the weekly parts bound together in a colour-printed pictorial wrapper at fourpence. It was originally owned and edited by E. Harrison of Salisbury Court, but was taken over by its printers, Maddick & Portage, Crane Court, Fillet Street, as their account remained unpaid. It was in this magazine that *The Adventures of Sixteen-String Jack* were first recounted.

Good Words for the Young, the junior version of the magazine *Good Words*, was published monthly from 1868 to 1872, and then continued as *Good Things for the Young of All Ages*, 1872–7. The standard of the wood-cut illustrations was particularly high, derived in part from its adult companion which employed the talents of many of the leading 'Sixties' artists of the day. Starting life under the editorship of Dr Norman Macleod, from 1870 to 1872 the chair was occupied by George Mac-Donald, and two of his most famous stories appeared there as serials: *At the Back of the North Wind* and *Ranald Bannerman's Boyhood*, both with illustrations by Arthur Hughes.

The Boy's Own Paper survived without a change of name from the first issue, published on Saturday, 18 January 1879, until its final appearance eighty-eight years later in February 1967. *The Boy's Own Annual*, published in pictorial cloth-bindings at the end of each year, was issued regularly until the outbreak of World War II, but there was then a break of twenty-six years until it restarted at Christmas 1964. In its heyday it was the most popular boy's magazine, outselling its many rivals by thousands of copies a week, and employing as regular contributors nearly every well known writer for juveniles. The full-page colour-printed plates by Edmund Evans were a speciality.

It was due to the popularity of *The Boy's Own Paper* that *The Union Jack* failed to command a similar market. It started just that much behind, having allowed its rival a full twelve months' lead, its first issue appearing in January 1880 as a penny weekly magazine. Alternatively, it could be bought monthly at sixpence (2½p), giving as an extra a large portrait photograph of a well known children's author. Edited by W. H. G. Kingston when he was already a dying man, the chair passed to G. A. Henty for the nineteenth weekly issue in May 1880. His tale, *Facing Death, a Tale of the Coal Mines*, had started as a serial the previous month. R. M. Ballantyne contributed *Fighting the Salmon in Norway*, Jules Verne *The Steam House* and Manville Fenn *The Ensign and the Middy*. Several of Henty's best-known tales eventually found a place in its pages. Yet it managed to survive for only four volumes, finishing its life as a magazine with the issue dated 25 September 1883.

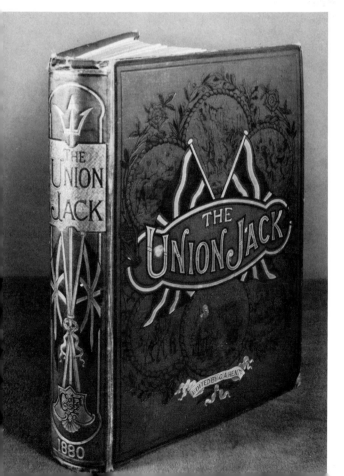

Four cloth-bound volumes were issued during 1880–3, but none is now easy to find in anything approaching acceptable condition as generations of boys thumbed their way through its pages. Height: 28cm

Magazines for girls, and for younger children, were the province of women editors. *Aunt Judy's Magazine for Young People*, a monthly published 1866 to 1885 in half-yearly, Christmas and midsummer volumes, was established by Mrs Gatty, and included among its contributors such famous names as Lewis Carroll and Hans Andersen. The first periodical specially devised for teenage girls was *Every Girl's Magazine*, a monthly published from 1878 to 1888 and edited by Alicia Amy Leith. It appeared as *Every Girl's Annual* at the end of each year. Kate Greenaway was responsible for some of the colour-printed frontispieces, as she was for those in *Little Wide-Awake*, edited by Mrs Lucy Sale Barker, a monthly magazine which ran from 1875 to 1892, with an annual of the same name.

The most famous of the magazines for girls was undoubtedly *The Girl's Own Paper*, which ran continuously (with various later changes of name) from 1880 to 1948. It appeared at the end of each year as *The Girl's Own Annual*, and in its time consumed the talents of nearly every female writer for schoolgirls in Britain. It was published by the proprietors of a successful adult magazine *The Leisure Hour*, 1852–1905, who were also responsible for *The Boy's Leisure Hour*, which commenced publication in January 1884 as a penny weekly, but was also issued (from October 1887) in monthly parts, each containing the previous four weekly numbers, bound in illustrated colour-printed paper wrappers at fourpence a copy. Annuals of this publication did not appear, but it is famous for having seen the appearance of such delights of Victorian childhood as 'Three-Fingered Jack', 'Cheeky Charlie', 'Sweeney Todd the Demon Barber', 'Jack Sheppard', 'Broad Arrow Jack', 'Spring-Heeled Jack' and 'The Adventures of Ching Ching'. So popular did this little Chinese boy become that *Ching Ching's Own Magazine* came into being in June 1888, and continued until June 1893.

By this time the stationers and bookshops had their counters crowded with a bewildering array of children's magazines. *Comic Cuts* started in May 1890; *Comic Pictorial Nuggets* in May 1892, continuing as *Nuggets* from November 1892 until it ceased publication in March, 1905; *The World's Comic*, 1892–1908, was followed by the famous *Chums* in September 1892. From that time onwards we come to the age of the 'comics' of our own boyhood, with names like *The Magnet*, *The Gem*, *The Bulls-eye*, *Tiger Tim's Tales*, *The Champion*, *Chatterbox*, *Hotspur*, *The Jester*, *The Marvel*, *Merry and Bright*, *Pluck*, *The Rover*, *The Triumph* and *The Wild West Weekly*.

One other class of paper-bound reading matter which children in their teens found irresistible was the 'penny dreadfuls', the 'bloods' of the period extending from 1840s to the 1900s. The earlier titles, such as *The Royal Rake*, 1842, by Leman Rede (1802–47), who that same year

A four-volume set, and extremely rare in their original printed paper-covered boards, dated 1822. The publisher, John Arliss, started one of the first juvenile libraries. Height: 13cm

had started the magazine *Judy* as a rival to *Punch* (only two numbers appeared), were satirical romances rather than true blood-and-thunder thrillers, although the vivid descriptions of such characters as John Rann, alias 'Sixteen-String Jack', and his henchman Kit Clayton, as well as the graphic woodcut illustrations of bloody deeds and highway robberies, pointed the way to the lurid sequels that were to follow from other hands. By the 1850s, the publishers of 'penny parts', to be known all too soon as 'penny dreadfuls', had settled to their task of providing sorely needed escapism for those of the indigenous poor who had learned to read.

Edward Lloyd (1818–90), founder of *Lloyd's Newspaper*, was one of the first to see the possibilities of this market, and during the 1840s he started to put out an increasingly wide range of penny-a-week gibbety horror stories, using as *dramatis personae* the more accomplished of the upholders of the *laissez-faire* principle listed in the *Newgate Calendar, or Malefactors' Bloody Register*. Some of the tales he wrote himself, but he also gathered around him a stable of specialist hack writers of the calibre of Edward Viles and John Frederick Smith, who themselves employed even more threadbare and undernourished minor hacks to

(Above left) *Typical of the 'public school' magazines of the early part of the twentieth century,* The Captain *was issued monthly, and in book form twice a year, starting in 1899. Height: 25cm.*
(Above right) *Issued at 'one halfpenny weekly',* Dark Deeds of Old London *was typical of the 'bloods' of the 1870s*

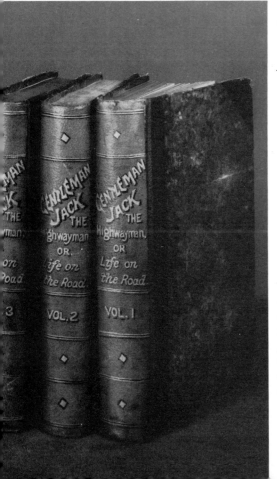

A distinctive private binding from the library of the late Barry Ono, Clapham Common, London, who described himself as 'The Penny Dreadful King'. Gentleman Jack, *1852, by Edward Viles, was published by Edward Lloyd, London, and regaled its readers with the bloodthirsty adventures of Claude Duval in a series of 205 weekly penny parts. Height: 22.5cm*

help in churning out the hundreds of thousands of words needed weekly. *Gentleman Jack; or Life on the Road*, 1852, was typical of the long-running serials issued at a penny a week, 'No's 2, 3, & 4, presented gratis with No. 1'. *Vileroy; or, The Horrors of Zindorf, The Black Monk; or, The Secret of the Grey Turret* and *The Castle Fiend* paved the way for one of Lloyd's most successful publications, *Varney the Vampire*, by James Malcolm Rymer.

None of these titles was meant primarily for the juvenile market, but it did not take adolescents long to discover the blood-curdling excitement to be had for the price of a penny. Thomas Frost, in his *Forty Years' Recollections*, 1860, tells how he met Lloyd's manager, 'a stout gentleman of sleek costume and urbane manners', in the hope of selling him a story for publication. It was admitted to him:

> Our publications circulate among a class so different in education and social position from the readers of three-volume novels that we sometimes distrust our own judgment and place the manuscript in the hands of an illiterate person—a servant, or machine boy, for instance. If they pronounce favourably upon it, we think it will do.

So children took as their own such stories as *Almira's Curse, The Ranger of the Tomb, The Maniac Father* and *Geralda the Demon Nun*; these last two titles from the pen of the indefatigable Thomas Peckett Prest, the creator of that undying tale of private enterprise slightly over-stepping the mark: *Sweeney Todd; the Demon Barber of Fleet Street*, first published by Lloyd under the unlikely title of *The String of Pearls*.

Edward Viles made full use of the fictional Robin Hood attributes of the notorious Dick Turpin by producing *Black Bess; or, The Knight of the Road*, a serial published by E. Harrison which ran to the aston-ishing total of 254 weekly parts. But even this paled into insignificance beside the series of 'Jack Harkaway' stories, written by Bracebridge Hemyng. The first adventure in *Boys of England Magazine*, published by Edwin J. Brett (1828–95), as a penny weekly which commenced pub-lication in November 1866 and continued until June 1899. The youth-ful hero of ten thousand fights and several hundred hair's-breadth escapes from death made his bow in the issue for July 1871, and his subsequent exploits boosted the sales and profits of the paper to the point where the proprietor named his newly acquired premises Harkaway House.

By 1890 the market was saturated with the paper-bound products of scores of printing and publishing firms which had mushroomed into prominence in attempts to satisfy the public appetite for blood-and-thunder. By this time there were probably fifty or more new titles to

This weekly magazine was published at one penny a copy from November 1866 until June 1899, edited, after the first nine numbers, by E. J. Brett. It was here that the first 'Jack Harkaway' stories appeared in July 1871. 14.5 × 17.5cm

The long series of Books for the Bairns *commenced publication in 1896. They were excellent value at an old-fashioned penny a copy.* 18.2 × 12cm

choose from each week. Such firms as the Aldine Publishing Company issued lists of four hundred available numbers from which their young readers could take their pick. Tales such as *The Wolf Demon, Tiger Dick* or *Fire-eye, the sea Hyena* sometimes continued in weekly serials for as long as as a year and seemed only to whet the appetite of their subscribers for more. Fortunes were made out of a single author's series of tales: Hogarth House, Bouverie Street, London, carried many of the successful George Emmett stories, and found a money-spinner in *The Blue Dwarf*, by Percy B. St John (1821–89), a lurid and blood-stained tale of Dick Turpin's fictional hunchback confederate. It was continuously reprinted, with variations, for over thirty years. *The Quarterly Review* was complaining in 1890, in the most vigorous term, that stories such as *Broad-Arrow Jack*, by Edwin Burrage, were 'a class of literature which has done much to people our prisons, our reformatories, and our colonies with scapegraces and ne'er-do-wells'.

Fortunately, not all the paper-bound periodicals for juveniles were devoted to the interests of the lowest common denominator and the constant devourer of the horror story. In 1896 publication commenced of a monthly series of slim little booklets, each of sixty-two pages of text and pictures, which were issued in pictorially printed pink paper wrappers, at a price of only one old-fashioned penny a copy. *Books for the Bairns*, edited by the journalist and social reformer W. T. Stead (1849–1912), who later perished in the *Titanic* disaster, were an immediate success, far exceeding their owner's expectations. They were published at first by *The Review of Reviews* office, and later, when each printing of a new number ran into hundreds of thousands of copies, by Stead's Publishing House, an enterprise set up specially to cope with the demand. The first title to be issued was *Aesop's Fables*, with no less than two hundred illustrations, and this set a standard that could only be profitably maintained by selling up to and exceeding 50,000 copies a week. The price of one penny a copy stayed constant throughout the lifetime of the periodical. All the well known fairy- and folk-tales were printed, and when these were exhausted the editor turned to historical tales, biographies, mythology, pictures and stories from foreign lands, digested versions of literary classics, and a host of other easy-to-read works for young people to enjoy. In fact, *Books for the Bairns* represented the first serious attempt to supply a cheap form of reading matter for the tens of thousands of poor children who could now, thanks to the passing of the Education Act, at last experience the long-denied pleasure of reading for their own instruction and entertainment.

SELECT BIBLIOGRAPHY

The bibliographical works listed below form a selective reference background which a collector of early children's books needs to consult. Specialist collections and some of the best-known writers for juveniles have their own individual bibliographies which can be bought and consulted separately as your interest dictates. These are not included in this general list. Some of the titles given below have been reprinted and are available in new editions.

Annals of English Literature, 1475–1950. Oxford University Press, Oxford, 1961

Boys will be Boys, E. S. Turner (magazines and penny dreadfuls). Collins, London, 1948

Cassell's Encyclopaedia of Literature, S. H. Steinberg (ed.) (2 vols). Cassell, London, 1953

Children's Books in England, F. H. Darton. Cambridge University Press, Cambridge, 1932 (third edition, revised, 1982)

Children's Books of Yesterday, P. James. Special issue of *Studio Magazine*, September 1933

Children's Books of Yesterday, P. H. Muir. National Book League, London, 1946

Collector's Book of Books, Eric Quayle. Studio Vista, London, 1971

Collector's Book of Boys' Stories, Eric Quayle. Studio Vista, London, 1973

Collector's Book of Children's Books, Eric Quayle. Studio Vista, London, 1971

Early American Children's Books, A. S. W. Rosenbach. Southworth Press, Portland, USA, 1933

Early Children's Books and their Illustrators, Gerald Gottlieb. Pierpont Morgan Library & Oxford University Press, New York, 1975

English Children's Books, P. H. Muir. Batsford, London, 1954

Key Books of British Authors, Andrew Block. Archer, London, 1933

John Harris's Books for Youth, 1801-1843, Marjorie Moon. Five Owls Press, Cambridge, 1976

Les Livres de L'Enfance (2 vols). Compiled by Gumuchian & Cie, Paris, 1930

Miniature Books, Louis W. Bondy. Sheppard Press, London, 1981

Newbery, Carnan, Power, S. Roscoe. Dawsons of Pall Mall, London, 1966

Nineteenth-Century Children, Gillian Avery. Hodder & Stoughton, London, 1965

Osborne Collection of Early Children's Books, 1476–1910, Judith St John (ed.) (2 vols). Toronto Public Library, Canada, 1975

Oxford Dictionary of Nursery Rhymes, I. and P. Opie. Clarendon Press, Oxford, 1951

Pages and Pictures from Forgotten Children's Books, Andrew W. Tuer. Leadenhall Press, London, 1898

Stories from Old-Fashioned Children's Books, Andrew W. Tuer. Leadenhall Press, London, 1899

'Studio' Special Winter Number 1897–'98, Gleeson White (ed.).

Written for Children, J. R. Townsend. Miller, London, 1965

XIX Century Fiction, Michael Sadlier (2 vols). Constable, London, 1951

INDEX

Figures in bold type refer to illustrations